THE
PESHITTA
OF THE
TWELVE PROPHETS

THE
PESHIṬTA
OF THE
TWELVE PROPHETS

BY

A. GELSTON

CLARENDON PRESS · OXFORD

1987

Oxford University Press, Walton Street, Oxford OX2 6DP
Oxford New York Toronto
Delhi Bombay Calcutta Madras Karachi
Petaling Jaya Singapore Hong Kong Tokyo
Nairobi Dar es Salaam Cape Town
Melbourne Auckland
and associated companies in
Beirut Berlin Ibadan Nicosia

Oxford is a trade mark of Oxford University Press

Published in the United States
by Oxford University Press, New York

© A. Gelston 1987

All rights reserved. No part of this publication may be reproduced,
stored in a retrieval system, or transmitted, in any form or by any means,
electronic, mechanical, photocopying, recording, or otherwise, without
the prior permission of Oxford University Press

British Library Cataloguing in Publication Data
Gelston, A.
The Peshitta of the Twelve Prophets.
1. Bible. O.T. Minor Prophets—Criticism,
Textual
I. Title
224'.90663 BS1560
ISBN 0-19-826179-9

Library of Congress Cataloging in Publication Data
Gelston, A.
The Peshitta of the Twelve Prophets.
Bibliography: p.
Includes index.
1. Bible. O.T. Minor Prophets. Syriac. Peshitta.
2. Bible. O.T. Minor Prophets—Manuscripts, Syriac.
I. Title.
BS1560.A4G442 1985   224'.9043   85-13608
ISBN 0-19-826179-9

Set on a Lasercomp
at Oxford University Computing Service
Printed in Great Britain
at the University Printing House, Oxford
by David Stanford
Printer to the University

PREFACE

THE scope and purpose of this monograph and its relation to other work on the Peshitta are indicated in the Introduction. It is necessary here to say something about the format of its presentation.

The time is not yet ripe for a definitive study of the Peshitta of the Dodekapropheton. The main purpose of this monograph is to make available to other students of the text of the Hebrew Bible and particularly of the Peshitta version of the Old Testament the data which have emerged from my collation and evaluation of the biblical Mss of the Peshitta of the Dodekapropheton for the Leiden EDITION. The emphasis therefore falls on the direct presentation of primary evidence and of the inferences which may be drawn from it. The detailed and technical nature however of much of this material presents formidable obstacles in the way of achieving a readable presentation. Considerable efforts therefore have been made to minimize the use of abbreviations and esoteric terminology. Footnotes have been eschewed and necessary references to secondary literature kept to a minimum. Most of the latter are in the form of the author's surname in capitals, with a page reference where necessary, full bibliographical details being supplied together with notes of other abbreviations after the table of contents. Familiarity with the presentation of *Vetus Testamentum Syriace* and its nomenclature of the Peshitta Mss has had to be presupposed, and it is assumed that the reader of this monograph will have a copy of the EDITION to hand.

The indexation of this monograph has also presented particular problems. The table of contents indicates where material about particular Mss may be found and where particular topics are discussed. A comprehensive index to references to the Dodekapropheton has not been thought practicable or desirable. Instead a series of separate indexes to chapters 3–8, in varying but self-explanatory form, has been provided in an attempt to facilitate reference to passages already classified under the headings of the subjects treated in those chapters. The search for discussion of a particular variant can thus be kept separate from that for an evaluation of the Peshitta of a particular passage in relation to MT,

LXX or T. The indices to chapters 6–8 are selective, in that passages where minor details are examined have not been included, and this has kept them within a reasonable compass. No index has been provided to the secondary literature. It is impossible to write about the textual problems of the Dodekapropheton without constant reference to such works as those of RUDOLPH and SEBÖK and the more detailed studies of particular parts of the text such as that of GERLEMAN. Almost always the relevant material will be found *ad loc* both in these works and in the present monograph. References to the secondary literature have generally been restricted to instances where original suggestions have been either adopted or disputed; it would have been cumbersome and tedious to document every agreement and disagreement with the secondary literature.

Considerations of space have necessitated a selective approach to much of the material, and in a number of places further examples could be given. It is hoped that nothing of major significance has been overlooked, and that the selection of material has not led to an unrepresentative picture of the evidence. Inevitably work of this nature demands a great deal of time, and this monograph marks the completion of almost exactly twenty years of research on the Peshitta of the Dodekapropheton. From time to time fresh perspectives alter one's judgement about details, and the fortuitous timing of other publications prevents a monograph of this kind from being fully up to date. Review copies of Owens' monograph on the Genesis and Exodus Citations of Aphrahat and of Balentine's "The Hidden God" enabled me respectively to add the appended note to chapter 4 and to modify my judgement on Mi iii 4 between writing chapters 5 and 6 (*cf* pp 127, 151). Had B. Grossfeld's article in ZAW 96, 1984, pp. 82–101, appeared before the writing of chapter 6 I should have taken note of it in the relevant paragraph on p. 142, but it did not seem necessary subsequently to introduce any modifications into my presentation there of the evidence of the Peshitta of the Dodekapropheton. Since the completion of this monograph I have prepared a collation of two further biblical Mss of the Peshitta of the Dodekapropheton, 9d2 and 11d2, and on the 30th August, 1985, I read a paper at the Peshitta Symposium in Leiden entitled 'Some readings in the Peshitta of the Dodekapropheton'. Both of these are to be published in the Symposium Volume, which will be no. 4 of the Monographs of the Peshitta Institute, Leiden, and which is expected to appear in 1986. They will serve to supplement the present work. Further pertinent studies may well have appeared by the time this monograph is published, and the interim nature of this investigation has been emphasized at several points. For a magisterial survey of the wider aspects of Peshitta research reference may be made to the article by P.A.H. de Boer entitled, 'Towards an Edition of the Syriac Version of the Old Testament' (VT 31, 1981, pp. 346–357).

It is a pleasant duty to record my gratitude to several scholars who have given me practical assistance. I am indebted particularly to Dr. R.P. Gordon for the loan of a copy of his thesis, which alerted me particularly to several agreements between the Targum and the Peshitta in Malachi which I had overlooked in my preliminary study, to the Rev. D.J. Lane for an advance copy of his review of the EDITION, and to Dr. M.P. Weitzman both for an advance copy of his article and for a private communication informing me about the pattern of relationships of Peshitta Mss in other Books of the Old Testament. Dr. S.P. Brock provided me with information about the reading of the Peshitta Mss in Is ii 3f., and Dr. S.C. Reif kindly verified a reading in the Paris Polyglot. The authorities of the Bodleian Library at Oxford allowed me to consult the Ms 17a3, and the Research Fund of Durham University covered my expenses in doing so. Professors P.A.H. de Boer and W. Baars gave me much help and advice in preparing the EDITION, and Professor J. Barr has given advice about the publication of this monograph. I am most grateful to the Delegates of the Oxford University Press for accepting this work for publication, and to their staff, especially Mr. J.K. Cordy, for much practical help and advice during the process of publication. The specialist reader of the Press and Mr. K. Jenner of the Peshitta Institute kindly drew my attention to a few details requiring emendation or modification. I am grateful too to the Oxford University Computing Service and in particular to Mrs C.M. Griffin, and also to Mr. S.V. Cope for overcoming the problems of setting a complicated manuscript in type. A generous subvention towards the cost of publication was made by the Hall-Houghton Trustees, and I am particularly grateful to the chairman of the Trustees, Professor E.W. Nicholson, for his help in this respect. My greatest debt is to my wife for her constant encouragement, and also for practical assistance in checking the typescript and the proofs.

Durham
16 November, 1985

A. GELSTON

CONTENTS

Abbreviations and Bibliographical References	xi
Introduction	xv
Addenda and Corrigenda to the Edition	xxiii

PART I
THE TRANSMISSION OF THE PESHIṬTA TEXT

1. DESCRIPTIONS OF THE LATER BIBLICAL MANUSCRIPTS	3
2. FAMILIES AND GROUPS	26
A 9a1 *fam*: (12a1) (16/)9a1 17a6–9.11	28
B 14a1 *fam*: 14a1 17a1–5.10	38
C 16g6 19g5.7	45
D 15d2 *fam* (15d2 17d4 19d2.3) 17d3 19d4 (19/17d1)	49
E 16d1 17d2 18d1 18g1	53
F 17d5 18d2 19d1	61
3. DISTINCTIVE READINGS OF THE OLDEST MANUSCRIPTS	65
1. The oldest manuscripts and the standard text	65
2. Agreed readings of the oldest manuscripts	67
3. Agreed readings of two or more of the oldest manuscripts	71
4. Readings peculiar to each of the oldest manuscripts	76
5. Some general considerations	85
4. TOWARDS THE ORIGINAL PESHIṬTA	92
1. The Text of the Edition	92
2. Some readings not printed in the Edition	93
3. Inner-Syriac corruptions	98
4. Syrohexaplaric influence	101
5. Conclusion	104
APPENDED NOTE TO CHAPTER 4	106

PART II
The Peshiṭta as a Version

5. The Hebrew Text Behind the Peshiṭta	111
1. Introduction	111
2. Non-Masoretic readings	113
3. Variants within the Masoretic tradition	118
4. Further evidence for a consonantal *Vorlage* distinct from MT	125
5. Conclusion	129
6. The Peshiṭta as a Version of the Hebrew	131
1. Stylistic modifications	131
2. Lexical equivalents	139
3. Exegetical and theological modifications	147
4. Conclusion	156
7. The Peshiṭta and the Septuagint	160
1. Introduction	160
2. The dependence of the Peshiṭta on LXX	162
3. The use of LXX by the Peshiṭta translators	166
4. Some further agreements between LXX and the Peshiṭta	171
5. Conclusion	176
8. The Peshiṭta and the Targum	178
1. Introduction	178
2. Stylistic modifications	180
3. Lexical agreements	183
4. Exegetical traditions	186
5. Conclusion	189
9. The Origins of the Peshiṭta	191
Indexes	199
Readings discussed	199
References to the Dodekapropheton	201

ABBREVIATIONS AND BIBLIOGRAPHICAL REFERENCES

SOME abbreviations used in *Vetus Testamentum Syriace*, Leiden (*cf* General Preface pp. XXIIf., I i pp. XIIf.) have also been used in this monograph. It may be useful to point out that Sa is the abbreviation used for Zechariah. In addition to those listed the term *cal curr* (= *calamo currente*) has been used to denote errors corrected by the original copyist before proceeding.

Primary Sources

MT	the Masoretic Text of the Hebrew Bible, as in *Biblia Hebraica Stuttgartensia* (BHS).
LXX	the Septuagint. For the Dodekapropheton the Göttingen edition of J. Ziegler (1967) has been used, and for other Books the fifth edition of A. Rahlfs' *Septuaginta* (1952).
LXX^{Barb}	the Barberini version of Hb iii.
A	Aquila
Th	Theodotion
S	Symmachus
	For the above F. Field, *Origenis Hexaplorum Quae Supersunt*, Oxford (1875), reprinted Hildesheim (1964) has been used, supplemented by Ziegler's edition of the LXX of the Dodekapropheton.
V	the Vulgate, as in *Biblia Sacra iuxta Vulgatum Versionem*, Stuttgart (1969).
T	the Targum, as in A. Sperber, *The Bible in Aramaic*, Leiden (1959-1973).

The Greek New Testament has been consulted in the second edition of the Bible Society's text (1958) and the New Testament Peshitta in the Bible Society's *The New Testament in Syriac* (1950). The Old Syriac Gospels have been consulted in F.C. Burkitt, *Evangelion da-Mepharreshe*, Cambridge (1904).

EDITION	*Vetus Testamentum Syriace* III, 4. For parts of the Old Testament Peshitta other than the Dodekapropheton *Vetus Testamentum Syriace* has been used wherever it is available, and otherwise the 1954 reprint of the edition of the Trinitarian Bible Society (the Urmia edition).
LIST	*List of Old Testament Peshitta Manuscripts* (Preliminary Issue), Peshitta Institute, Leiden (1961).

Syh   the Syrohexapla. The edition of A.M. Ceriani, *Codex Syro-Hexaplaris Ambrosianus photolithographice editus* (= *Monumenta sacra et profana*, vol VII), Milan (1874) has been used.

The Qumran texts have been consulted whenever possible in E. Lohse, *Die Texte aus Qumran*, Munich (1964), and otherwise in the sources listed in J.A. Fitzmyer, *The Dead Sea Scrolls—Major Publications and Tools for Study*, Montana (1975).

CD   the Damascus Document.

Ancient and Mediaeval Commentators

Theodore   *Theodori Mopsuesteni Commentarius in XII Prophetas*, ed. H.N. Sprenger, Wiesbaden (1977).

Isho'dad   *Commentaire d'Išo'dad de Merv sur l'Ancien Testament IV. Isaïe et les Douze*, ed. C. Van den Eynde, CSCO 303 (Scriptores Syri 128) (1969).

Barhebraeus   *Gregorii Barhebraei In Duodecim Prophetas Minores Scholia*, ed. B. Moritz, Leipzig (1882).

Modern Studies

BALENTINE   S.E. Balentine, *The Hidden God*, Oxford (1983).

BARR   J. Barr, *Comparative Philology and the Text of the Old Testament*, Oxford, 1968.

BARTHÉLEMY   D. Barthélemy, *Les Devanciers d'Aquila*, Vetus Testamentum Supplement X (1963).

BROWNLEE   W.H. Brownlee, *The Text of Habakkuk in the Ancient Commentary from Qumran*, JBL Monograph Series XI (1959).

CERIANI   A.M. Ceriani, *Le Edizioni e i Manoscritti delle Versioni Siriache del Vecchio Testamento* (Memorie del Reale Istituo Lombardo di scienze e lettere, Classe di lettere e scienze morale e politiche, Vol XI, fascicolo II), Milan (1869).

CHILTON   B.D. Chilton, *The Glory of Israel*, JSOT Supplement Series 23, Sheffield (1983).

DIETTRICH   G. Diettrich, *Ein Apparatus Criticus zur Pešitto zum Propheten Jesaia*, BZAW 8 (1905).

DI LELLA   A.A. di Lella, Introduction to Proverbs in *Vetus Testamentum Syriace* II, v (1979).

DIRKSEN   P.B. Dirksen, *The Transmission of the Text in the Peshiṭta Manuscripts of the Book of Judges*, Monographs of the

ABBREVIATIONS AND BIBLIOGRAPHICAL REFERENCES

	Peshiṭta Institute, Leiden, vol 1 (1972).
EMERTON	J.A. Emerton, *The Peshitta of the Wisdom of Solomon*, Studia Post-biblica, vol 2, Leiden (1959).
GERLEMAN	G. Gerleman, *Zephanja textkritisch und literarisch untersucht*, Lund (1942).
GORDON	R.P. Gordon, *Targum Jonathan to the Minor Prophets from Nahum to Malachi*, unpublished Ph. D. thesis, Cambridge (1973).
HAYMAN	A.P. Hayman, Review of KOSTER in JSS XXV (1980), pp. 263–270.
JANSMA	T. Jansma, *Inquiry into the Hebrew Text and the Ancient Versions of Zechariah IX–XIV*, Leiden (1949).
JELLICOE	S. Jellicoe, *The Septuagint and Modern Study*, Oxford (1968).
KAHLE	P.E. Kahle, *The Cairo Geniza*, second edition, Oxford (1959).
KBL	L. Koehler & W. Baumgartner, *Hebräisches und Aramäisches Lexikon zum Alten Testament*, third edition, Leiden (1967–).
KOSTER	M.D. Koster, *The Peshiṭta of Exodus*, Studia Semitica Neerlandica 19, Assen (1977).
LANE	D.J. Lane, Review of EDITION in JBL 103 (1984), pp. 107f.
LEVI DELLA VIDA	G. Levi della Vida, *Ricerche sulla formazione del più antico fondo dei Manoscritti Orientali della Biblioteca Vaticana*, Studi e Testi 92 (1939).
NÖLDEKE	T. Nöldeke, *Kurzgefasste Syrische Grammatik*, second edition, Leipzig (1898).
OTZEN	B. Otzen, *Studien über Deuterosacharja*, Acta Theologica Danica VI, Copenhagen (1964).
PAYNE SMITH	R. Payne Smith, *Thesaurus Syriacus*, Oxford (1879–1901).
RUDOLPH	W. Rudolph, *Kommentar zum Alten Testament* XIII, Gütersloh (1966–1976).
RYSSEL	V. Ryssel, *Untersuchungen über die Textgestalt und die Echtheit des Buches Micha*, Leipzig (1887).
SAEBØ	M. Saebø, *Sacharja 9–14, Untersuchungen von Text und Form*, Wissenschaftliche Monographien zum Alten und Neuen Testament, vol 34, Neukirchen (1969).

Sebök	M. Sebök (Schönberger), *Die syrische Uebersetzung der zwölf kleinen Propheten*, Breslau (1887).
Sperber	A. Sperber, *The Bible in Aramaic*, Leiden (1959–1973).
Vollers	K. Vollers, *Das Dodekapropheton der Alexandriner*, ZAW 3 (1883), pp. 219–272, 4 (1884), pp. 1–20. The reference on p. 162 *infra* is to vol 3, p. 244.
Weitzman	M.P. Weitzman, *The Origin of the Peshitta Psalter*, in edd. J.A. Emerton & S.C. Reif, *Interpreting the Hebrew Bible*, Essays in honour of E.I.J. Rosenthal, University of Cambridge Oriental Publications 32, Cambridge (1982), pp. 277–298.
Wright	W. Wright, *Catalogue of Syriac Manuscripts in the British Museum*, Part 1 (1870).
Ziegler	J. Ziegler, *Duodecim Prophetae*, Septuaginta XIII, second edition, Göttingen (1967).

Periodicals

BZAW	Beihefte zur Zeitschrift für die Alttestamentliche Wissenschaft.
CSCO	Corpus Scriptorum Christianorum Orientalium.
JBL	Journal of Biblical Literature.
JSOT	Journal for the Study of the Old Testament.
JSS	Journal of Semitic Studies.
VT	Vetus Testamentum.
VTS	Supplements to Vetus Testamentum.
ZAW	Zeitschrift für die Alttestamentliche Wissenschaft.

INTRODUCTION

> There is no other Syriac text which can be compared in importance with the Old-Testament Peshitta. Not only is this the one direct non-midrashic translation of the Hebrew Bible into a language closely related to Hebrew and therefore invaluable to the study of the Bible text; it is also practically the oldest and best-attested text in Syriac, with an influence second to none on the development of that language.
>
> M.H. Goshen-Gottstein, *Scripta Hierosolymitana* 8, 1961, p.26.

THE publication of a critical text of the Peshitta, which is now well under way, makes possible a new stage in the study and use of this ancient version of the Old Testament. Until now scholars have been able to use the Peshitta only in one of the printed editions or in Ceriani's lithographic reproduction of the Ambrosian Codex at Milan, except for individual Books for which a limited critical apparatus was available. It has become clear not only that the various printed editions are based on a limited number of (often very poor) Mss, but that the Ambrosian Codex itself contains a considerable number of readings peculiar to itself, rendering it hardly a safe tool for textual criticism if used in isolation from other Mss. Readings quoted confidently in commentaries as those of the Peshitta prove on occasion to be no more than the idiosyncrasies of a single Ms! It is unfortunate that earlier generations of Peshitta scholars appear not to have recognized the supreme importance of the preparation of a critical text of the Peshitta before any valid conclusions can be drawn, and have not given this task the priority it logically required.

This omission is now being made good by the publication of *Vetus Testamentum Syriace* under the auspices of the International Organization for the Study of the Old Testament by a team of scholars under the general direction of the Peshitta Institute of the University of Leiden, The Netherlands. When this work is complete a major step forward will have been taken in Peshitta studies. In the meantime further studies must be based on the fascicles already published. Since it has already become clear that the Peshitta does not present a uniform picture in the several Books of the Old Testament, it is in any case prudent that in the early stages of the next chapter of Peshitta research attention should be addressed separately to different Books of the Old Testament. Such a method has also the practical advantage that a scholar who has already edited the Mss of a particular book for the critical edition of the Peshitta text has in the process become aware of some of the special problems requiring attention in that Book. Significant monographs have already been published by P.B. Dirksen on Judges and M.D. Koster on Exodus. While the scope of the present monograph differs from that of either of these it is offered as a further contribution to Peshitta research.

The Peshitta text of the Dodekaporpheton used as the basis of this monograph is that printed in the Leiden Edition: *Vetus Testamentum Syriace* III, 4 (1980), hereafter referred to as the EDITION. That text was prepared according to the rules of the Peshitta Institute, which required that the text of 7a1 (the Ambrosian Codex) was to be printed except where it was clearly erroneous or lacked the support of at least two of the older Mss. Some account of the modifications of the text of 7a1 in the text as printed is to be found in the Introduction to the EDITION; further attention is given to some of them in chapter 3 of this monograph. It is of interest that the rules governing the relationship of the Basic Text of the EDITION to 7a1 resulted in the printing of the reading of 7a1 as the Basic Text on three occasions when it is the inferior reading, and the relegation of the reading of 7a1 to the Apparatus on seventeen occasions when it is the superior reading! A list of Addenda and Corrigenda to the EDITION is prefaced to this monograph.

The collation of the Biblical Mss of the Dodekapropheton for the EDITION was undertaken by the present writer. In addition to the material published in the EDITION the following material, prepared according to the format of *Vetus Testamentum Syriace* II, 4 (1976), which for financial reasons had to be excluded from subsequent fascicles, has been deposited at the Peshitta Institute:

(a) Headings and Subscriptions in Mss later than 12d3
(b) An Elenchus Omissionum in three parts:
    (1) Mechanical omissions in all Mss
    (2) Non-mechanical omissions judged to be erroneous in Mss to 12d3 (these were partially included in the Introduction to the EDITION at a late stage in its preparation)

(3) All non-mechanical omissions in Mss later than 12d3
(c) A list of later Mss sharing readings noted in the Second Apparatus (indicated in the Apparatus by an arrow)
(d) A list of shared readings in Mss later than 12d3
(e) A list of shared errors in all Mss (part of this was also included in the Introduction to the EDITION at a late stage)
(f) A list of errors peculiar to each Ms
(g) A list of readings peculiar to each Ms later than 12d3
(h) An Index Nominum
(i) An Index Orthographicus, containing the nominal as well as the verbal orthographic variants in all Mss, set out according to the General Preface (1972) of *Vetus Testamentum Syriace*.

It should be explained that the criterion for distinguishing readings from errors in (d)–(g) was simply that of intelligibility; a number of variants classified as readings are in all probability to be regarded as inner-Syriac corruptions (*cf* chapter 4, section 3), but wherever the variants yielded an intelligible text it seemed right to give them the initial benefit of the doubt.

Much of the material deposited at the Peshiṭta Institute is utilized in Part I of the present monograph. What is significant for the description and evaluation of the individual Mss and for the examination of their inter-relationships is presented as clearly and objectively as possible. For complete details however it is necessary to apply to the Peshiṭta Institute.

Part I of the present monograph is concerned with the transmission of the Peshiṭta text. First of all a brief description is provided of all the Biblical Mss of the Dodekapropheton later than 12d3, to complete the set of descriptions of the earlier Mss printed in the Introduction to the EDITION (chapter 1). There follows an examination of the relationships of certain Mss to one another (chapter 2).

Attention is next directed to the quest for the original Peshiṭta text. Here a close examination is made of the distinctive readings of the earliest Mss, particularly those held by some or all of them in common. These readings are evaluated especially from the standpoint of transcriptional probability and from that of their relative closeness to the Hebrew text. Some assessment of the value of each of these earliest Mss is also attempted. Some consideration is also given to the relationship between these earliest Mss and what we have called the "Standard Text" (chapter 3). In the light of these investigations an attempt is made to determine which readings in the First and Second

Apparatus of the EDITION are probably to be preferred to those of the Basic Text. A few readings attested only in later Mss and not printed at all in the EDITION are also introduced at this point. Some consideration is given to the question of inner-Syriac corruptions originating earlier than the oldest extant Mss, and to the possible scope of Syrohexaplaric influence on the Mss of the Peshitta (chapter 4). The first part of the monograph concludes with a general assessment of the present state of knowledge of the Peshitta text of the Dodekapropheton. An appended note to chapter 4 offers some preliminary soundings on the citations from the Dodekapropheton in Aphrahat and Ephrem.

Part II of the monograph is concerned with an attempt to evaluate the Peshitta of the Dodekapropheton as a version of the Hebrew original. An examination of the relation of the Peshitta to the Hebrew is concerned to establish first the character of the Hebrew *Vorlage* of the Peshitta and its relation to the Masoretic Text (chapter 5), and then the nature of the Syriac translation with the bearing of this on the limitations of the possibility of reconstructing the Hebrew *Vorlage* (chapter 6). There follows an examination of the relation of the Peshitta to the Septuagint (chapter 7) and Targum Jonathan (chapter 8). Agreements with these versions are carefully sifted in an attempt to determine whether they indicate direct influence, dependence on a common *Vorlage* distinct from the Masoretic Text, or dependence on common exegetical traditions. Significant agreements with other versions are examined in chapter 5. In the last chapter some attention is paid to wider questions, such as the date and provenance (Jewish or Christian) of the Peshitta, and an assessment of its value for both the textual criticism and the exegesis of the Hebrew text of the Dodekapropheton.

Tribute must be paid to the pioneering work of SEBÖK on the relation of the Peshitta of the Dodekapropheton to the Hebrew, Septuagint and Targum. My indebtedness to his work is apparent throughout Part II and also in chapter 4, section 3. I have often profited from his insights, though I have also often found other explanations more convincing than his. For instance I accept his suggestion of an inner-Syriac corruption in Hb i 12, but offer a quite different judgement from his on the question of the identity of the *Vorlage* behind the word in question (see pp 99, 119). After almost a century it is not surprising that his work is dated in many respects. The Qumran discoveries in particular have taught textual critics of the Old Testament to be far more cautious in conjectural emendation than was customary in his day. Attention may be drawn here to two further defects in his work. His method—a survey of detailed points *seriatim*, prefaced by a very concise Introduction, where the lists of references are not always accurate—makes it difficult to use his monograph otherwise than as a verse-by-verse commentary, and in particular to assess the overall results of his investigations. Unfortunately he nowhere indicates specifically which edition of the Peshitta he uses. At the bottom of p. 53 he refers to both Lee's edition of 1823 and the London Polyglot, while on p. 51 he cites Ceriani and the Syrohexapla for the reading ܐܬܪܝ in Mi v 4, a reading which occurs in no Biblical Ms of the Peshitta. On p. 56 he cites the reading ܘܡܒܘܥܐ in Na ii 5, which is peculiar among the Biblical Mss to 17a5, where it has been touched up (see pp 97f. *infra*). This Ms was used as the basis of the Syriac text of the Paris Polyglot, which in turn was reproduced in the London Polyglot, whence Sebök presumably derived the reading in question. These criticisms must not however detract from the lasting value of much of his work.

Attention should be drawn at this stage to certain topics which are not covered in the present monograph. The readings of Lectionary Mss were collated for the EDITION by the staff of the Peshitta Institute and the microfilms of these Mss were not seen by the present writer. For this reason, and because the excerpting of biblical passages for lectionary purposes always involves the possibility of minor modifications to suit the liturgical context, no study of the readings of these Mss has been included in the present work. The readings of these Mss printed in the Second Apparatus of the EDITION have however all been examined, and attention is directed on p. 93 to the one reading attested only in a Lectionary Ms which is considered significant. Readings of the so-called Massoretic Mss have also been ignored. In addition to the brief note on the citations of the Dodekapropheton in Aphrahat and Ephrem, the text citations in the commentaries of Isho'dad and Bar Hebraeus have been scrutinized and reference is made to them where this is considered appropriate.

Two kinds of variant have been practically ignored in this study. One is the purely orthographic variant, which is of interest for the study of the Syriac language but affords little insight into the nature of the Peshitta itself. The other is that of variants in the use of diacritic points, which have only occasionally been taken into consideration. The reason for this is not that they are considered to be unimportant, but that practice varies so much between different Mss that it is often difficult if not impossible in our present state of knowledge to determine the significance of a particular diacritic point.

No attempt has been made in the present monograph to evaluate the several printed editions of the Peshiṭta. Some work has already been done in this area and it would seem worthwhile to postpone a definitive study until after the completion of *Vetus Testamentum Syriace*.

A final area in which the present study may be thought defective is that of the evaluation of the Peshiṭta translation in relation to the Talmudic principles of exegesis on the lines of Ch. Heller, *Untersuchungen über die Peschiṭta zur gesamten Hebräischen Bibel*, Teil 1 (Berlin, 1911). All his examples from the Dodekapropheton have been examined, and some of them appear to be of a rather trivial nature and capable of less specific explanations such as stylistic modifications or simply a certain freedom on the part of the translator. Any worthwhile study of this aspect of the Peshiṭta however requires a familiarity with the principles and practice of Talmudic exegesis to which the present writer cannot lay claim.

One aspect of this study to which attention must be drawn is the possibility at many points of more than one interpretation of the data. A particular reading of the Peshiṭta may for instance be interpreted variously as reflecting a Hebrew *Vorlage* distinct from the Masoretic Text, reflecting the influence of the Septuagint, or merely representing the Syriac translator's interpretation of the Hebrew. The agreement in a distinctive reading of two or more Mss may be the result of coincidence as well as of a direct or indirect relationship between these particular Mss in the transmission of the Peshiṭta. Caution must always be exercised. We have tried to follow the general trend of the evidence, but inevitably much of it concerns relatively minor details and in many individual cases there is room for differences of interpretation and judgement. What is least likely to be helpful is the merely statistical approach, and this has been eschewed except in cases where the evidence is overwhelming in its quantity.

It is clear that Peshiṭta studies are still in their relative infancy. The critical study of the extant Mss in connection with the preparation of *Vetus Testamentum Syriace* is making possible for the first time an objective study of this ancient version of the Old Testament. To what extent the expectations voiced by Goshen-Gottstein in the passage quoted at the beginning of this Introduction will be realized will become apparent only as Peshiṭta studies advance on a broader front.

At the present stage it is possible only to make advances within the study of individual Books of the Old Testament. Attention has been drawn to some areas where further research is still required. The conclusions drawn from the evidence presented in this monograph may well have to be modified in the light of further and more broadly based studies in the future. It seems worthwhile however to present this monograph as a contribution to the ongoing study of the Peshiṭta of the Old Testament, and as an aid to the critical use of the EDITION of the Dodekapropheton in *Vetus Testamentum Syriace*.

ADDENDA AND CORRIGENDA TO THE EDITION

p.IX   *sub* 7a1, paragraph 2:
line 3—for 'Ml iii 6' read 'Ml iii 1.6'.
line 12—for 'forty-six' read 'forty-five'.

p.X   line 2—for 'Mi ii 4, iii 1.2' read 'Mi ii 4, iii 2'.
line 11—for 'sixty-eight' read 'sixty-seven'.

p.XI   line 6—after 'corrected).' insert:
'There is also a *rasura* at the end of Sa i 16, which appears to be the deletion *cal curr* of an additional ܐܡܪ ܗܘܐ.'

p.XV   line 4—for 'six' read 'seven'.

sub 12a1, paragraph 3:
line 5—for 'Twelve' read 'Thirteen'.
line 6—for 'nine' read 'ten'.

p.XXI   *sub* 18d1—for 'Ms Oo i. 18' read 'Ms Oo I. 18'.

LIST OF UNIQUE UNCORRECTED ERRORS IN MSS TO 12D3—add footnote:
'Errors concerning the addition or omission of *seyāmē* are not included in this List, although they have been reckoned in the total numbers of errors given in the descriptions of the Mss.

p.XXIII   *sub* 12d1—delete the error recorded in Sa x 4, since this has been corrected in the Ms.

p.XXXI   line 24—for 'journies' read 'journeys'.

p.22   app II 14—delete '10d1' and '12d1 (*vid*)' and replace with: '9d1 11d1 12a1 12d2.3→: *l.n.* 8j1'.

p.28   text, line 1—add *seyāmē* to the fifth word (ܕܢܚܐ); also in the *lemma* in app II. Delete the *seyāmē* in ܕܛܠܝܐ.

p.30   text, line 14—add *punctum* below *dalath* in the fourth word (ܘܠܝܕܐ).

p.32   text, bottom line—delete the stop at the end of the line.

p.43   app II 7 1°—for '12d1-3' read '12d1.3'.
app II 7 2°—insert '11d1'.

p.47	app II iii 1—insert as first variant: '܏ܗ]*om* 7a1 8a1*'.
p.54	text, line 5—add *seyāmē* to the fourth word (ܫܠܗ̈ܝ).
p.58	text, line 16—delete the stop at the end of the line.
p.65	app II 18$^{2°}$—for '12d1–3' read '12d1.3'.
p.77	text, line 9—transfer the stop from the first to the second word. text, line 13—the second word should be ܕܚܝܐ, not ܕܚܝܐ.
p.79	app I—the penultimate letter in the reading of 7a1 is *nun*, not *yudh*.
p.93	app II—after first *lemma* bracket insert: '*om* 12a1→'.
p.98	text, line 1—the first letter of the first word is *lamadh*.

PART I

THE TRANSMISSION OF THE PESHIṬTA TEXT

1
Descriptions of the Later Biblical Manuscripts

DESCRIPTIONS of the Biblical Mss to the twelfth century are provided in the Introduction to the EDITION. A list of the remaining Biblical Mss with occasional brief notes is given there on pp. XX–XXI. Descriptions of these Mss and of the later supplements to 8a1, 9a1 and 11d1 are presented in this and the following chapter. Each Ms is given in this chapter a brief description in respect of contents, script, marginal additions, etc. Where known from the colophon or elsewhere the date of the Ms and the name of the copyist are given. The sources of this information are for the most part indicated in the LIST, and it has not been thought necessary to repeat them here. These later Mss were studied in photographs (in the case of 14/8a1 and 16/9a1) or photographs made from microfilms supplied by the Peshiṭta Institute, supplemented in the case of 14/8a1, 16/9a1 and 17a3 by an autopsy.

All but seven of the later Mss find a place in one or other of the six families and groups surveyed in the following chapter. It is convenient to defer most of the textual description of these Mss to that chapter. All that is given here is some indication of the quality of each Ms, with special reference to omissions and peculiar readings and, where appropriate, some indication of the extent to which it has later been corrected. In the case of the remaining seven Mss (13a1, 13d1, 14d1, 15d1, 15d3, 17d1 and 18<13dt1) a somewhat fuller textual description is given in this chapter.

A few general remarks may be useful by way of explanation. The Mss have been classified solely by script, and the tables in NÖLDEKE have been used as a standard. None of these Mss has been found to adhere strictly to the forms given in the Nestorian column, and the term Nestorian Estrangela has been used to describe Mss with a preponderantly Nestorian script, but where the *taw* and often also the final *caph* conform to the Estrangela shape for these letters.

At the time when the material was originally being prepared for the EDITION the rules required a distinction between mechanical and non-mechanical omissions. Those of the latter in the Mss to the twelfth century positively considered to be errors were listed separately, while the others were recorded in the Second Apparatus. All non-mechanical omissions in the later Mss were to be deemed errors, and were so listed in a separate section of the Elenchus Omissionum. One mechanical omission in Sa iii 4 ($^{2°}$ܐܪ̈ܥ ... ܘܐܪܥܐ) occurs in all Mss except 6h9, 7a1, 8a1* and 19g7; it was partly supplied in 19g5[1]. This omission has been included in the totals given for individual Mss in the descriptions below, but has not generally been taken into account in assessing the evidence for families and groups. On this reading see pp 70, 128, 134 *infra*.

In addition to readings found already in the Second Apparatus, whose presence in one or more of the later Mss was indicated by an arrow, there was to be a list of Shared Readings in two or more of the later Mss, a list of Shared Errors (other than omissions) in all Mss (the part of this which concerned the older Mss was reproduced in the Introduction to the EDITION), and lists of readings and errors peculiar to each of the later Mss (except 18 < 13dt1). In classifying variants into readings and errors for these lists the sole criterion adopted was that of intelligibility. In the initial preparation of the material for the EDITION it seemed right to give the benefit of the doubt to any reading, however improbable, which was not patently erroneous. It has however become clear in the preparation of this monograph that many variants, classified as readings simply because they are intrinsically intelligible, are as a matter of fact Inner-Syriac corruptions or simple miscopyings. This became very clear in cases (such as 17a3) where there is positive evidence to identify the exemplar used. It is however in the light of the original classification of the variants that such phrases in the following descriptions of Mss as "*x* readings, of which *y* are certainly erroneous" should be understood.

Finally it should be noted that when the number of readings in the Second Apparatus found in a particular Ms is given, this usually excludes those readings which are found in all or almost all the later Mss, since these represent the standard text of the Peshiṭta and are of no significance in assessing the quality of an individual Ms.

Note. It is no part of the purpose of this monograph to investigate the lectionary notations given in the Biblical Mss of the Dodekapropheton. Reference is made however, both in the Introduction to the EDITION and in the present chapter, to a basic division of the Dodekapropheton into twenty-five lections in thirty-

DESCRIPTIONS OF THE LATER BIBLICAL MANUSCRIPTS 5

five Mss. It may be of interest to note the verses at which the lections usually begin:

Hs i 1, iv 1, vii 8, x 9, xiv 2, Jl ii 15, Am i 3, iv 1, vi 1, ix 1, Jon i 1, iv 9, Mi iii 9, vi 6, Na ii 1, Hb i 11, Zf i 1, iii 8, Hg ii 15, Sa iii 1, vi 9, viii 20, xi 10, xiv 6, Ml ii 3.

13a1 = Paris, National Library, Syr. Ms 9, fols. 281ª–301ª.

This Ms is unique among the Biblical Mss in that it contains not a continuous text of the Dodekapropheton but a catena of a hundred and eighty-five excerpts, ranging in length from a single word to one extract which includes the end of Obadiah, the whole of Jonah and the beginning of Micah. Details of the passages excerpted have been deposited in the Peshitta Institute. In the inscriptions and subscriptions of the individual books the preposition ܡܢ is generally used, but this was omitted by the original scribe in the subscriptions to Amos and Haggai.

The Ms is written in double columns in a neat Serta. One of its earliest owners wrote the date 1601 (i.e. A.D. 1290, cf. EMERTON, p. xxxi). There are large footnotes on the first page and at the end of Habakkuk and a number of small marginal notes. Prayers for the scribe are requested at the end of Hosea. A few short passages are obscure, and on a few pages the ends of lines are not legible. A number of suffixes and a few words are abbreviated.

There were originally twenty-eight omissions (seven of them mechanical) in this Ms; of these all but one are peculiar to the Ms and fourteen have been corrected. There are fifty-two readings peculiar to the Ms, twenty of which are certainly erroneous: ten of these are omissions of one or more letters. Five of these peculiar readings and four readings shared with other Mss could be explained as due to assimilation to the Syrohexapla. The Ms agrees with six readings of 7a1 in the second apparatus, two of these readings (Na ii 2, Zf ii 5) occuring also in 6h9, while at Sa xiv 9 the Ms agrees with 7a1 7k8 12d2 19g5.7 against all other Mss. A correction at Am ix 11 affords another agreement with 7a1. No relationship with any particular Ms is established, but the agreements with early Mss suggest that it derives directly or indirectly from an early exemplar and partially compensate for its somewhat careless character.

13d1 = Sharfet, Seminar Library, Fonds patriarchal, Ms R. 124, fols. 64^b–122^a.

This Ms contains an incomplete text of the Dodekapropheton, the following passages being missing: Hs i 7 ⟨syr⟩ ⟨syr⟩$^{1°}$–v 9 ⟨syr⟩, Jl i 13 ⟨syr⟩–iv 14 ⟨syr⟩, Am ix 5 ⟨syr⟩$^{1°}$–Ob 8 ⟨syr⟩$^{2°}$, Hg ii 18 ⟨syr⟩–Sa i 10 ⟨syr⟩, xi 17 ⟨syr⟩–xiv 10 ⟨syr⟩. Moreover the top corners are missing from Hs vii 5 to Jl i 5 and at Hg ii 2–3, 10–12, and a number of passages are indistinct. The date of the Ms is given in the LIST as A.D. 1218, but Sherwood (as cited in the LIST) gives it as A.D. 1206. The Ms is written in single columns in Serta. There is a tendency to elongate letters at the end of a line; alternatively the line is filled out with a dash or other device, or the beginning of the next line is anticipated. Several words are abbreviated, particularly ⟨syr⟩ to ⟨syr⟩ (e.g. Sa vi 13) and ⟨syr⟩ to ⟨syr⟩ (e.g. Sa viii 3). The usual twenty-five lectionary divisions are noted at the extant passages. There are several marginal notes, e.g. a gloss about Hosea's origin and burial at the end of Hosea.

There were originally thirteen omissions (eight of them mechanical) in this Ms; of these eleven have been corrected and ten are peculiar to this Ms. There are firty-three readings peculiar to the Ms, of which thirty-one are certainly erroneous; six have been corrected. Most of the peculiar readings concern the omission, addition, alteration or metathesis of single letters or the presence or absence of *seyāmē*; there are four dittographs and five cases of *adiunctio*. There is a slight tendency to assimilate to neighbouring passages. No relationship with any particular Ms is established. It appears to be a moderate copy of a good exemplar.

14/8a1 = Paris. National Library, Syr. Ms 341, fols. 176 and 184.

These two folios supplement 8a1 where it is not extant. They contain the following two passages: Jl i 10 ⟨syr⟩–Am ii 9 ⟨syr⟩ and Sa xi 6 ⟨syr⟩–Ml ii 8 ⟨syr⟩. The script is Nestorian Estrangela, and these folios like the rest of 8a1 are written with three columns to a page. The first letter of ⟨syr⟩ (Jl ii 19) is anticipated at the end of the previous line.

Five omissions (four of them mechanical) have been noted in this Ms, all of them peculiar to it and none of them corrected. There are twenty-five readings peculiar to the Ms, nineteen of which are certainly erroneous, mostly concerning single letters. No relationship with any particular Ms has been noted. This supplement is sadly inferior in quality to 8a1 itself.

14a1 = Paris, National Library, Syr. Ms 11, fols. 37ᵃ–67ᵃ.

This Ms contains a complete text of the Dodekapropheton. It is written in double columns in a neat Serta, with occasional Jacobite vowels. It is partially stained by water so that some words at the beginning or end of lines are obscured. The binding in some cases also obscures the beginning or end of a line. The usual division into twenty-five lections is noted in the margin. There are a number of corrections and some marginal notes, one at Na iii 8 being from Barhebraeus. At Am ii 14 the word ܪ̈ܚܡܝ is pointed with *reboṣo*, but a marginal note gives the pointing with *pethoḥo*. It is often not clear whether *shin* is preceded by *yudh* or not in this Ms.

This Ms belongs to 14a1 *fam* (see chapter 2, section B) and seems to have been the immediate exemplar for 17a1.3.4.5.10. There were originally seventeen mechanical and fourteen non-mechanical omissions in this Ms, but all except the common one at Sa iii 4 have been corrected. None of the others recurs outside 14a1 *fam*. There are four readings peculiar to the original Ms, of which the three that are certainly erroneous have all been corrected and the fourth is in any case an uncertain reading. One is a dittograph and the other three consist each of the omission of a single letter. As corrected this Ms offers a text very close to that of the main Peshitta tradition.

14d1 = Leiden, Peshitta Institute Ms 1, fols. 47ᵇ–87ᵃ.

This Ms contains a complete text of the Dodekapropheton, written in single columns in a neat Nestorian Estrangela, partly vocalized. It is dated A.D. 1306/7, and was copied from an exemplar at Mosul. The middle of each page is obscure and parts are often illegible. A space is often left before the final letter of a word at the end of a line. The plural ܫܢ̈ܝܐ is consistently written in this way with a single *mim*, and the proper name Nineveh is curiously written with *seyāmē*. Three words are combined into one at Sa xii 2. The word ܢܫܒܚܘܢܗ in the Inscr of Ob is abbreviated to ܢܫܒ. The usual twenty-five lectionary divisions are noted. There are several marginal notes, some of a massoretic character while two appear to be Carshuni glosses. One note at Am vi 14 seems to suggest revocalizing ܘܢܣܚܦܘܢ as an Aph'el. See further W. Baars' description in *VT* 13 (1963), pp. 260–264.

8   DESCRIPTIONS OF THE LATER BIBLICAL MANUSCRIPTS

Twenty-eight omissions, sixteen of them mechanical, were noted in this Ms; twenty-two are peculiar to the Ms, and twenty-four have been corrected. 14d1 supports ten readings in the Second Apparatus, five of them in company with many other Mss. At Zf i 12$2°$ it agrees with 8a1 and 12d2 against *ceteri* in a Syrohexaplaric reading. At Am iv 6 it agrees with 7a1 7k10 and 8a1 against *ceteri*, though the reading consists merely of the omission of *waw init*. In one case (Mi ii 13$2°$) the variant has been corrected.

Twenty-six readings peculiar to this Ms have been noted, of which sixteen are certainly erroneous (eight of them are dittographies) and nine have been corrected. Two of these readings appear to be assimilations to other passages: the addition of ܐܠܗܐ after ܡܪܝܐ in Jl ii 14 (cf Jon iii 9) and the reading ܒܝܬ ܐܠܗܐ for ܒܝܬܐ in Sa i 10 (cf i 11). The addition of *beth* before Bethel in Hs xii 5 is also found in the Syrohexapla. The reading of ܥܠ for ܥܡ in Mi vi 1 is found otherwise only in Barhebraeus' quotation of the text. The prefixing of ܐܝܟ to ܝܘܡܐ in Ml iii 19 is an interpretative gloss found also in the Targum Jonathan.

The Ms also has four readings shared with later Mss and four shared errors; the only one of any possible significance is the reading of ܥܠ before ܟܠ in Am ix 10, which occurs otherwise only in 16d1, but this could have arisen as a corruption of a dittograph. No significant relationship with any other particular Ms emerges from its agreements with other Mss. 14d1 may thus be regarded as a fairly good witness to the text, possessing some interesting readings peculiar to itself.

15/11d1 = London, British Library, Add. Ms 7152, fol. 77.

This is a supplement to 11d1, containing Ml iii 1 ܡܢ to the end. It is written in single columns but, unlikle the rest of 11d1, in Serta.

There is one non-mechanical omission peculiar to this Ms. There are also three readings, two of which are certainly erroneous, peculiar to it. Five readings, one of which is certainly erroneous, have been noted in which this Ms agrees with others. Each of these readings is found also in 19g5.7, and three of them also in 16g6, but two of the latter occur also in several other Mss, and there are several other readings in 16g6, 19g5 and 19g7 which do not occur in this Ms. Its exemplar probably belonged to the wider family to which 16g6 and 19g5.7 also belong (see chapter 2, section C).

DESCRIPTIONS OF THE LATER BIBLICAL MANUSCRIPTS

15d1 = Cambridge, University Library, Add. Ms 1965, fols. 57ᵇ–106ᵃ.

This Ms contains a complete text of the Dodekapropheton, written in single columns in a neat Nestorian Estrangela. It was written in A.D. 1493 by a scribe named Gabriel. The usual division into twenty-five lections is noted in the margin.

Apart from the common mechanical omission in Sa iii 4 only two omissions have been noted in this Ms: a mechanical one at Na i 5 shared exclusively with 15d3, and a non-mechanical one at Ml iii 13 peculiar to this Ms. The Ms supports three readings in the Second Apparatus and appears once in the list of shared readings in the later Mss. Eight readings peculiar to this Ms have been noted, of which six are certainly erroneous; one of the latter concerns the addition of *seyāmē* and the others all concern the omission, addition or alteration of single letters. One of the remaining peculiar readings is the substitution of *stat emph* for *stat abs*, and the other that of ܡܕܘܥܪ for ܡܕܘܥܪ in Ob 16.

It is clear from these data that this Ms is an unusually good witness to the standard text of the Peshiṭta, and that it has no particular affinity to any other Ms.

15d2 = Woodbrooke, S.O.C.L., Ming. syr. Ms 98, fols. 49ᵃ–100ᵇ.

This Ms contains a complete text of the Dodekapropheton, written in single columns in a very clear and handsome Nestorian Estrangela, with some Nestorian vowels. It was written in A.D. 1454. The usual division into twenty-five lections is noted in the margin. At Hs ii 17 a word is begun at the end of a line, and begun again on the new line. There is a marginal device at Sa ix 15.

The Ms is the common ancestor of 15d2 *fam*, itself part of a wider family including also 17d3 and 19d4 (see chapter 2, section D). There is only one mechanical omission peculiar to 15d2*, and this has been corrected. There are five readings peculiar to the Ms, four of them errors which have been corrected and the fifth the prefixing of *waw* to ܚܝ in Hs x 9. This Ms is therefore a careful copy, and in its corrected form presents a text fairly close to the main Peshiṭta tradition.

15d3 = Aqra, Chald. Bishopric, Ms I, 2°, fols. 54ᵃ–82ᵇ.

This Ms contains an incomplete text of the Dodekapropheton, the extant text beginning at Hs x 2 ܡܫܘܒܐ and ending at Sa xiii 9 ܐܪܡܠ. It is written in double columns in a neat Estrangela, though the Greek *theta* is sometimes used in place of *taw* (e.g. Hs x 10). The Ms is damaged at Sa viii 10–11, ix 8–10 and the photograph is in many places difficult to read. A device is occasionally used at the end of a line, and on six occasions a word is divided over two lines. The usual division into twenty-five lections is noted in the margin.

There are twenty omissions (eleven of them mechanical) in this Ms; sixteen are peculiar to the Ms, and nine have been corrected in more than one later hand. There are fifty-four readings, thirty-three of which are certainly erroneous, peculiar to this Ms; eight of the errors have been corrected, and one introduced by a corrector. Eight of these peculiar readings consist of the metathesis of two adjacent words. 15d3 supports six readings in the Second Apparatus and has six readings shared with one or more later Mss and five shared errors. No significant relationship has emerged with any particular Ms.

This Ms thus appears to be a rather poor and unintelligent copy of a fairly good but perhaps not very legible exemplar.

16/9a1 = Florence, Biblioteca Medicea Laurenziana, Or. Ms 58, fols. 141^a–145^b.

This is the completion in a sixteenth-century hand of the Dodekapropheton in 9a1 after the expiry of 9a1 itself at Hs xiv 6. Like 9a1 itself this Ms is written in double columns in a vowelless Serta in a small cramped hand. The Ms is uncertain or illegible in a number of places. Two words are joined at Jl ii 2. There is an abbreviation at Zf iii 17. A letter is extended to fill a line at Jl i 19, and there is a tendency to begin a word at the end of a line and to begin it again on the next line. At Mi iv 3 the word ܪܘܚܐ appears as a long dash ending in *'alaph* with the correct form supplied above. There are some marginal corrections.

This supplement does not reproduce the lost text of 9a1 but is copied from 12a1 or a Ms fairly closely related to 12a1 (see chapter 2, section A). The poor quality of this Ms is at once evident from its ninety peculiar erroneous readings, some of which are grotesque, e.g. the metathesis of ܠܐ ܗܘܐ in Mi i 1. There are seventeen further peculiar readings. There were fifty omissions (twenty of them mechanical) in the original Ms, thirteen of which have been corrected and three others marked by a *lacuna*. This Ms is of importance only as the main link between 12a1 and 17a6 *fam.*

16d1 = Rome, Vatican Library, Vat. sir. Ms 4, fols. 57ª–102ᵇ.

This Ms contains a complete text of the Dodekapropheton, written in single columns in a Nestorian Estrangela with some Nestorian vowels. It was written in A.D. 1556 by the presbyter Jacob. The Ms is obscured in a number of places. Line-fillers were sometimes used, while occasionally the final letters of a word were written in the margin. Many corrections have been made, a number of them by the original scribe *cal curr*. The usual division into twenty-five lections is noted in the margin, though the sixth is at Jl ii 12 instead of ii 15. There is a gloss on f. 58ᵇ.

This Ms belongs to the group 16d1 17d2 18d1 18g1 (see chapter 2, section E). There were originally fourteen omissions in this Ms, ten of them mechanical, but all except the general omission in Sa iii 4 have been corrected. There are sixty readings, of which fifty-four are certainly erroneous, peculiar to this Ms; twenty-nine of these have been corrected. The omission of one or more letters, especially at the end of a word, is common. There is also a slight tendency to add occasional words. As originally written therefore this Ms was a rather careless copy.

16g6 = Woodbrooke, S.O.C.L., Ming. syr. Ms 279, fols. 284ª–307ᵇ.

This Ms contains a complete text of the Dodekapropheton, written in double columns in a neat vowelless Serta. There are historical notes at the beginning of most of the Books, and a number of glosses (many in Carshuni). One at Na ii 6 is from Barhebraeus. Some of the usual lectionary divisions are noted; one is at Jl ii 23 instead of ii 15. A few letters are decorated. A line-filler is used in the middle of a line at Sa xi 5. ܡܣܟܢܐ is abbreviated to ܡܣܐ at Sa vii 1. *Beth* and *qoph* are sometimes hard to distinguish in this Ms. The photograph suggests that the Ms is damaged in a few places.

There are forty-three omissions (twenty-six of them mechanical) peculiar to this Ms, of which fifteen have been corrected. There are a hundred and eleven readings, seventy-one of them certainly erroneous, peculiar to this Ms, of which twelve have been corrected and two introduced by the corrector. A number of further errors were corrected *cal curr*. Despite a few agreements with the oldest Mss this Ms is thus of rather poor quality. Its relationship to 12a1 and to 19g5.7 is examined in chapter 2, section C.

17a1 = London, British Library, Egerton Ms 704, fols. 219ᵃ–234ᵇ.

This Ms contains a complete text of the Dodekapropheton, and was written according to the colophon by Abraham bar Jeshua from Qoṣur. No date is given in the colophon. The Ms is written in double columns in a small neat Serta with occasional Jacobite and Nestorian vowels. The usual division into twenty-five lections is noted in the margin. A device is sometimes used to fill out a line, while occasionally the beginning of a word is anticipated at the end of the previous line. At the end of Micah and Zephaniah the scribe adds a reference to the prayer of the prophet. The point over *rish* is omitted in ܪܥܝܗ in Zf i 4.

This Ms belongs to 14a1 *fam* (see chapter 2, section B) and is the best of the seventeenth century copies of 14a1. It has no significant relation with any particular Ms outside this family. There were originally ten mechanical and eleven non-mechanical omissions in this Ms, only three of which have been corrected, and twelve of which are peculiar to this Ms. The omissions tend to be of single words, whose absence makes nonsense of the remaining text. There are forty-five readings (of which twenty-two are certainly erroneous) peculiar to this Ms, of which only three have been corrected. Many of these peculiar readings concern the presence or absence of *seyāmē*, confusion between *dalath* and *rish*, or the omission, addition, alteration or metathesis of single letters. One marked characteristic is the replacement of a noun with a pronominal suffix by the noun in *stat emph*, often followed by ܕܝܠ with a suffix.

17a2 = Milan, Ambrosian Library, Ms A.145 Inf., fols. 238ᵃ–275ᵇ.

This Ms contains a complete text of the Dodekapropheton, written in double columns in a neat vowelless Serta. The part of the Ms containing the Dodekapropheton was written according to the colophon by Elia of Eden in A.D. 1615. The usual division into twenty-five lections is noted in the text. A few corrections have been made. A line-filler is used about thirty times. Occasionally the beginning of a word is anticipated at the end of the previous line. Suffixes are sometimes abbreviated. At Na iii 13 ܠܚܦܕܠܗܝܢ is divided over two lines after *dalath*.

This Ms belongs to 14a1 *fam* (see chapter 2, section B) and seems to have been copied directly from 17a4. There are fourteen mechanical and ten non-mechanical omissions in this Ms, of which only one has been corrected and nine are peculiar to this Ms. There are thirty-three readings (of which twenty-four are certainly erroneous) peculiar to this Ms, only one of which has been corrected. The vast majority of these peculiar readings concern the omission, addition, alteration or metathesis of single letters, or the presence or absence of *seyāmē*.

17a3 = Oxford, Bodleian Library, Bod. Or. Ms 141, fols. 367ª–391ᵇ.

This Ms contains a complete text of the Dodekapropheton, written in double columns in a neat Serta with occasional Nestorian vowels. It was completed in A.D. 1628. An examination of the handwriting of parts of this Ms where the scribe is identified demonstrates that the Dodekapropheton was written by Joseph and not by his assistant Cyriacus. The usual division into twenty-five lections is noted in the margin, though some of these notations are only partly visible, three seem to be missing, and that at Na ii 1 occurs two verses early. A later hand has noted some omissions, and added some variant readings (identified as *Greg*) and scholia of Barhebraeus. The scribe uses a number of devices to fill out a line, and occasionally attaches a flourish to a letter at the top or bottom of a column. He often anticipates the beginning of a word at the end of the previous line. The *dalath* following ܡܠܟ is often attached to it instead of to the following word. In Na i 11 ܡܘܬܒܗ is divided over two lines after *taw*. Several corrections have been made *cal curr*.

This Ms belongs to 14a1 *fam* (see chapter 2, section B) and seems to be a direct copy of 14a1. There are forty-four mechanical and forty non-mechanical omissions, of which only seven have been corrected and sixty-seven are peculiar to this Ms. There are no less than two hundred and seventy-nine readings peculiar to this Ms, of which one hundred and sixty-eight are certainly errors, and only twenty-three have been corrected. Two of the peculiar readings occur in alterations to the original text. These statistics confirm the poor reputation of this Ms.

17a4 = Oxford, Bodleian Library, Poc. Ms 391, fols. 436ª–457ᵇ.

This Ms contains a complete text of the Dodekapropheton, and was written according to the colophon by Elia of Eden in A.D. 1614. It is written in double columns in a fairly neat vowelless Serta. It has been corrected in a number of places probably by the original scribe before he copied 17a2 from it. The usual division into twenty-five lections is noted in the text. There are some Carshuni and massoretic notes in the margins. A line-filler is used on a number of occasions and also sometimes a device at the side of the page (e.g. at Jl ii 14). The beginning of a word is occasionally anticipated at the end of the previous line. ܘܡܫܠܡܐ is divided over two lines after *dalath* at Hs viii 3.

This Ms belongs to 14a1 *fam* (see chapter 2, section B), and seems to have been the immediate exemplar for 17a2. The relatively small number of readings peculiar to this Ms needs therefore to be balanced by the readings shared exclusively with 17a2. There were originally twelve mechanical and eight non-mechanical omissions in this Ms, but eight have been corrected. There are ten readings (of which six are certainly erroneous) peculiar to this Ms, and four of these have been corrected. Six of these peculiar readings concern the omission, addition, alteration or metathesis of single letters, two the metathesis of adjacent words, one the addition of ܫܠܝܛ after ܡܪܐ, and one the addition of *seyāmē*.

17a5 = Paris, National Library, Syr. Ms 6, fols. 343ª–368ᵇ.

This Ms contains a complete text of the Dodekapropheton, written in double columns in a neat Serta with some Jacobite vowels. It is tightly bound with the result that the beginnings and ends of some lines are not visible on the photograph. Some of the usual notes of the division into twenty-five lections occur in the margin; doubtless the others are concealed by the binding. The Ms has been carefully corrected in many places by a later hand. There is a marginal gloss at Mi i 1 on the name "Morashtite", explaining it as Lachish. A line-filler is occasionally used.

This Ms belongs to 14a1 *fam* (see chapter 2, section B). There were originally twenty-six mechanical and seven non-mechanical omissions in this Ms, twenty-four being peculiar to it; sixteen have been corrected. There are forty-five readings (of which twenty-six are certainly erroneous) peculiar to this Ms. Nine of these have been corrected, but three occur in alterations to the original Ms. Nine of the peculiar readings concern initial *waw* (usually added), and three of the errors are dittographs.

17a6 = Paris, National Library, Syr. Ms 8, fols. 80ᵇ–97ª.

This Ms contains a complete text of the Dodekapropheton, written in double columns in a neat vowelless Serta. The hypothesis that it was written by Sergius Risius (*cf* EMERTON, p. xxiv) is confirmed, as in the case of Exodus (*cf* KOSTER, p. 24), by a comparison of its handwriting with that of 17a7-9. A line-filler is sometimes used. Space has been left for the inscriptions and subscriptions to the individual Books, but these have not been supplied. The first word of a page is sometimes anticipated at the foot of the previous page, and occasionally (e.g. Jl i 7) not then repeated at the top of the new page. The photograph of Hs ii 5-20 is very obscure.

This Ms belongs to 9a1 *fam*, and a full textual description is given in chapter 2, section A6.

17a7 = Rome, Biblioteca Casanatense, Ms 194, fols. 363^a-380^b.

This Ms contains a complete text of the Dodekapropheton, written by Sergius Risius in double columns in a neat vowelless Serta. The tops of some of the pages are obscure in the photograph. The beginnings of two or three lines are missing at Ml ii 13-14. There is an extensive apparatus of variant readings in the lower margin. Some of the usual lectionary divisions are noted; one is at Sa viii 18 instead of at viii 20. There are some explanatory glosses. A line-filler is used a number of times. There is a tendency to attach *dalath* to ܡܠܟܐ instead of the following word.

This Ms belongs to 9a1 *fam*, and a full textual description is given in chapter 2, section A4.

17a8 = Rome, Vatican Library, Vat. sir. Ms 7, fols. 424^a-441^b.

This Ms contains a complete text of the Dodekapropheton, written by Sergius Risius in double columns in a neat vowelless Serta. The photograph is obscure in a number of places, particularly at the top of the page. There is an extensive apparatus of variant readings in the lower margin. The usual lectionary divisions are noted in the margin; as in 17a7 one is at Sa viii 18 instead of at viii 20. There are some explanatory glosses. The Subscription to Sa was omitted in the text and added in the side margin, while that to Ml was relegated to the lower margin, though the General Subscription was included in the text. There is a line-filler at Sa xii 8. At Hs xi 4 ܐܘܪ is filled out to complete the line thus: ܐܘܪ‌ܐ. There is a correction *cal curr* at Zf iii 8. Words are twice divided over two lines, and abbreviations are occasionally used in the Subscriptions.

This Ms belongs to 9a1 *fam*, and a full textual description is given in chapter 2, section A3.

17a9 = Rome, Vatican Library, Vat. sir. Ms 8, fols. 318ᵇ–333ᵃ.

This Ms contains a complete text of the Dodekapropheton, written by Sergius Risius in double columns in a neat vowelless Serta. It subsequently belonged to Abraham Ecchellensis the Maronite. An extra page (f. 359ᵃ) duplicates Sa ix 12 ܪܬܐܘܣܐ.–xi 5 ܝܐܝܡ, and is designated 17a9 *bis*. The photograph is in many places obscure and some readings are uncertain. Space has been left for the inscriptions and subscriptions to the individual Books, but these have not been supplied.

This Ms belongs to 9a1 *fam*, and a full textual description is given in chapter 2, section A5.

17a10 = Rome, Vatican Library, Vat. sir. Ms 258, fols. 345ᵃ–366ᵇ.

This Ms contains a complete text of the Dodekapropheton, written in double columns in a neat vowelless Serta. Nothing is known of the provenance of this Ms beyond the fact that it was transferred to new ownership in A.D. 1697. The Ms as it appeared on the microfilm was obscured by many offsets, which resulted in a number of readings not being clear. The usual lectionary divisions are noted in the margin. A line-filler is occasionally used. ܡܫܘܬܐ is abbreviated to ܡܫܘ in the inscription to Ob. Words are sometimes wrongly divided: e.g. at Sa viii 19 ܘܠܐܪܬܐ is divided over two lines after the first *dalath*, while at Am iii 14 ܥܠ ܡܕܒܚܐ is written as a single word.

This Ms belongs to 14a1 *fam* (see chapter 2, section B). There were originally thirty-nine omissions (twenty-seven of them mechanical) in this Ms; twenty-five are peculiar to this Ms, and seven have been corrected in a handwriting similar to or identical with that of the original copyist. The correction at Zf i 14 contains the reading ܬܒ in place of ܠܒ, a reading attested otherwise only in 17a2.4. This suggests that after making his copy from 14a1 the scribe may have checked it against 17a2 or 17a4 and supplied from that source a few of the passages he had originally omitted. There are a hundred and twenty-three readings (a hundred of which are clearly erroneous) peculiar to this Ms, as well as two further peculiar readings introduced by a later hand. The relatively large number of omissions and peculiar readings indicates the poor quality of this Ms.

DESCRIPTIONS OF THE LATER BIBLICAL MANUSCRIPTS   17

17a11 = Rome, Vatican Library, Vat. sir. Ms 461, fols. 372ª–388ᵇ.

This Ms contains a complete text of the Dodekapropheton, written in double columns in a neat vowelless Serta. It is however sometimes difficult to distinguish respectively between *beth* and *ʿe* and between *qoph* and *shin*. The Ms was written at Rome in A.D. 1666 by Niʿmat Ḥaṣruni. The copy is careless, but some corrections have been made *cal curr*. A line-filler is frequently used.

This Ms belongs to 9a1 *fam*, and a full textual description is given in chapter 2, section A5.

17d1 = Berlin, German State Library, Ms. or. fol. 2695, fols. 42ᵇ–74ᵇ.

This Ms, apart from two *lacunae* (Jl ii 19 ܚܝܘܬܐ–Am iii 2 ܐܪܝܐ and Sa viii 18 ܝܬܒܝ–Ml *fin*) contains a complete text of the Dodekapropheton, written in A.D. 1691. It is written in single columns in a neat but rather small Nestorian Estrangela with some Nestorian vowels. The Ms is obscured by discoloration in a number of passages. Much of Jon iii 7–8 is lost, where a large patch seems to have been stuck over the Ms. There are a number of abbreviations (indicated by a point below rather than a dash above), and a number of corrections have been made *cal curr*. The usual lectionary divisions are noted in the margin.

There were originally thirty-four omissions (sixteen of them mechanical) in this Ms; twenty-seven are peculiar to the Ms, and five have been corrected. There are forty-six readings (of which thirty-six are certainly erroneous) peculiar to this Ms; ten have been corrected. There are seven dittographies and eight transpositions of adjacent words; several other peculiar readings consist of additional words. The Ms agrees with eight readings in the Second Apparatus, and figures six times in the list of shared readings in the later Mss and five times in the list of shared errors. There is no pattern of agreement with any particular Ms; the omission of *mim* in ܣܘܣܘܬܐ in Jl i 5, found otherwise only in 17d4*, is probably a coincidence. The Ms is thus a rather poor copy, with no particular affiliation to any of the families or groups surveyed in chapter 2.

The two *lacunae* in 17d1 have been supplied by a later hand (19/17d1), and 19d3 was probably used as the exemplar for this supplement (see chapter 2, section D5). This supplement also is written in Nestorian Estrangela with some Nestorian vowels.

17d2 = Cambridge, University Library, Ms. Oo I.7, fols. 49ᵃ–89ᵃ.

This Ms contains a complete text of the Dodekapropheton, written in single columns in a clear Nestorian Estrangela with some Nestorian vowels. It was written by a scribe named George in A.D. 1682. The usual lectionary divisions are noted in the margin, while chapter divisions are also noted in the text. The latter sometimes occur in strange places, e.g. in Mi iii 1 after the opening ܐܡܪܒ, while chapter eight of Amos begins at vii 7! Several corrections have been made *cal curr*, while other corrections have been made in a small neat later hand, which has also added some explanatory glosses.

This Ms belongs to the group 16d1 17d2 18d1 18g1 (see chapter 2, section E), and is the best representative of the group. There were originally nine omissions (six of them mechanical) in this Ms; six have been corrected, and all except the general omission in Sa iii 4 are peculiar to the Ms. There are twenty-six readings (all but three of which are certainly erroneous) peculiar to this Ms; nine have been corrected. One additional peculiar reading has been added as a marginal variant by the later hand. Most of the peculiar readings consist of the omission, addition or alteration of single letters, though in two cases a word has been added.

17d3 = Baghdad, Library of the Chaldean Patriarchate, Ms 119, fols. 38ᵇ–78ᵃ.

This Ms contains an incomplete text of the Dodekapropheton, lacking Hs i 1 ܒ¹°–ii 15 ܫܒܝܘ̈ܗܝ and xii 10 ܐܟܬܒܘ–xiv 9 ܐܒܝܘܢܐ܆, and Ml i 10 ܠܟ–iii 3 ܚܡܝܪܐ and iii 10 ,ܒܝܬܝ–14 ܚܝܠܬܢܐ. The text is also slightly obscured by a tear at Hs vii 6–10 and viii 4–8. The Ms is written in single columns in a small neat Nestorian Estrangela with some Nestorian vowels. The usual lectionary divisions are noted in the margin.

This Ms is closely related to 15d2 *fam* (see chapter 2, section D). There are seven omissions (four of them mechanical) peculiar to this Ms, of which only one has been corrected. There are nine readings (all but one certainly erroneous) peculiar to this Ms; three of them have been corrected. Most of the peculiar readings concern the omission or alteration of single letters or a suffix or the transposition of adjacent words; two are dittographies.

17d4 = Woodbrooke, S.O.C.L., Ming. syr. Ms 64, fols. 40ᵇ–72ᵃ.

This Ms contains a complete text of the Dodekapropheton, except for Am i 8 ܒܝܘܡ ܗܘ ... iii 4 ܕܐܬܐ which has been supplied by a later hand (18/17d4). The original Ms was written by the deacon Sunday, but the part of the colophon which presumably contained the date has been deliberately obliterated. The Ms is written throughout in single columns in a small neat Nestorian Estrangela with some Nestorian vowels. The photograph is obscure in a number of places, and the beginnings or ends of lines are in places sewn into the binding. The copyist had a tendency to omit individual letters, which are then added above. At Am ix 4 ܨܠܡܝܗܘܢ is divided over two lines after *dalath*. The usual lectionary divisions are noted in the margin. Some of the names of the individual prophetic Books at the top of the page are incorrect, e.g. the page beginning at Am iii 5 is headed Joel! There is an Arabic note on f. 48ᵃ.

This Ms belongs to 15d2 *fam* (see chapter 2, section D). There are nineteen omissions (seven of them mechanical) peculiar to this Ms; seven have been corrected. There are also forty-four readings (all but seven certainly erroneous) peculiar to the Ms; twenty-one of these have been corrected. Most of the peculiar readings concern the presence or absence of *seyāmē*, or the omission, addition, alteration or metathesis of single letters. This Ms is thus a poor copy of a relatively good Ms (15d2).

There are very few textual data to make it possible to evaluate the supplement 18/17d4. Its sole peculiar reading is an apparent substitution of *beth init* for *dalath init* in ܢܚܠܐ in Am i 13. One can only infer that the supplementer was a careful copyist.

17d5 = Woodbrooke, S.O.C.L., Ming. syr. Ms 489, fols. 43ᵈ⁽ˢⁱᶜ⁾–81ᵇ.

This Ms contains a complete text of the Dodekapropheton, written in single columns in a clear and elegant Nestorian Estrangela, fully vocalized with Nestorian vowels. The Ms was written in Alḳosh by the priest Israel and completed in A.D. 1674. It was renovated by the deacon Abraham in the mid-nineteenth century. The inscriptions and subscriptions to the individual prophetic Books are for the most part written in slightly larger characters than the text. The usual lectionary divisions are noted in the margin. There is a line-filler at Sa ix 9, but a space is sometimes left before the final letter of the last word in a line.

Discoloration has obscured part of Sa iv 4–Ml i 5. There is an explanatory gloss at Hs iii 3 and a massoretic note at the end of most of the individual prophetic Books.

This Ms belongs to the group 17d5 18d2 19d1 (see chapter 2, section F), and has no significant relationship with any other particular Ms, though it does contain several readings attested also in the oldest Mss but not attested in 18d2 or 19d1. There were originally twenty-five omissions (fourteen of them mechanical) in this Ms; nine have been corrected and thirteen are peculiar to this Ms. There are eighty-six readings (of which forty-four are certainly erroneous) peculiar to this Ms; nine of these have been corrected. There is a tendency to alter the usual word order, and there are four dittographies. There is a good deal of carelessness in this Ms, but some of its distinctive readings are certainly not the result of carelessness (see examples in chapter 2, section F).

18d1 = Cambridge, University Library Ms OO I.18, fols. 253^b–312^a.

This Ms contains a complete text of the Dodekapropheton, written in single columns in a small Nestorian Estrangela with Nestorian vowels. The inscriptions and subscriptions to the individual prophetic Books are written in large characters and ornamented; they are however missing after the inscription to Micah, though space has been left for their insertion. Chapter divisions are noted, but not lectionary divisions. *Seyāmē* are often omitted, though sometimes the vocalization shows that a plural is intended. A number of errors have been corrected *cal curr*. Spaces are often left in the middle of words; the place name ܐܫܟܢܙ at Zf ii 4 is divided over two lines after the *'alaph*. It is often difficult to distinguish between *lamadh* and *'e* or between *dalath* and *waw*. A line-filler is occasionally used. The marginal corrections at Hs i 6–7 probably and at Jon iv 5 certainly were made by a later hand.

This Ms belongs to the group 16d1 17d2 18d1 18g1 (see chapter 2, section E). There are eight omissions (two of them substantial mechanical omissions) peculiar to this Ms, of which two have been corrected. There are forty-five readings (of which thirty-three are certainly erroneous) peculiar to this Ms; eleven of these have been corrected. A further peculiar reading was introduced by the corrector. Most of the peculiar readings concern the omission, addition or

DESCRIPTIONS OF THE LATER BIBLICAL MANUSCRIPTS 21

alteration of single letters, three are metatheses of adjacent words and two are dittographies.

18d2 = Baghdad, Library of the Chaldaean Patriarchate, Ms 113, fols. 59ª–108ª.

This Ms contains a complete text of the Dodekapropheton, written in single columns in a small neat Nestorian Estrangela with some Nestorian vowels. It was written in A.D. 1701. The usual lectionary divisions are noted in the margin. There are also a number of massoretic notes, including one at the end of each prophetic Book. Some explanatory glosses in the margin are encircled. A line-filler is occasionally used. The names Israel and Judah are usually spelt without prosthetic *'alaph*, but this has been intermittently added above.

This Ms belongs to the group 17d5 18d2 19d1 (see chapter 2, section F). There were originally twenty-two omissions (thirteen of them mechanical) in this Ms; seventeen have been corrected and twelve are peculiar to this Ms. The only reading peculiar to this Ms occurs in the correction of one of these omissions (that of ܡܒܥܐ 2° at Am v 18), where an apparently later hand supplied ܡܗܝ (*vid*). Apart from the omissions this is a careful copy.

18g1 = Amsterdam, University Library, Ms 47 (I F 19), fols. 70ª–179ª.

This Ms contains a complete text of the Dodekapropheton, written in single columns in a large clear Nestorian Estrangela with Nestorian vowels. Hs viii 11–14 and Am iii 8–11 are written in elongated characters. The Ms gives the impression of having been copied from an exemplar which was sometimes not very clear by a scribe who was unfamiliar with the language. There are chapter divisions (that at Mi iii 1 occurring after the opening ܐܡܪܘ) but no lectionary divisions. A line-filler is sometimes used. The first word on a page is often a repetition of the last word on the previous page. *Seyāmē* are often omitted, though the vocalization often indicates that a plural is intended. Words are sometimes divided over two lines. A number of errors have been corrected *cal curr*; the correction of an error at Na iii 11 at least is by a later hand.

This Ms belongs to the group 16d1 17d2 18d1 18g1 (see chapter 2, section E). There are four omissions (two of them mechanical) peculiar to this Ms; three of them have been corrected. There are ninety-nine readings (of which eighty-one are certainly erroneous) peculiar to this Ms; twenty-two of these have been corrected. Many concern the omission, addition or alteration of single letters; there are also a number of dittographies.

18 < 13dt1 = Manchester, John Rylands Library, Rylands Syr. Ms 4, fols. 28ᵃ–61ᵃ.

This Ms contains a complete text of the Dodekapropheton, written in single columns in a neat vowelless Nestorian Estrangela. It was written in Peking in A.D. 1727 and copied from a thirteenth century Ms. now lost. Gottstein (B.J.R.L. 37, p. 431) claims that the copy was made carefully, but the many solecisms and erratic use of diacritic points suggest both that the copyist's grasp of the language was very limited and that his exemplar was in places difficult to decipher and perhaps faded. *Beth, qoph* and *shin* seem to be confused at times. The usual lectionary divisions are noted in the margin. There is a line-filler at Ob 8 and a large device in the margin at Am viii 1. Words are sometimes wrongly divided. Some of the more bizarre readings are: ܟܣܝܢܐ for ܟܣܝܐ (Hs ii 20), ܗܝܐ for ܗܘ (Am i 4), ܐܡܪ for ܐܡܪ (Am vii 8), ܒ ܢܝܢܘܐ for ܢܝܢܘܐ (Jon i 2), ܚܕ for ܚܕ (Jon iv 8), ܘܢܗܪܘܢ for ܢܗܪܐ (Na ii 4), ܣܡܐ for ܣܡܝܐ (Sa i 17). In view of readings of this nature it was decided that only those readings in this Ms which occur in at least one other Ms should be recorded, and for this reason it is impossible to provide an analysis of omissions and readings peculiar to this Ms. The photograph is obscure in places, especially at the top of some pages.

Only two omissions are recorded for this Ms: the common mechanical omission at Sa iii 4 and a non-mechanical omission (of the word ܬܘܒ at Am vii 13) shared with 17d1. The Ms supports seven readings in the second apparatus, and figures eight times in the list of shared readings in the later Mss and ten times in the list of shared errors. Fifteen of these readings are simply cases of the absence of *seyāmē*. No significant relationship with any particular Ms emerges from these data. This is a very poor Ms, the worst Biblical Ms of the Dodekapropheton.

19d1 = Berlin, German State Library, Ms or. fol. 3122, fols. 56ᵃ–103ᵇ.

This Ms contains a complete text of the Dodekapropheton, written in single columns in a clear Nestorian Estrangela with full Nestorian vocalization. The Ms was written in A.D. 1813. The usual lectionary divisions are noted in the margin. There is a massoretic note at the end of each prophetic Book. There are also some massoretic notes and explanatory glosses in the margin. Some corrections have been made *cal curr*. A line-filler is used before the last word in the line at Sa xi 12. The names Israel and Judah are usually spelt without prosthetic *'alaph*, but this has been intermittently added above.

This Ms belongs to the group 17d5 18d2 19d1 (see chapter 2, section F); it is probably the best representative of the group. There were originally five omissions in this Ms; three have been corrected and two are peculiar to the Ms. There are eight readings (of which six are certainly erroneous) peculiar to this Ms; three have been corrected. Two of these readings concern the alteration of a single letter, two the addition of an extra word, two the addition of *seyāmē*, and two are dittographies. The relatively low numbers of peculiar omissions and readings indicate that this is a fairly good Ms.

19d2 = London, British Library, Add. Ms 7151, fols. 44^b–80^b.

This Ms contains a complete text of the Dodekapropheton, written in single columns in Nestorian Estrangela with some Nestorian vowels. The Ms was written in A.D. 1812 by two copyists: Joseph wrote most of the Dodekapropheton, but his pupil Simon wrote the last four folios (from Sa x 11 ܡܫܪܐ). The pupil's work is not only in a smaller hand, but he writes the name Israel with prosthetic *'alaph* unlike his master. There is an ascription of praise and a prayer for the scribe at the end of Ml. The usual lectionary divisions are noted in the margin.

This Ms belongs to 15d2 *fam* (see chapter 2, section D). There were originally twenty-four omissions (twelve of them mechanical) in this Ms; eighteen have been corrected and twelve are peculiar to this Ms. There are twenty-nine readings (fourteen of which are certainly erroneous) peculiar to this Ms; six have been corrected. Some of these peculiar readings are distinctive (see chapter 2, section D4). This Ms is thus a rather poor copy.

19d3 = London, British Library, Or. Ms 4395, fols. 50^b–90^b.

This Ms contains a complete text of the Dodekapropheton, written in single columns in a large clear Nestorian Estrangela with practically full Nestorian vocalization. It was written in A.D. 1813. A few words in Ml iii 14–15 have perished, and there are a few corrections in a later hand. The usual lectionary divisions (omitting however those at Hs xiv 2 and Jon i 1) are noted in the margin. Two words are divided over two lines: ܡܙܕܟܝܢܗ after the second *waw* at Na ii 13 and ܡܬܬܒܪܝܢ after the second *taw* at Sa xii 10. ܒܢܝܗ is abbreviated to ܒܢܝ. in the inscription to Ml.

This Ms belongs to 15d2 *fam* (see chapter 2, section D). There are fifteen omissions (nine of them mechanical) peculiar to this Ms, of which nine have been corrected. Three others (two of them mechanical) recur only in 19/17d1, which was probably copied from this Ms (see chapter 2, section D5). There are nine readings (four of them certainly erroneous) peculiar to this Ms, none of which have been corrected. Most of them concern the omission, addition or alteration of single letters. This Ms is thus of only moderate quality.

19d4 = Woodbrooke, S.O.C.L., Ming. syr. Ms 427, fols. 51ª–92ᵇ.

This Ms contains a complete text of the Dodekapropheton, written in single columns in a neat Nestorian Estrangela with fairly full Nestorian vocalization. It was written in A.D. 1825 by the priest Gabriel, who adds a doxology (ܘܠܗ ܫܘܒܚܐ) at the end. The usual lectionary divisions are noted in the margin. Occasional corrections have been made *cal curr*. The last four words of Am i 8 are lost in damage to the text, and there is some corresponding loss and obscurity at Am ii 5f. There are marginal glosses in a later hand at Sa ix 9 and xi 13 referring respectively to the triumphal entry of Jesus and to Judas Iscariot. The first seven words of Am v 12 (at the top of f. 64ª) are written again above without any variants in a later very bad hand!

This Ms is closely related to 15d2 *fam* (see chapter 2, section D). There are nine omissions (four of them mechanical) peculiar to this Ms; three have been corrected. There are eight readings (all but one certainly erroneous) peculiar to this Ms; one has been corrected and three are dittographies.

19g5 = Rome, Vatican Library, Borg. sir. Ms 116, fols. 152ª–183ᵇ.

This Ms contains a complete text of the Dodekapropheton, written in single columns in a clear Serta with occasional Jacobite and Nestorian vowels. It was written in A.D. 1868. Line-fillers are occasionally used, and a word is sometimes divided over two lines with a mark underneath each half to indicate continuity. There are extra scribal notes at the beginning and end, and a request for prayer for the wretched scribe at the end of Micah! There are a number of entries in more than one later hand, though they are not always easy to distinguish and all are written in Serta (with occasional Jacobite or Nestorian vowels). These supply omissions or alter readings in 19g5*; in a number of cases alternative readings are introduced by ܣܐ, indicating that they are derived from another exemplar.

There are thirty-three omissions (sixteen of them mechanical) peculiar to this Ms; twenty-five have been corrected. There are eighty-eight readings (of which sixty-three are certainly erroneous) peculiar to this Ms; twenty-five have been corrected, and five were introduced by the correctors. The poor quality of this Ms is enhanced when the large number of omissions and readings shared exclusively with 19g7 is also taken into account. The relationship of this Ms to 16g6 and 19g7 is examined in chapter 2, section C.

> 19g7 = Woodbrooke, S.O.C.L., Ming. syr. Ms 63, fols. 189^b–218^b.

This Ms contains a complete text of the Dodekapropheton, written in double columns in a clear Serta with occasional Jacobite and Nestorian vowels. It was written by the deacon John in A.D. 1821. The photograph is obscure at a number of points in Mi, Na, Hb and Zf. Not infrequently the last two or three letters of a word at the end of a line are written above. Words are sometimes divided over two lines. A word is sometimes begun at the end of a line and begun afresh at the beginning of the next line. There are occasional ornamental devices in the margin or attached to e.g. a final *lamadh*. Some corrections have been made in a later Serta hand. There are explanatory glosses from Barhebraeus at Hs iii 2, Jl Inscr and Mi iv 8. There are also some Carshuni glosses.

There are eighteen omissions (four of them mechanical) peculiar to this Ms; six have been corrected. There are sixty-eight readings (of which forty-nine are certainly erroneous) peculiar to this Ms; eight have been corrected. The Ms is thus a slight better copy than 19g5 of their common exemplar, but it has received less correction than 19g5. The relationship of this Ms to 16g6 and 19g5 is examined in chapter 2, section C.

2
Families and Groups

ALL but seven of the later Mss belong to one or other of the six families and groups considered below. Two of the pre-thirteenth century Mss, 9a1 and 12a1, also belong to the first of these families. A few preliminary remarks will be appropriate before we examine the relationships between the several Mss.

An exhaustive survey of the evidence for the relationships between the several Mss in these families and groups has not been attempted here. For one thing the sheer bulk of the evidence would make such a survey cumbersome. A more positive reason is that the textual significance of some agreements may be very small indeed. The same mechanical omission for instance may very well occur in two unrelated Mss for no other reason than the ease with which it can arise in the process of copying. Orthographic variants and variants in the spelling of proper names may often reflect the habitual practice of the copyist rather than reproduce his exemplar. Variations in the use of diacritic points are subject to the further disadvantage that it is often by no means a simple matter to determine their significance. Variants of these kinds have therefore been largely ignored in this chapter.

What criteria have been used to determine relationships between Mss? Shared omissions, particularly of a non-mechanical nature, are often indicative of a relationship. In fact, a group of common omissions is usually found in Mss related in a *fam*, though exceptions may be found in Sections B and E. The greatest value of omissions is however sometimes of a negative kind, in that a Ms containing uncorrected omissions cannot readily be held to be at any rate the sole exemplar of another Ms in which these omissions do not occur.

Shared readings of a distinctive kind, particularly non-mechanical errors, may also point strongly to a direct relationship, and occasionally an error can only be explained satisfactorily in terms of dependence on a particular exemplar. This may be seen in the evidence for the dependence respectively of 17a3 on 14a1 and of 17d4 on 15d2 set out in Sections B3 and D3. Conversely a distinctive reading can prove that a Ms cannot have been the sole exemplar of another Ms which preserves the ordinary reading.

In general a number of shared omissions, particularly of a non-mechanical nature, and distinctive readings, particularly of an erroneous nature, found exclusively in common in two or more Mss points strongly to a direct relationship between them. This however has to be qualified in two directions. In the first place the common ancestor of a *fam* may prove difficult to identify if its quality is good, or if it has been corrected early and carefully. An example of this may be seen in the case of 14a1. On the other hand even a large number of common omissions and distinctive readings does not prove direct dependence of one Ms on another. Each case has to be considered on its merits, and each apparent case of direct dependence tested for uncorrected omissions and distinctive peculiar readings in the putative exemplar which would disprove direct dependence. Examples may be seen in the relationships between 19g5 and 19g7 and between 18d1 and 18g1 considered respectively in Sections C3 and E3.

The term *fam* has been used sparingly in this chapter, and so far as possible restricted to cases where the dependence of all other members of a *fam* on the ancestor can be demonstrated beyond reasonable doubt. The other groups consist of Mss which almost certainly belong to a *fam* whose ancestor is no longer available to us, and which is probably considerably larger than the group under consideration. The term 16d1 *fam* for instance has not been used to describe the Mss considered in Section E, because it is clear that although 16d1 is the oldest Ms of this group available to us it cannot itself be the ancestor of any of the other Mss in the group. On the other hand 15d2 *fam* denotes a branch within a larger but fairly close-knit *fam* which also includes 17d3 and 19d4; the ancestor however of this larger *fam* is not available to us.

The Mss considered in Sections A, B and C have already been examined in relation to other books of the Old Testament. The evidence of the Dodekapropheton tends to confirm and supplement conclusions already reached by other scholars concerning these Mss. The Mss considered in Sections D, E and F on the other hand for the most part contain only the prophetic books. Some of these, in particular three of the four considered in Section E, were examined in relation to Isaiah by DIETTRICH. He examined also two of the Mss considered in Section D (19d2 and 19d3), noting that they had thirty readings in common. While however this is consistent with the close relationship noted between these two Mss in the Dodekapropheton in Section D4, its significance can hardly be assessed in isolation from the remaining Mss in the group and particularly within 15d2 *fam*. None of the Mss considered in Section F was examined by Diettrich.

A. 9a1 *fam*: (12a1) (16/)9a1 17a6–9.11

1. Introduction

Fundamental work has been done on these Mss by DIRKSEN (pp. 59–70) and KOSTER (pp. 404–427). There were however unusual factors in both Judges and Exodus, and this is the case also in the Dodekapropheton. In Judges 17a6 is missing and 17a11 has a different textual affiliation, but the basic relationship between 17a7–9 and 9a1 is clear: 17a8 was copied from 9a1, and both 17a7 and (slightly later) 17a9 were copied from 17a8. In Exodus 9a1 itself is missing, and the basic source of 17a6–9.11 is 16b3. In the Dodekapropheton 9a1 is extant only for Hs i 1–xiv 6, though the remainder of the text has been supplied by a later hand (16/9a1) in a text-form closely related to that of 12a1.

The four Mss 17a6–9 were all copied by Sergius Risius. 17a8, particularly in its uncorrected form, has a number of exclusive agreements with (16/)9a1, making it practically certain that as in Judges 17a8 was copied directly from (16/)9a1. The copy however was not made uncritically. Risius noted a considerable number of variant readings at the foot of the page (17a8^{mg}), and some of these in fact record the reading of (16/)9a1 when he has preferred to follow another exemplar in his text. Each of Risius' other copies (17a6.7.9) contains a number of peculiar readings (specially omissions) which make it impossible for it to have been the exemplar of any of the others; each of these must therefore be regarded as a copy of 17a8. 17a11 on the other hand, which was copied twenty-eight years after Risius' death, has a number of exclusive agreements with 17a9, which make it probable that it was copied from that Ms.

The five Mss 17a6–9.11 have an overwhelmingly common text-form. They have fifty-seven readings exclusively common to themselves, a further eighty-seven exclusively common to themselves and (16/)9a1, and a further thirty-three exclusively common to themselves, 12a1 and 16/9a1. These figures would be nearly doubled by the inclusion of passages where these Mss have a common reading found also in Mss outside the *fam*, and of passages where one or occasionally two of the seventeenth century Mss deviate from the reading of the *fam*. In the preparation of the EDITION the siglum 17a6 *fam* was used to denote readings common to 17a6–9.11 from the cessation of 9a1 at Hs xiv 6, and within Hs i 1–xiv 6 when they clearly differed from that of 9a1. This siglum was adopted for convenience only, without prejudice to the question of the mutual relationship of Mss within 17a6 *fam*; it is now clear that 17a8 is to be regarded as the parent of 17a6 *fam*. With regard to the seventeen variants in Hs i 1–xiv 6 included under the siglum 9a1 *fam* (9a1 *l.n.*) or 9a1 *fam* (9a1 *vid*) (cf. EDITION, p. XV), it may now be noted that in eleven of these passages (Hs ii 25, iv 4, 13, 14, viii 1, 2, x 6, 15$^{1°}$, xi 1, 8 *bis*) 17a8^{mg} gives the usual reading. There is thus a presumption that the *fam* reading in 17a8^{txt} was also the reading of 9a1. For the six remaining passages (Hs v 10 *bis*, 11, vii 16, x 15$^{2°}$, xi 11) there are no variants recorded in the margin of 17a8. One can only note that in general within Hs i 1–xiv 6 17a8 agrees certainly with twenty and probably with another six unusual readings of 9a1, while it diverges from 9a1 clearly fifteen times and probably once more. It seems therefore that the six readings in question have a slightly greater chance of being those of 9a1 than not, though there can of course be no certainty in any particular case.

A complete analysis of the distinctive readings of this *fam* is neither necessary nor practical. What follows is a brief examination of the relationship between 12a1 and 16/9a1, an examination of 17a8^{txt} and 17a8^{mg} and of the exemplars used by Risius in writing this Ms, and a brief examination of the remaining Mss in the *fam*.

2. The relationship between 12a1 and 16/9a1

The many passages in both these Mss where the reading is illegible prevent a complete analysis of the relationship between them, but there is sufficient evidence to make the relationship clear beyond serious doubt.

In Hs i 1–xiv 6, where 9a1 is extant, each Ms has a substantial number of readings which do not occur in the other. The only reading they have in common is at Hs iv 15, where they agree with *ceteri* in reading ܐܝܢܘܗܝ against the ܐܢܘܗܝ of 7a1 8a1 and 12d1. There is clearly no evidence for any relationship between 9a1 and 12a1.

After the expiry of 9a1 at Hs xiv 6 the picture is quite different. Seven of the nine uncorrected omissions in 12a1 recur in 16/9a1. There are also ninety readings common to the two Mss, including the thirty-three exclusively common to these Mss and 17a6 *fam*. The remaining uncorrected omissions in 12a1 (ܟܝܐ ... ܟܐܘܡ in Am i 9 and ܟܐܪ ܒܚܡܣ in Hb i 6) would be immediately apparent to a copyist following the sense of the passage, and the first in particular could very easily be supplied from the context. There are a few unusual readings in 12a1, where 16/9a1 has the usual reading:

Hs xiv 9	ܘܒܐܘܝ ܟܣܒܠܐ]	*c. sey* (*bis*)
Am vii 12	ܘܐܡܪ] *om waw*	(The recurrence of this reading in 17a6–8 is probably a coincidence.)
Jon i 7	ܟܝܐ] ܢܐ	
Mi iii 8	ܘܐܟܠܐ] *c. sey*	
Mi iv 14	ܒܬܝ] ܒܬܝ	
Na iii 19	ܥܠ] ܠܗ	
Sa viii 18	ܣܐܠܬܐ] *om*	
Ml ii 9	ܘܡܟܚܕܝܢ] ܘܡܟܚܕܝܢ	

These variants are not of such a kind as to require the presence of another exemplar for 16/9a1, particularly when we recall the one hundred and seven readings peculiar to 16/9a1 and the sixty-eight readings exclusively common to 16/9a1 and 17a6 *fam*. It is clear therefore that the exemplar of 16/9a1 was at least closely related to 12a1, and there seems no insuperable difficulty in the way of identifying it with 12a1, though this cannot be proved conclusively.

3. 17a8[txt] and 17a8[mg]

A complete analysis of the variants between the text and margin of 17a8 is excluded, partly by illegibility (including illegibility in (16/)9a1) in some instances, and partly because some of the variants concern only matters of orthography or diacritic points. The vast majority of the variants however admit of a fairly simple classification, which leaves the main conclusion in no doubt.

It is clear in the first place that (16/)9a1 was the main exemplar for 17a8. Twenty-three out of thirty-six uncorrected omissions in 16/9a1 recur in 17a8*, while a further five also recur in 17a8 and the rest of 17a6 *fam* and one at Sa v 6 recurs in 17a7.8. A lacuna in 16/9a1 draws attention to three of the remaining omissions (at Am iii 4, vi 3 and ix 5; it is interesting to note that in 12a1 the first and last of these passages have perished completely, while the second contains a word of the right length which is almost illegible and may already have presented difficulties to the copyist of 16/9a1). In any case, as we shall see, Risius had access to at least two other Mss. Ninety-seven unusual readings of (16/)9a1 recur in 17a8^{txt}, the usual reading being recorded as a variant in 17a8^{mg}; this figure may be increased by the addition of nine further passages where the reading of (16/)9a1 is only probable.

Risius however did not use (16/)9a1 uncritically as an exemplar. In fifty-three passages clearly, and possibly in a further eight, he relegated the reading of (16/)9a1 to the margin. In twenty-one (or twenty-three) of these passages the reading of (16/)9a1 is unusual; in the remaining thirty-two (or thirty-eight) it is the common reading. These figures show that Risius made a careful comparison between (16/)9a1 and his other exemplars, and made a judgement in each case which readings to adopt into the text and which to relegate to the margin. He rejected a few readings of 9a1 (Hs i 2, vii 15, xii 3) without even recording them in the margin.

We must now ask which other exemplars in addition to (16/)9a1 Risius used in writing 17a8. The answer cannot be given quite as simply as in the case of Exodus and Judges. For the only other biblical text mentioned in the receipt cited by LEVI DELLA VIDA (pp. 362ff., n.4) besides the two Mss identified with 16b3 and 16c1 is an Arabic version of Tobit. The Biblia Reggia which Risius also borrowed from the Vatican Library was identified by Levi della Vida with the Royal Polyglot of Antwerp, which did not contain a Syriac text of the Old Testament. Levi della Vida's first quotation from the Archive of the Vatican Library pertaining to Sergius Risius (*ibid.*) however records the latter's request to be allowed to consult the Syriac and Arabic books in the Vatican Library pertaining to Holy Scripture, in order to "collate them with the Syriac and Arabic texts which he has (conferirli con li testi syri et Arabi, che esso ha)". Now it is clear that 16d1 was already in the Vatican Library by about 1574 (cf. LEVI DELLA VIDA, pp. 187–189, 193), and it is virtually certain that this was one of the Mss used by Risius. Not only do eighteen of the variants in 17a8^{mg} occur in 16d1 (some of them otherwise peculiar to that Ms and perhaps its later distant relatives, cf. Section E), but 16d1 was almost a companion volume of 16b3 and 16c1 which we know Risius used respectively for Exodus and Judges (LEVI DELLA VIDA, p. 180). This Ms may well have been the source of usual readings set in the text or margin of 17a8 alongside unusual readings of (16/)9a1, but no less than twenty-six of the variants in 17a8^mg occur in no other biblical Ms available to us, while four are attested in various Mss other than (16/)9a1 and 16d1. Risius must therefore have used at least one other exemplar, and it seems reasonable to look for it (or them) among the texts in his own possession mentioned in the quotation from the Vatican Library Archive given above. While many of the 'usual' readings could have been derived from a Ms of 14a1 *fam* (cf. KOSTER, p. 427), the only distinctive reading of that *fam* to occur in 17a8^txt or 17a8^mg is the substitution of *waw* for *dalath* in ܪܘܚܐ in Sa vii 9, which could well be a coincidence. There is no real evidence that Risius used a Ms of 14a1 *fam* in the Dodekapropheton of 17a8.

The priority of 17a8 within 17a6 *fam* is shown firstly by the exclusive agreements between (16/)9a1 and 17a8*, secondly by the absence of any distinctive readings exclusively common to 17a6.7.9.11, and thirdly by the nature of the few readings in which 17a8 in its corrected form differs from the rest of the *fam*:

Hs ix 9	ܪܚܝܢ] *c. sey* (*vid*)	
Jl ii 16	ܢܒܘܪ1°] ܢܒܘܢ	(The dittograph is obvious.)
Jon i 2	ܒܐܕܢܝܗܘܢ] ܒܐܕܢܝܗ	
Mi ii 6	ܢܛܝܦܘܢ] ܢܛܝܦܝܢ	(Perhaps recognized as an error.)
Na iii 12	ܒܥܘܒܐ] ܘܥܘܒܐ	
Sa v 6	ܗܘ2°] *om*	(This recurs only in 17a7, but ܗܘ could have been added spontaneously in 17a6.9.)
Ml ii 16	ܣܢܐ ܐܠܗܐ] *tr*	(An obvious error in the context.)

All of these except Jl ii 16 are agreements with (16/)9a1 which were not perpetuated in the rest of the *fam*. Only Mi ii 6 positively suggests recourse to another exemplar. In Na iii 12 Risius seems to have copied the reading ܘܥܘܒܐ of 16/9a1 and then to have correctd it *cal curr* by prefixing *beth*, but without deleting the *waw*, thus producing an erroneous conflate form; in his later copies he rightly adopted only the *beth*. None of these readings is a serious obstacle to 17a8 having been the immediate exemplar of 17a6.7.9, though it is curious that Risius did not correct 17a8 especially at Mi ii 6.

4. 17a7^{txt} and 17a7^{mg}

17a7 is the only other Ms of Risius to be furnished with a critical apparatus like that of 17a8. As far as choice of variants for the text and margin is concerned there is very little difference between 17a7 and 17a8 in the Dodekapropheton. There are only a few passages where Risius seems to have reversed his judgement. At Jl ii 23 17a8^{txt} seems to have the peculiar reading ܚܘܪܒܐ, while 17a8^{mg} originally had the usual reading ܚܘܒܐ, though subsequently a *dalath* was added above. 17a7^{txt} reads ܚܘܒܐ and 17a7^{mg} ܚܘܪܒܐ. Was the correction in 17a8^{mg} made *cal curr* or at the time when 17a7 was being copied? Perhaps the most likely sequence is that Risius adopted the original reading of 17a8^{mg} into the text of 17a7, relegating the reading with *dalath* to the margin. But on looking again at 17a8 he may have thought that the real difference between text and margin that Ms was the deletion of the medial *'alaph* and accordingly adjusted 17a8^{mg} by adding the *dalath*, thus bringing about complete agreement between 17a7^{mg} and 17a8^{mg} in this passage. At Sa ii 15 17a8^{txt} seems to read ܩܫܬܗ, while 17a8^{mg} reads ܩܫܬܗ, the reading of 12a1 16/9a1 (*vid*) as well as of 7a1 *et ceteri*. In 17a7^{txt} the reading ܩܫܬܗ is adopted, and ܩܫܬܗ (whose only other possible occurrence is in 17a9 (*frt*)) is relegated to the margin. At Sa x 1 the reading in 17a7^{txt} is ܟܣܘܝ, while *seyāmē* are added to the word in 17a7^{mg}; in 17a8 however the word is found with *seyāmē* in both text and margin. The reading without *seyāmē* is found otherwise only in 16/9a1. Here it seems that Risius has added the second dot in 17a8^{txt} at the time when he was copying 17a7 or even 17a9, thus confirming the reading he had originally relegated to the margin. Perhaps one should also add here the variant in Mi i 8, where the orthographic *yudh fin* is omitted in 17a7^{mg}.

The remaining differences between 17a7^{mg} and 17a8^{mg} are by way of omissions and additions. Ten readings in 17a8^{mg} do not recur in 17a7^{mg}. Two of these seem simply to be clarifications of 17a8^{txt}, while a third presents no apparent difference from it. One is the addition of *seyāmē* to ܒܢܝܟ in Sa vii 5 in a marginal reading where the main variants are different. In the case of the remaining six 17a7^{txt} agrees with 17a8^{txt} and the variant in 17a8^{mg} is simply omitted, whether by oversight or deliberate rejection. There are four additional variants in 17a7^{mg}. At Am iv 9 the same variant is given as in 17a8^{mg} followed as an alternative reading by what appears to be identical with the reading in the text! The other three are real variants, two of them peculiar to 17a7ᵐᵍ, while the third (the prefixing of *waw* to ܐܪ in Sa xiv 18) is found also in 6h9 7k8 and a few later Mss. In each of these cases 17a7ᵗˣᵗ agrees with 17a8ᵗˣᵗ. There are also four erroneous readings peculiar to 17a7ᵐᵍ introduced in the process of copying from 17a8ᵐᵍ, and the omission of *seyāmē* in another reading may also come under this category.

As far as the text of 17a7 is concerned there are four uncorrected omissions peculiar to this Ms (Hs vii 9 ܟܣܡ, Am vii 4 ܠܝ, Sa ix 8 ܟܣܬܝܚ and Sa xiv 19 ܐܠܐ), which alone make it improbable that 17a7 was the exemplar of 17a6 or 17a9. There are six uncorrected readings peculiar to 17a7, and two passages where 17a7 deviates from readings characteristic of the *fam*:

Am vii 13	ܘܒܐܪܐ ܐܟܠ] ܘܐܪܐ ܐܟܠ	The additional *beth* may have been omitted by haplography in 17a7.
Sa ix 10	ܘܣܐ⁴°] om *waw*	The *waw* may have been added spontaneously in 17a7.

Three other readings where 17a7 finds partial support in the *fam* may be mentioned:

Am iii 8	ܢܣܗܡ] ܢܣܗܡ	(Also in 17a9.11.) This is probably an assimilation to the reading of 17a6–9 in Am iii 4.
Sa xii 6	ܠܡܐܟܠܐ] *c. sey*	(Also in 17a9.11.)
Ml iii 22	ܚܒܪ,] *om*	(Also in 17a6*.)

These are probably all coincidences except for the agreements of 17a11 with 17a9. The absence of any other shared omissions peculiar to 17a6 and 17a7 reduces the significance of Ml iii 22. Finally there are five readings in which 17a7 agrees with Mss outside the *fam*; these concern changes of suffixes, *seyāmē*, *waw init* and *adiunctio*, and are of no real significance.

Dirksen's hypothesis that some of the corrections in 17a8 were made at the time when 17a7 was copied from it and some later is borne out for the Dodekapropheton, where 17a7 agrees with 17a8* four times (Hb iii 9, 17, Hg i 14, Sa iv 14) and with 17a8¹ three times (Hs i 6, ii 25, Hg ii 7).

5. 17a9 and 17a11

These Mss have eleven readings exclusively common to themselves, of which four are omissions. They have a further eight common readings, three of which are omissions, shared only with Mss outside the *fam*. On five occasions they deviate from readings characteristic of the *fam*, but in two of these (Hs xii 12, Mi iii 8) they follow readings in 17a7^{mg}.8^{mg}:

Hs xii 12	ܐܪܒܐ] *pr beth*	
Am vii 12	ܐܟܡܐ] *om waw*	
Mi iii 8	ܢܘܗܪܘ] ܢܘܗܪܘ	(Here 17a7^{txt}.8^{txt} follow the usual reading.)
Na iii 1	ܚܠܐ] *c. sey*	
Sa xii 1	,ܗܒܠܠܬܗ] ,ܗܒܠܠܬܗ	

On five other occasions they agree with one other *fam* or related Ms:

Am iii 8	ܢܝܚܡ] ܢܝܚܡ	(Also in 17a7.)
Mi v 7	ܐܗܒ] *om dalath*	(Also in 17a6.)
Hb iii 11	ܐܫܝܕܒ] *om dalath*	(Also in 16/9a1.)
Sa xii 6	ܠܐܪܣܝܐ] *c. sey*	(Also in 17a7.)
Ml iii 1	ܠܘܚܠܡ] *pr* ܠܡ	(Also in 17a6.)

These are probably all coincidences.

These twenty-nine common readings prove that there is a close relationship between these two Mss, and suggest the possibility that 17a9 was the exemplar of 17a11. Are there any readings in 17a9 which would make this improbable? The only uncorrected omission peculiar to 17a9 (that of ܠܟ in Zf i 12) was probably supplied by the scribe of 17a11 by emendation of the following ܠܗ, which he omits (*cf infra*). At Hs xiv 4 and Mi vi 11 17a9 follows 17a8^{mg} in reading *seyāmē* where they are omitted in 17a6–8.11, but the omission in 17a11 is probably a secondary corruption. 17a9 has six erroneous readings peculiar to itself, but two of these are dittographies, one the omission of *seyāmē*, one the omission of a single letter, and the remaining two the addition of *waw init* and *beth init* respectively. All of these could easily be corrected without recourse to another exemplar. Clearly then there is no serious difficulty in the way of regarding 17a9 as the exemplar of 17a11 in the Dodekapropheton.

Before leaving 17a9 it is worth noting that in the duplicate of Sa ix 12–xi 5 17a9 *bis* agrees with 17a7^{mg}.8^{mg} at Sa ix 13 against the reading ܒܬܢܝܢ[1°]*pr beth* found in 16/9a1 and 17a6 *fam* (including 17a9). This appears to be the only difference between 17a9 and 17a9 *bis*.

There are eighteen omissions, only one of which has been corrected, peculiar to 17a11, and a further four (all mechanical) shared only with Mss outside the *fam*. The Ms has seventy-six readings (of which nine have been corrected) peculiar to itself, and a further seventeen shared only with Mss outside the *fam*. Although these figures illustrate the poor quality of this Ms, their chief significance is to set in perspective the twelve passages where 17a11 deviates from agreed readings of 17a6–9:

Hs iv 11	ܢܣܒܗ] ܢܣܒܘ	17a11 has merely ܢܣܒ.
Hs vii 4	ܟܬ̇ܢܘܪ] ܟܬ݂ܢܘܪ	
Jl ii 6	ܕܩܕܪ̈ܐ] ܕܩܕܪܐ	
Am iii 4	ܢܗܡ] ܢܢܗܡ	
Am vi 1	ܘܟܠܗܘ] ܘܪܟܠܗܘ	17a11 has ܘܕܟܠܗܘ.
Am vii 10	ܟܠܗܘܢ] ܟܠܗ	17a11 has merely ܟܠ.
Mi v 4	ܕܐܪܥܐ] *c. sey*	This word occurs in a passage omitted in 17a11.
Mi v 11	ܚܪ̈ܫܐ] *s. sey*	
Zf i 12	ܟܒܪ̈ܐ] *pr* ܟܠ	The immediately preceding ܟܠ was omitted in 17a9, and 17a11 probably represents a correction of the ܟܠ of 17a9 into the ܟܠ required in the context.
Sa ix 2	ܕܬܠܒ] *om dalath*	17a11 has the peculiar erroneous reading ܬܘܒ.
Ml ii 6	ܐܗܦܟ] ܗܦܟܘ	17a11 has merely ܗܦܟ.
Ml ii 17	ܕܟܠ] *om dalath*	The *dalath* could easily have been added spontaneously in 17a11 after ܐܡܪܝܢ ܐܢܬܘܢ.

None of these readings in 17a11 is incompatible with the use of 17a9 as exemplar, and the cases where 17a11 agrees with the usual reading against the rest of the *fam* (especially in Jl ii 6, Am iii 4) could easily have arisen by accident! The one exclusive agreement between 17a6 and 17a11 (the addition of *seyāmē* to ܕܐܪܝܘܬܐ[1°] in Na ii 12) is probably a pure coincidence.

It seems likely then that in the case of the Dodekapropheton 17a9 was the sole exemplar of 17a11.

6. 17a6

This Ms has nineteen omissions, five of which have been corrected, peculiar to itself; one further mechanical omission (also corrected) is found also in two Mss outside the *fam*. There are twenty-three readings (sixteen of which are certainly erroneous and two of these have been corrected) peculiar to this Ms, and eight further readings shared only with Mss outside the *fam*. The two passages where 17a6 deviates from the agreed reading of the rest of the *fam* are:

Jon i 6   ܢܝܗܢ] ܢܝܗܢ
Hb iii 9   ܐܬܘܬܐ] ܐܬܘܬܐ

The second of these is interesting. 17a6* read ܬܘܬܐ, which is clearly a corruption of the *fam* reading. But 17a6¹ read , ܐܬܘܬܐ, which appears to be also the reading of 17a8¹, a correction which is not found in 17a7 or 17a9. Unfortunately this affords no evidence for the relative date of the original copying of 17a6. There is one exclusive agreement between 17a6 and 17a8 as far as the *fam* is concerned:

Na ii 13   ܐܬܒ] c. sey   (Also in 12a1 16/9a1 17a5 (*vid*).)

There may be another, but the reading is only probable in 17a6:

Na ii 14:   ܘܩܝܢܝ] ܘܩܝܢ ܝܢ

This Ms is clearly the poorest of the four copied by Sergius Risius, but like 17a7 and 17a9 it appears to have been copied directly from 17a8.

7. Conclusion

The pattern of relationships has now emerged with reasonable clarity and probability. 9a1 was supplemented after its expiry at Hs xiv 6 from either 12a1 itself or a Ms closely related to it. The resultant (16/)9a1 was the primary exemplar used (but not uncritically) by Sergius Risius as he wrote 17a8. He also used 16d1 and at least one other Ms not available to us. His three remaining Mss seem each to have been copied directly from 17a8. The first to be copied was evidently 17a7, in view of the two passages in which it agrees with 17a8* while 17a6 and 17a9 agree with 17a8¹ (Hg i 14, Sa iv 14); at Hb iii 9, 17 17a6 and 17a9 (17a6 essentially at Hb iii 9, *cf supra*) also agree with 17a8*. There is no evidence therefore to indicate whether 17a6 or 17a9 was the next to be copied, but perhaps the decline in quality in 17a6 suggests that it was the last. Finally, twenty-eight years after Risius' death, 17a11 was copied, and there seems good reason to suppose that it was copied directly from 17a9. Before we take our leave of 17a6 *fam* we should note that Risius' critical work in the writing of 17a8 ensured that the text of 17a6 *fam*, while far from good, is a great deal better than that of 16/9a1, its main exemplar for nearly four fifths of the Dodekapropheton.

B. 14a1 *fam*: 14a1 17a1-5.10

1. Introduction

The fullest and most recent discussion of these Mss is that of KOSTER (pp. 255 ff.). He has argued convincingly that 15a2 and (15/)14a1 together form a single complete Bible, within which the Prophets form an original nucleus (14a1) which was enlarged to a pandect by a fifteenth century copyist. The fifteenth century part of this pandect is dependent on 12a1, but this is not the case with the prophetic nucleus of 14a1. The complete pandect was the source of 17a1-5.10. An examination of four major *lacunae* together with information derived from the colophons of 17a2.3.4 enables Koster to list the seventeenth century Mss in the following chronological order: 17a1.2.4.5.3.10. Each of these is directly dependent on 15a2 except 17a4, which is a direct copy of 17a2.

Koster's conclusions for Exodus are supported, with only minor variations, by the evidence of the Dodekapropheton. It is clear here too that 17a1-5.10 are dependent on 14a1, but since in the Prophets 14a1 is independent of 12a1 the family has no relation to that Ms in this Book. Koster's chronological order of the seventeenth century Mss (in particular the priority of 17a1) is compatible with the internal evidence of the Dodekapropheton, with the sole exception that in this part of the Old Testament 17a2 is a copy of 17a4 and not *vice versa* (as Koster himself indicates on p. 261). As in the case of Exodus the number of variants peculiar to each of the seventeenth century Mss precludes the possibility of any but 17a2 being a direct copy of any of the others. The direct dependence of 17a3 on 14a1 (*cf* KOSTER, pp. 261 f., 320) finds clear confirmation in the Dodekapropheton in two erroneous readings of 17a3 which are best explained as miscopyings of 14a1.

2. The dependence of 17a1–5.10 on 14a1

The textual evidence for this dependence, though not very extensive, seems to be conclusive. 14a1 had evidently been carefully corrected before it was used as the exemplar of the seventeenth century Mss, and in its corrected form it is a good representative of the main tradition of the Peshiṭta of the Dodekapropheton. There are thus only relatively few distinctive readings by which the dependence of the seventeenth century Mss on 14a1 may be proved. They fall into three main categories:

(a) Readings common to 14a1 and 17a1–5.10 and found in no other Ms.

Mi iv 13	ܐܬܪܒܘ] *om waw*	
Hb i 2	ܘܡܢܐ] ܡܢܐ	
Hb ii 15	ܪܘܚܬܢ] *stat emph*	
Sa viii 2	ܘܒܚܬܐ] ܒܚܬܐ	This reading is only probable in 14a1; in 17a5 it has been corrected.
Sa x 3	ܐܬܘܬܐ] ܐܬܪܬܐ	
Sa xiv 8	ܘܦܪ] *pr waw*	This has been deleted in 17a5.
Ml i 10	ܘܠܐ] *om waw*	

The fourth of these readings is undoubtedly an error since it results in nonsense. The second and fifth, though they yield an intelligible sense, are probably also to be reckoned as errors. These three readings seem to be instances of miscopying one or two letters. The remaining variants are minor and significant only because their attestation is confined to these Mss.

To this list may perhaps be added the omission of ܠܗ at Hs ii 11 in 17a1–5.10, where 14a1 is illegible. This omission occurs also in 19g5.7*.

(b) Passages where 14a1 offers alternative readings which are adopted by different Mss within 17a1–5.10.

These may conveniently be subdivided into two categories:

(i) Passages omitted in 14a1* but supplied by the corrector:

Hs ii 9	ܐܬܚܒ ... ܐܪ 3°	The correction was missed in 17a1*.
Jl iv 17	ܠܐܝܐ	The correction was missed in 17a3.
Am vii 8	ܡܪܝ 2°	The correction was missed in 17a3.
Am vii 13	ܗܘ 2°	The correction in 14a1 was made in a very small hand above the ∴ at the

		end of the verse, and was missed in 17a1.5.10.
Jon iii 8	ܘܡ] om waw	The correction was missed in 17a10.
Hg i 8	ܒܗ 2°	The correction was missed in 17a1*.3.
Sa iv 13	ܘܐܡܪ ... ܗܠ	The correction (at the top of the column) was missed in 17a3.10.
Sa v 9f.	ܒܝܢ ... ܠܐܠܗܐ	The correction was missed in 17a10*.
Sa xiv 19		The whole verse was omitted in 14a1*. The marginal correction read *stat emph* for ܝܘܠܕܗ, a reading found in 17a1–5.10 but in no other Ms.

(ii) Passages where there is a variant reading in the margin of 14a1:

Hs ix 4	ܕܫܡܝܢܗܘܢ] add ܐܠܐ	14a1¹ 17a1.2.4.10. Here 17a3.5 follow the (usual) reading of the text.
Hs xii 9	ܟܢܥܢܝܐ] ܟܢܥܢܝܐ	14a1¹ 17a3.10. Here 17a1.2.4.5 follow the (usual) reading of the text.
Jon iv 8	ܠܢܘܚܐ	Here ܠܢܘܚܐ is inserted in the margin of 14a1 without the corresponding correction of *lamadh* to *dalath* in the text. 17a1.2.4 made this obvious further correction in adopting the marginal reading of 14a1.
Sa xi 10	ܕܐܒܠܐ] ܕܢܒܠܐ	14a1¹ 17a1.2.4.5.10. Here 17a3 follows the (usual) reading of the text, while the other Mss prefer the otherwise unattested variant of the margin.
Ml ii 7	ܒܦܘܡܗ] ܒܦܘܡܗ	14a1¹ 17a1–5. Here 17a10 follows the (usual) reading of the text, while the other Mss prefer the otherwise unattested variant of the margin.

Two further passages may be considered here:

Hs xiii 15	ܬܫܩ	The tail of the final *qoph* in 14a1 could be read as a *yudh*. This word is

		written with a final *yudh* in 17a1.2.4.5.10, but not in 17a3.
Mi iv 5	ܠܥܠܡ ܘܠܥܠܡ ܥܠܡܝܢ	This is abbreviated to ܠܥܠܡ ܘܠܥܠܡܝܢ in 14a1 and 17a5 and abbreviated further to ܠܥܠܡ ܥܠܡܝܢ in 17a1–4.10.

(c) Readings found in only five of the seventeenth century Mss:

Hs ix 10	ܒܗ] ܒܠܗ	14a1 17a1–4.10.
Sa vii 9	ܢܩܘܫܬܐ] ܕܩܘܫܬܐ	14a1 17a1–4.10 (also 17a6 *fam*).

Here at first sight 17a5 seems to be independent of 14a1 *fam*. But a closer examination of the photograph suggests that the Ms has been skilfully corrected in these passages and that it originally shared the reading of the rest of the family. The second of these readings, while yielding a tolerable sense, is best regarded as either an inner-Syriac corruption or an assimilation to Sa viii 19 *ad finem*; in either case it may well have occurred independently in 17a6 *fam*.

Hg ii 15	ܗܘ] om	17a1–5.

This word is obscured by a blot in 14a1. The omission has been made good by the corrector of 17a5. In 17a10 the word occurs at the end of the line and could also be a later supplement, in which case the word would have been omitted also in 17a10*.

Jl iv 6	ܘܬܒܘ¹°] *om waw*	17a2–5.10.

In 14a1 this word occurs at the beginning of the line where the text is obscured by the binding. The *waw* is not visible on the photograph, but the alignment suggests that it was there. Its presence in 17a1 alone of the seventeenth century Mss lends support to Koster's suggestion (p. 260) that 14a1 had not been bound in its present position within (15/) 14a1 at the time when 17a1 was copied from it.

The evidence of the four passages in this last category is thus seen to corroborate the dependence of the six seventeenth century Mss on 14a1.

The twenty-eight passages considered in this section have all been examined in 12a1. The Ms has either perished or is illegible in eight passages; it certainly agrees with the main tradition against 14a1 *fam* in twelve passages and appears to do so also in the remaining eight. In no case does it clearly agree with 14a1 *fam*. The only readings common to 12a1 and 14a1 are either found in several other Mss as well (Hs iv 14, Jon ii 3, Mi v 1) or are to be regarded as a coincidence (the omission of ܐܠܗܐ in Am vi 8 exclusively common to 12a1* and 14a1*). 14a1 *fam* seems thus to be independent of 12a1 in the Dodekapropheton.

3. Evidence for the direct copying of 17a3 from 14a1

Two erroneous readings in 17a3 are best explained as miscopyings of 14a1.

At the end of Hs x 8 after the ❖ is the single word ܚܠܛܐ, followed by another ❖. This has been twice marked as an error, first by a stroke through the *lamadh*, and secondly by encircling the word in red. The word occurs in ix 16, and it is significant that in 14a1 Hs ix 16 and x 8 are in parallel columns on the same page, ܚܠܛܐ being exactly opposite ܚܛܗܝ, the last word in x 8.

At Sa i 15 17a3 prefixes a *waw* to ܝܠܕ. This is nonsense in the syntax of the verse. The corrector of 14a1 however uses a sign very like a *waw* to indicate the point in the text at which a word should be inserted from the margin. There is a clear example of this at Sa vi 6, where the sign is prefixed to ܩܘܡ in the margin as well as used to indicate the point in the text where it should be inserted. The same thing has happened in Sa i 15, where the sign before ܝܠܕ indicates the point at which ܒܪܗ in the margin should be inserted into the text. The copyist of 17a3 has mistaken the sign for a *waw*.

4. Evidence for the direct copying of 17a2 from 17a4

Koster has set out the basic facts about the relationship between 17a2 and 17a4 (p. 261). 17a4 was written by Elia of Eden in 1614. The second part of 17a2, to which the Dodekapropheton belongs, was written by the same scribe in the following year. An examination of the handwriting shows that it is indeed identical, and that where omissions in the text of 17a4 have been supplied in the margin (e.g. Hs vii 14, Sa vii 13–14) this has been done in the same handwriting.

The textual evidence points to 17a2 being a direct copy of 17a4 in the case of the Dodekapropheton. The two Mss agree in a number of readings peculiar to themselves. These comprise five mechanical and two non-mechanical omissions, and forty readings of which eighteen certainly and the remainder probably are erroneous. The more interesting of these readings include the substitution of *zain* for *dalath* in

ـܟܪܝܢܗܘܢ (Zf i 9) and of *qoph* for *shin* in ܘܫܢܝܚܝ (Sa v 11), and the omission of the negative in ܬܬܟܫܘܢ ܘܠܐ (Mi vi 15), where the *waw* is retained and prefixed directly to the verb.

Two erroneous readings in particular point to the priority of 17a4. The first three words of Hs ii 12 were omitted in the text of 17a4 and supplied in the margin, where the *'alaph init* in ܐܠܬܐ is omitted. The erroneous reading ܠܬܐ occurs in the text of 17a2, suggesting that the supplement had already been added to 17a4 at the time when 17a2 was copied from it. The transference of *dalath* before ܠܐ in Am iv 7 to precede ܚܕܐ³° in both Mss is best explained by the fact that in 17a4 ܚܕܐ is exactly one line above ܠܐ and both words are at the beginning of the line; the misplacing of *dalath* is thus a mechanical error in 17a4 which has been copied into the text of 17a2.

17a2 has no less than nine uncorrected omissions and thirty-two readings (of which twenty-three are certainly erroneous) peculiar to itself. These would suffice to prove that 17a4 could not have been copied from 17a2, even if this possibility were not excluded by the dates given in the colophons.

The few readings in 17a4 which are not reproduced in 17a2 are such that the scribe may well have made the appropriate adjustment as he made the copy. For instance, in the original text of 17a4 there was a *homoeoteleuton* from the first to the third ܥܠ in Hs vii 14; the omission was supplied in the margin, but the scribe failed to attach the necessary *waw init* to the ܥܠ in the text. This has been supplied in 17a2, but would be felt to be required by anyone following the sense of the passage as a whole. The fact that such corrections were not made in 17a4 at the same time suggests that those corrections which were made in 17a4 were made prior to the copying of 17a2.

One error in 17a4 has been inadvertently corrected in 17a2! 17a4 substitutes *dalath* for *rish* in ܠܥܝܢܝ in Hs vii 4 in company with 7a1, 14a1 and a number of other Mss. But it so happens that the point belonging to *dalath* in ܘܡܙܕܠܗܒܢ occurs in the line above immediately over the *dalath* in ܠܥܝܢܝ. Moreover the point belonging to this *dalath* is near the tip of *ṭeth* in ܒܛܠ in the line below and could easily have been missed. It seems that Elia misread his own writing in 17a4 and thus unconsciously produced the correct reading ܠܥܝܢܝ in 17a2!

These data point strongly to the conclusion that Elia wrote 17a4 and corrected it before writing the second part of 17a2, in the copying of which he used only the corrected 17a4.

5. Evidence for the mutual independence of 17a1.3.4.5.10

The possibility that any one of these five seventeenth century Mss could have been copied directly from another is excluded at once by the fact that each of them has several uncorrected omissions peculiar to itself (or in the case of 17a4 shared exclusively with 17a2). Such agreements as occur within these Mss are thus most probably due to accidental coincidence. A few readings shared in each case exclusively (except where 17a2 follows 17a4) by three of these Mss are given here as an illustration; it will be noted that only two combinations of Mss occur more than once (for two and three readings respectively).

Hs ii 14	ܒܪܐ] *pr dalath*	17a3.5.10.	The synonym ܒܪܗ occurs in ii 20.
Hs ii 17	ܘܢܣܒܘܗ] *om waw init*	17a3.5.10.	
Hs x 14f.	ܐܝܬ ܒܝܬ ... ܒܢܝܗ] *om*	17a3.5.10.	This is a *homoeoteleuton*. In 14a1 ܐܝܬ ܒܝܬ occurs twice at the beginning of the line two lines apart. The three copyists have made the same mechanical error.
Am iv 5	ܢܝܚ] *s. sey*	17a1.5.10.	
Am iv 8	ܘܡܬܟܢܫ] *om waw*	17a(2.)4.5.10.	
Zf i 3	ܐܡܪ̈] ܐܡܪܝܢ	17a(2.)4.5*.10.	The correct form has been mistaken for an abbreviation.
Hg i 15	ܟܗܢܐ] *stat emph*	17a1.3.5*.	The *'alaph* at the beginning of the following word is written close to the *mim* in 14a1 and could easily have led to this reading.

In all these passages except Hs x 14f. and Hg i 15 14a1 is obscure. This may have led to several scribes making the same "improvements".

6. Conclusion

The relations between the seven Mss in 14a1 *fam* may be set out as follows. 14a1 seems to have been the direct exemplar of five of the seventeenth century Mss (17a1.3.4.5.10), while 17a2 was copied directly from 17a4. The evidence of Jl iv 6 suggests that 17a1 was the first of the five Mss to be copied from 14a1. We know from the colophons that 17a4 was copied in 1614, 17a2 in 1615 and 17a3 in 1628. There is nothing in the Dodekapropheton to confirm or contradict Koster's hyopthesis that 17a5 was copied before and 17a10 after the copying of 17a3 in 1628. There is no dependence in the Dodekapropheton of 14a1 *fam* on 12a1 or any other known Ms.

C. 16g6 19g5.7

1. Introduction

The most thorough recent discussion of these Mss is that of DI LELLA (pp. XVIII–XXIII, XXV, XXXII). He thinks that 12a1 and 16g6 are "independent witnesses to a standard pre-twelfth-century text-type of Proverbs" and that "since 19g5 and 19g7 have many unique variants in common, it seems best to consider these Mss as a separate mini-group. But these Mss also witness to a mixed text-type." He concludes that 19g5 and 19g7 have a common source but that neither is a copy of the other. DIRKSEN (pp. 55f.) draws attention to the fact that 19g4 (of which 19g5 is the continuation) and 19g7 were both written in Beth Khudaida, where also 16g6 was supplemented (18/16g6). EMERTON (p. lxx) finds that the Jacobite correction of 19g5 is closely related to 16g6. The evidence of these three Mss in the Dodekapropheton is consistent with these findings.

2. Agreements between 16g6 and 19g5.7

The exclusive agreements between these three Mss comprise three omissions (mechanical omissions of a single word in Jon i 12 and of three words in Na i 2, and a non-mechanical omission of a single word in Jon iv 7) and thirty-one readings, of which three are certainly erroneous. The most distinctive of these readings are:

Hs x 10	ܚܫܒܐ] *pr* ܒܠܡܐ
Jl ii 8	ܐܘܪܚܐ] ܐܘܪܚܐ,
Am ix 9	ܠܬܚܬ] ܠܐܪܥܐ
Ob 19	ܠܛܘܪܐ] *pr* ܛܒܝܬܐ

To these must be added a further thirty readings, of which one is certainly erroneous, common to these three Mss and one or more other Mss. Six of these readings (Hs iv 14, Am ii 8, Jon ii 3, iv 8$^{2°}$, Mi v 1, Na ii 11) occur also in 12a1, but none of these readings is distinctive and all are found also in other Mss. At least four and probably six of the other twenty-four readings occur in 16/9a1 in passages where 12a1 itself is illegible, and there may be some presumption that they occurred in 12a1. There are however no omissions common to 12a1 and all three of these Mss, though there are four omissions common to 12a1 and 16g6, of which two have been corrected in 16g6.

At first sight one might expect these three Mss to form a family in view of the relatively large number of agreements between them. It is clear however from a more detailed examination that no one of these Mss can derive directly from any other. It is also clear from what has already been said that although these Mss have some readings in common with 12a1 there is little evidence to suggest that they are directly descended from it.

A stronger case may be made for a direct relationship between 16g6 itself and 12a1. In addition to the four common omissions already mentioned they have twenty-four common readings, of which two (Jon iv $8^{1°}$ and Sa x 11) are distinctive and three (Hs ix 13, xiii 1 and Ml ii 9) are exclusive to these two Mss. The possibility however that 16g6 is descended directly from 12a1 is excluded by the seven uncorrected omissions in 12a1 which do not recur in 16g6, although all but two of them recur in 16/9a1 (*cf* Section A above). The thirty readings common to 12a1 and 16g6 have also to be compared with the ninety common to 12a1 and 16/9a1. The evidence of the Dodekapropheton therefore confirms Di Lella's conclusion for Proverbs, that 12a1 and 16g6 are independent witnesses to the same text-type.

It is also clear that, despite the agreements between the three Mss, 16g6 cannot be the direct ancestor of either 19g5 or 19g7. There are no less than seventeen mechanical and eleven non-mechanical omissions peculiar to 16g6, none of which has been corrected, and nine of which consist of several words. Moreover there are at least forty-five readings shared by 16g6 and other Mss which do not recur in either 19g5 or 19g7, and no less than a hundred and eleven readings peculiar to 16g6, of which seventy-one are certainly erroneous, twelve have been corrected and two introduced by the corrector. This evidence is too extensive to need detailed examination, and excludes any possibility of 19g5 or 19g7 having been copied from 16g6. On the other hand the agreements between these three Mss are sufficient to suggest their derivation from an ultimate common ancestor.

3. Agreements between 19g5 and 19g7

These two Mss have a very extensive measure of agreement. In addition to the three omissions they have exclusively in common with 16g6, 19g5.7 in their uncorrected form have forty further common omissions, twenty-eight of which are exclusively common to these two Mss. In their uncorrected form 19g5.7 have also a hundred and thirty-two readings (of which thirty-nine are certainly erroneous) exclusively in common, and a further forty-seven common readings (of which nine are certainly erroneous) which occur also in other Mss.

Despite this large measure of agreement, however, neither 19g5 nor 19g7 can be a direct copy of the other. The relative dates in any case preclude such dependence on the part of 19g7, but each Ms has a number of uncorrected omissions and readings peculiar to itself which exclude the possibility of it having been the exemplar of the other. There are eight uncorrected and twenty-five corrected omissions and fifty-eight uncorrected readings peculiar to 19g5, not to mention the twenty-five which have been corrected and the five introduced by the corrector. There are twelve uncorrected and six corrected omissions and sixty uncorrected readings peculiar to 19g7, in addition to the eight which have been corrected. The number of omissions and readings peculiar to each of these Mss demonstrates their poor quality, 19g5 being the poorer of the two though also the more extensively corrected.

The measure of agreement between these two Mss however is so great as practically to require their derivation from a common exemplar, and the number of exclusive agreements between 19g5 and 19g7 indicates that their common exemplar must also have been of rather poor quality. What further may be said about it? We have already observed that 16g6 has a number of agreements with 12a1 which do not recur in 19g5.7, and it is worth adding that there is only one reading common to 19g5.7 and 12a1 (Am iv 1) which does not occur also in 16g6. We may therefore conclude that the common exemplar of 19g5.7 is a more distant relative of 12a1 than 16g6.

The remarkable fact is that fourteen of the common readings of 19g5.7 are found also in the ancient Mss, and five of them (Hs ix 15, Hb i 13, Sa xi 7, xii 4 and xiv 10) in no other Ms. Other scholars have noted agreements between 19g5.7 and the ancient Mss, and this not only confirms Di Lella's judgement that 19g5.7 witness to a mixed text-type, but also draws attention to the possibility that ancient readings may be preserved almost uniquely in very late and poor Mss.

4. The corrections in 19g5

Nine passages in 19g5 are marked for deletion by a line drawn above them; six of these are omitted otherwise only in 16g6, and the remaining three in no other Ms known to us. None of the other thirty-nine uncorrected omissions in 16g6 are marked for deletion in this way in 19g5. Twenty of the readings introduced in 19g5[1] occur also in other Mss; sixteen occur in 16g6, six of them in no other Ms, but four of them also in 12a1 and two others in 16/9a1 in passages where 12a1 itself is illegible. One reading occurs otherwise only in 12a1 and one otherwise only in 19g7. To these must be added the six peculiar readings introduced by the corrector. Five of these (the exception being at Sa vi 9 where an omission was at first supplied in an incorrect form) and some but by no means all of the other readings introduced by the corrector are designated by ܟ, indicating that another exemplar has been used. It is clear from this survey that not all the corrections can have been made with reference to 16g6, and there has certainly been no serious attempt to revise 19g5 to conform consistently with 16g6. It is more natural to suppose that the exemplar used by the corrector was slightly more closely related to 16g6 than the common exemplar of 19g5*.7, but still fairly distant from it.

It is not easy in the Dodekapropheton to distinguish the corrections in 19g5 as those respectively of a Jacobite and a Nestorian corrector (*cf* EMERTON, p. xxvii) since the rare passages where Nestorian vowels occur (e.g. the omission supplied at Na iii 14) are actually written in Serta, and a number of the marginal notes are vowelless. All corrections have therefore been designated 19g5[1], though it remains possible that they are not all from one hand.

5. Conclusion

Despite the unusually large measure of agreement between these three Mss and particularly between 19g5 and 19g7 it has become clear that none of them can be derived directly from any other or from 12a1. As a group they are distant cousins of 12a1, to which 16g6 is somewhat closer than 19g5.7. The measure of agreement between 19g5* and 19g7 is so great that it is difficult to avoid the conclusion that they derive from a common exemplar. The exemplar used by the corrector of 19g5 seems to have been somewhat closer to 16g6.

Before leaving this section it should be remembered that the fifteenth-century supplement to 11d1 has five readings in Ml iii in common with 19g5.7, three of them occurring also in 16g6. The supplement is too brief to admit of any certain classification, and it should be noted that there are ten other readings in one or more of these three Mss in Ml iii which do not occur in 15/11d1. It is reasonable however at least to conclude that the exemplar used by the supplementer of 11d1 belonged to the wider family to which these three Mss also belong.

D. 15d2 *fam* (15d2 17d4 19d2.3) 17d3 19d4 (19/17d1)

1. Introduction

Most of the readings common to 15d2 *fam* occur also in 17d3 (where it is extant) and 19d4, and there can be no doubt that all six Mss belong to a single family, within which 15d2 *fam* forms a subsidiary branch. 19/17d1 is not an independent Ms but a supplement to fill two *lacunae* in 17d1, and it is closely related to 19d3. It will be convenient to consider first the evidence for the existence of the larger family, next that for the dependence of 17d4 and 19d2.3 on 15d2, then the relationship between 19d2 and 19d3, and finally that between 19d3 and 19/17d1.

2. Readings common to 15d2 *fam*, 17d3 and 19d4

These six Mss have two non-mechanical omissions (ܐܠܡܐ in Hb ii 14 and ܠܐ in Zf i 11) exclusively in common, and one mechanical omission (of the last six words of Zf ii 2) which occurs otherwise only in 17d1. They also have seven exclusively common readings, although 17d3 is not extant for the first two:

Hs ii 13	ܚܛܝ̈ܐ] ܚܛܝ̈ܬܐ	
Hs xiv 8	ܢܬܗܝ] ܢܬܗܝܘ	(This was later corrected in 17d4.)
Am iv 13	ܪܘܚܐ] ܪܘܚܗ	
Mi vi 12	ܚܛܗܝ̈ܟܝ] ܚܛܗܝܟܘ	
Zf i 9	ܟܠܗܘܢ] ܟܠܗܘ	
Zf iii 12	ܝܗܒܐ] ܝܗܒܬ	
Sa iv 7	ܐܝܟ] ܐܟ	

The second and fifth of these readings are sufficiently distinctive to constitute significant evidence of relationship.

Six further common readings, found also in one or more Mss outside the family, should be added:

Hs ix 2	ܐܪܝܐ]	c. sey	(Also in 12d2 17a1.2.4.)
Hs xiii 14	ܗܘܐ]	om	(Also in 12a1; 17d3 is not extant.)
Ob 13	ܕܢܗܘܘܢ]	c. sey	(Also in 7k10 17a5 19g7.)
Mi ii 13	ܬܗܝ]	add waw fin	(Also in 10d1 16/9a1 17a6 fam 19g5.7.)
Hb ii 18	ܘܟܠܗ]	om waw init	(Also in 17a7.)
Zf ii 6	ܢܬܝ]	s. sey	(Also in 19g5.7.)

These sixteen common readings, nine of them exclusive to these Mss, are probably sufficient to establish their membership of a single family. Four other readings, in each of which one Ms deviates from the others, should also probably be regarded as characteristic:

Hb iii 1	add ܠܐ ܕܒܝ	(Also in 6h9 7a1; not in 17d3.)
Hb iii 14	all except 19d4 follow the variant ܒܫܡܗܘܢ.	
Sa xiv 18	ܐܦ] pr waw	(Also in 6h9 7k8 17a7^{mg} 19/17d1; not in 19d2.)
Ml iii 22	ܐܬܪܝܢ] om waw fin	(Also in 13d1 19/17d1; not in 19d2.)

Before turning to 15d2 *fam* it is worth noting that 17d3 and 19d4* have one exclusively common reading—the omission of *beth* in ܒܐܪܥܐ in Sa xii 6. But since 17d3 has six uncorrected omissions and six other uncorrected readings peculiar to itself it cannot have been the exemplar of 19d4. It is just possible that the two Mss derive from a common exemplar, but much more likely that their agreement in Sa xii 6 is accidental, as is probably also the sole agreement which each has with 17d4 (in addition to the common readings of the family):

Hs viii 4	ܬܒܝܐ]	c. sey	17d3.4 (Also in 8a1 8j1 and fifteen later Mss.)
Jl i 17	ܐܣܟܘܬܐ]	c. waw fin	17d4 19d4 (Also in eight later Mss.)

All that can be said of 17d3 and 19d4 is that they derive from the same common ancestor as 15d2 *fam*, to which they are closely related.

3. The dependence of 17d4 and 19d2.3 on 15d2

The dependence of 17d4 and 19d2.3 on 15d2 emerges most clearly from a non-mechanical omission of three words (ܐܝܟ ܕܐܡܪ ܢܒܝܐ) from Jl ii 27 in the original text of 15d2. The *dalath* required by the sense of the passage after ܒܫܡܝ̈ is however retained, and attached to the second ܐܝܟ, which follows immediately after the passage omitted. Later an incomplete attempt was made to correct 15d2: ܢܒܝܐ was inserted above ܕܐܝܟ and ܕܐܡܪ was written in the margin, but the first ܐܝܟ was not supplied, nor was the (now superfluous) *dalath* prefixed to the second ܐܝܟ deleted. 17d4 gives an exact reproduction of 15d2 as corrected: ܕܐܝܟ ܕܐܡܪ ܢܒܝܐ ܒܫܡܝ̈, a nonsensical conflation explicable only as a direct copy of the corrected 15d2. 15d2 must therefore have received this correction before 17d4 was copied.

The original reading of 15d2, i.e. with the omission of the three words and the attachment of the *dalath* to the second ܐܝܟ, recurs in 19d2*.3 and 19/17d1. The last of these Mss is considered separately below. The exact agreement between 19d2*.3 and 15d2* points strongly to dependence of the immediate common exemplar of 19d2.3 (see next section) on 15d2 at some point before the latter was corrected. It only remains to add that the correction in 19d2 was complete; not only were the three words supplied, but the *dalath* prefixed to the second ܐܝܟ was deleted.

This conclusion is supported by a mechanical omission of six words (²° ܘܣܡܘ ... ¹°ܘܠܐ) from Jl ii 9, which occurs only in 15d2* 19d2*.3, but was supplied completely in the margin of 15d2, and thus left no trace in 17d4.

Neither of these omissions occurs in 17d3 or 19d4, and the incompleteness of the correction of 15d2 at Jl ii 27 excludes the possibility of either Ms being directly copied from 15d2. It would of course be possible to claim 17d3 and 19d4 as descendants of 15d2 if one posited an intermediate copy made from 15d2 before the latter was corrected, itself corrected completely at Jl ii 27 as was 19d2 at a later date. But it seems simpler to suppose that 17d3 and 19d4 were not directly descended from 15d2 at all.

The only uncorrected reading peculiar to 15d2 is the prefix of *waw* to ܠܐ in Hs x 9. As this does not afford a very likely sense it is easy to see how it could have been omitted by later copyists, and it does not therefore constitute any serious objection to the derivation of 17d4 and the common exemplar of 19d2.3 from 15d2.

4. The relationship between 19d2 and 19d3

These two Mss have seven (five of them exclusively) common readings, some of which have been subsequently corrected in 19d2. These comprise two mechanical omissions each of five words in Mi vi 15 and Sa v 5–6, a non-mechanical omission (the word ܕܝܢ) in Mi v 9, and the following readings:

Hs ix 14	ܠܗܘܢ 2°] *add* ܡܪܝܐ	(Also in 17a6.)
Mi iv 8	ܡܠܟܘܬܐ ܪܒܬܐ] *tr*	
Hg ii 22	ܕܡܠܟܘܬܐ 1°] *add* ܕܥܡܡܐ	
Sa iii 3	ܝܐܐ] *s. sey*	(Also in 16d1.)

At first sight these seven common readings might suggest that 19d2 is the exemplar of 19d3; the reverse relationship is excluded by the respective dates of the Mss as well as by the nine uncorrected omissions peculiar to 19d3 (and 19/17d1). This possibility too however is excluded by the divergence of 19d2 from readings of the *fam* at Sa xiv 18 and Ml iii 22, by the uncorrected omission of ܕܝܢ in Mi iv 12 peculiar to 19d2, and by twenty-three further uncorrected readings peculiar to 19d2, of which only two are immediately suspect as dittographies. The most serious of these are:

Jon i 8	ܘܡܢ ܐܝܢܐ ܐܢܬ ܥܡܐ] ܘܐܢܬ ܡܢ ܐܝܢܐ ܥܡܐ
Jon ii 8	ܢܦܫܝ] ܪܘܚܝ
Jon iii 6	ܡܠܟܗ] ܡܢ ܪܫܗ
Mi v 3	ܘܪܥܐ] *add* ܐܢܘܢ
Zf i 17	ܚܛܝܐ] ܚܛܐ
Sa viii 20	ܡܬܛܝܒܬܐ] ܚܫܝܒܬܐ

The agreements between 19d2 (particularly in its uncorrected form) and 19d3 are nevertheless sufficient to make it probable that they had a common exemplar.

5. The relationship between 19d3 and 19/17d1

19/17d1 comprises two supplements to 17d1, containing respectively Jl ii 19 ܠܟܘܢ–Am iii 2 ܡܛܠ and Sa viii 19 ܨܘܡܐ 1°–Ml *fin.*

Discounting the mechanical omission at the beginning of the second section, there are six mechanical and three non-mechanical omissions in 19/17d1; four of these are shared with 19d3 (the one at Jl ii 27 occurring also in 15d2* and 19d2*) and the remaining five are peculiar to 19/17d1. There are no further omissions in 19d3 within these passages. This constitutes strong evidence for 19d3 being the exemplar of 19/17d1. To this may be added six readings of 19d3 found also in 19/17d1, some of which (Jl ii 27, Sa xiv 18, Ml iii 22) have already been noted above. One exclusively common reading is the substitution of ܐܝܟ ܕܠܗܘܢ for ܐܝܟ ܠܗܘܢ in Jl ii 19.

There are seventeen readings, at least ten of them erroneous, peculiar to 19/17d1, and this sets in perspective the nine passages where 19/17d1 differs from 19d3 in agreement with one or more other Mss. No consistent agreement with any other particular Ms has emerged, and most of the agreements are probaby accidental. For instance, in Sa xiii 6 12d2 reads ܡܢ in place of ܒܡܐ and 19/17d1 reads ܡܢ ܒܡܐ; but the addition of ܡܢ is probably due to the initiative of the scribe of 19/17d1 rather than a deliberate conflation with the reading found otherwise only in 12d2.

There is only one distinctive reading within the relevant passages of 19d3 which does not recur in 19/17d1. This is the repetition of ܗܘܝܐ in Sa xi 4, which would be immediately obvious as a dittograph to the scribe of 19/17d1. There is thus no serious obstacle to the derivation of 19/17d1 from 19d3, and it is highly probable that 19d3 was in fact the exemplar used by the scribe who supplied the *lacunae* in 17d1.

6. Conclusion

The pattern of relationships between these Mss seems then to be fairly clear. 15d2 was the exemplar of 17d4 and, directly or indirectly, of the common exemplar of 19d2 and 19d3. In all probability 19d3 was the exemplar of 19/17d1. 15d2 *fam* comprises 15d2 and its descendants, but belongs to a larger family which includes also 17d3 and 19d4, and whose common ancestor is not available to us. This common ancestor would have been distinguished from 15d2 by not sharing the omissions at Jl ii 9, 27 (with the adjustment of the *dalath* in the latter passage) or the peculiar reading of 15d2 at Hs x 9.

E. 16d1 17d2 18d1 18g1

1. Introduction

There are no omissions common to the whole of this group of Mss, but there are a number of readings, some of them certainly and most of them probably erroneous, which point to a common tradition.

DIETTRICH (p. XVIII) noted thirty-three readings in Isaiah 15-66 common to 16d1, 17d2 and 18d1; 18g1 does not contain Isaiah, and did not therefore come within the purview of his study. In the Dodekapropheton each Ms has several readings peculiar to itself of such a kind as to make it difficult to believe that it can have been the sole exemplar of any of the others. It is most probable therefore that they all derive ultimately from a common ancestor which is not at present available to us, and that they are surviving representatives of a larger family. Within the group there is a much closer relationship, including some common omissions, between 18d1 and 18g1. This is examined separately below.

A number of readings characteristic of the whole group are found in $17a7^{mg}.8^{mg}$. These are most probably to be regarded as derived directly from 16d1. The only readings in $17a7^{mg}.8^{mg}$ which occur in Mss of this group but not in 16d1 itself (Hs x 1 in 18d1 and 18g1 and Am v 26 in 18g1) are explicable as derived respectively from 9a1 and 16/9a1 in $17a7^{mg}.8^{mg}$. Since 16d1 is only one of the sources of the variants noted in $17a7^{mg}.8^{mg}$ the latter Mss are not to be considered members of this group. They have been discussed in Section A above and will not be considered further here. In the following subsection however passages containing variants noted in $17a7^{mg}.8^{mg}$ are marked with an asterisk, and the term "exclusively" is used without respect to the occurrence of these variants in $17a7^{mg}.8^{mg}$.

2. The common tradition

The seven most distinctive readings exclusively common to 16d1 17d2 18d1 and 18g1 are:

Hs vi 6*	ܘܒܬܪܗܘܢ]	om beth
Hs ix 17*	ܐܠܗ,]	pr ܡܪܝܐ
Am ix 12*	ܫܪܟܐ]	add ܐܢܫܐ
Ob 4*	ܬܬܪܝܡ]	add ܐܝܟ (Probably assimilation to Mi v 8.)
Na iii 2*	ܪܟܫܐ]	ܪܓܠܐ
Sa vi 10	ܠܥܠ]	ܥܠ
Ml iii 14	ܡܪܝܐ 2°]	add ܐܠܗܐ

It is noteworthy that four of these readings consist of the addition of a single word. Two of the remainder (Na iii 2, Sa vi 10) are evidently miscopyings.

Seven less distinctive readings exclusively common to 16d1 17d2 18d1 and 18g1 are:

Hs ix 11	ܩܢܘ]	c. waw fin
Hs x 14	ܐܪܡ]	pr waw
Na iii 10	ܥܒܕܘܗܝ]	stat emph
Zf ii 5	ܕܩܠܬܗ]	s. sey
Zf iii 4*	ܡܪܗܝ]	c. 3 masc sg suff
Sa xi 13	ܒܝܬ 2°]	pr beth
Ml i 7*	ܕܝܠܝ]	om dalath

Four of these readings consist of the omission or addition of a single letter, and two consists of the addition or removal of a suffix.

Two readings not exclusive to the group should also be taken into account:

Hs i 6	ܕܒܝܬ]	pr ܒܝܬ	(Also in 17a6 *fam* except 17a8*.)
Hs xii 2	ܩܝܬܐ]	c. sey	(Also in 19d1.)

It remains to consider ten further readings attested only partially within the group. Readings shared exclusively by 18d1 and 18g1 are considered in the next subsection. Those to be examined here fall into two groups:

(a) Readings attested exclusively within the group:

Hs v 13	ܟܖܡܝܗܘܢ]	c. 3 masc pl suff	16d1 17d2*(vid) 18d1
Hs vii 14*	ܡܬܒܬܪ]	ܡܬܒܩܪ	16d1[1] 18d1
Jl i 10*	ܐܪܥܒܝ]	ܐܪܥܒܝ	16d1 17d2*
Am viii 5	ܡܬܩܠܐ]	s. sey	16d1 18d1 18g1
Mi iii 7	ܢܝܪܐ]	s. sey	16d1 18d1
Hg ii 20	ܟܪܝܟܐ]	ܟܪܒܐ	16d1 18d1* 18g1

(b) Readings attested also outside the group:

Jl iii 1	ܢܫܠܐ]	s. sey	16d1 18d1 18g1 (Also in 10d1 17a3.)
Ob 9	ܐܪܙܐ]	c. sey	16d1 17d2 (Also in 17a1.)
Mi iv 13	ܠܨܗܝܐ]	stat emph	16d1 18g1 (Also in 15d3 (vid) 17a2.4.6.)
Hb i 4	ܒܣܘܐܬܐ]	ܒܣܐܬܐ	16d1* 18d1 18g1 (Also in 6h9 18d2 19g5.7.)

Three of these readings concern the omission of *seyāmē* and are significant only for their absence from 17d2. A fourth concerns the addition of *seyāmē*; its absence from 18d1 and 18g1 is to be discounted by the marked tendency in both these Mss to omit *seyāmē*. In any case it is hardly more than an orthographic variant in this passage. Three readings (Hs v 13, Jl i 10 and Hg ii 20) are palpable errors of such a kind as a copyist might correct on his own initiative without recourse to another exemplar. Mi iv 13 is probably a case of assimilation to the occurrence of the same word in *stat emph* two words previously, and might also have been spontaneously corrected by a copyist. The remaining two (Hs vii 14 and Hb i 4) are probably genuine variants, though the latter of itself could easily arise through corruption. It could be an alternative rendering of לנצח giving the noun the meaning usually ascribed to it by Aquila, or it could be an assimilation to Is xlii 3f. in the form in which it is quoted in Mt xii 20 (Old Syriac and Peshiṭta). The reading in Hs vii 14 is deliberately substituted for the usual reading in 16d1 and was thus clearly regarded as a variant to be preferred; it may possibly have originated as an explanatory gloss suggesting the sense in which the usual reading was to be understood.

The distribution of these ten partially attested readings within the group is interesting. All ten occur in 16d1, while only three are found in 17d2 and two of these have been corrected. Seven occur in 18d1 and five in 18g1; four of these are common to the two Mss. These figures suggest two conclusions. The first is that 17d2 stands somewhat apart from the rest of the group. The second is that there is a closer relationship between 16d1 and 18d1 than between any of the others. But this needs to be balanced by the large amount of exclusive agreement between 18d1 and 18g1 to be considered in the next subsection.

It seems in fact hardly possible that 16d1 was the sole direct exemplar of any of the others. Although it has no uncorrected omissions, it has no less than thirty-one uncorrected readings peculiar to itself. Many of these are indeed such as a copyist might easily have corrected on his own initiative without recourse to another exemplar, but two in particular consist of the addition of a word (ܟܠܗ after ܘܚܡܪܐ in Sa ix 3 and ܪܒܐ after ܟܗܢܐ in Ml iii 16) which a copyist was hardly likely to discard unless he was checking 16d1 carefully against another exemplar. In any case it is clear that 16d1 was already in Rome in 1569 (LEVI DELLA VIDA, pp. 187–189), and can hardly therefore have been accessible to the copyists of the later Mss in this group.

Similar considerations make it highly unlikely that 17d2 was the sole direct exemplar of either 18d1 or 18g1. There is in fact one passage which might suggest the dependence of 18g1 on 17d2. At Hs xiv 3 the original text of 17d2 read ܥܠܝܗܘܢ in place of ܥܠܝܟܘܢ. This was corrected by a *caph* written above the *he*, possibly by the original scribe. In 18g1 the scribe wrote ܥܠܝܗܘ and then corrected it to ܥܠܝܟܘܢ *cal curr.* But this is probably a coincidence. The two uncorrected omissions in 17d2 (ܐܝܟ in Hs ii 1 and ܠܐ 2° in Am v 5) and many of the seventeen uncorrected readings peculiar to the Ms could no doubt have been spontaneously corrected by a copyist. But it is hard to see why a copyist should reject the addition of ܕܫܠܗܒܝܬܐ before ܕܡܒܥܪܬܐ in Jl ii 5 or the *lamadh* prefixed to ܥܡ̈ܡܐ 1° in Jl iv 12 unless he were carefully checking 17d2 against another exemplar. In any case the derivation of 18d1 or 18g1 from 17d2 would leave unexplained the readings the former Mss have in common with 16d1 which do not occur in 17d2.

3. 18d1 and 18g1

In addition to readings already considered in the last subsection these two Mss have a number of readings in common:
(a) two substantial mechanical omissions in Jon iv 5 and Hb ii 3.
(b) four non-mechanical omissions, each of a single word. The most striking is ܠܡܦܨܝܘ in Zf i 18.
(c) fifty-five readings, of which twenty-seven are certainly erroneous, peculiar to themselves. A great many of these are simply omissions of *seyāmē*, a characteristic of both these Mss. But the following are of more than usual interest:

Jl i 6	ܠܐܪܥܝ] ܠܐܘܪܥܝ	
Am viii 10	ܩ̈ܘܕܝܬܐ] ܩܘܪ̈ܝܬܐ	(= Syh)
Mi i 11	ܡܢܟܘܢ] ܡܢܗܘܢ	
Mi vii 2	ܟܡܢ̈ܝܢ] ܟܡ̈ܢܝܢ	
Hb iii 10	ܬܗܘܡܐ] ܬܝܘܡܐ	
Hb iii 11	ܘܒܢܘܗܪܐ] ܘܒܢܘܪܐ	
Zf iii 20	ܒܙܒܢܐ 1°] ܒܝܘܡܐ	
Sa viii 12	ܘܫܝܢܐ] ܒܫܝܢܐ	

(d) twenty-nine readings, of which thirteen are certainly erroneous, found also in some other Mss. The most interesting of these are:

Jl i 4	ܕܐܘܬܪ 3°] ܕܐܬܘܪ	(Also in 17a2*.)
Am vi 11	ܘܠܒܕ̈ܩܘܗܝ] ܘܠܒܪ̈ܩܘܗܝ	(Also in 17a3.)

Despite such a remarkable correspondence between these two Mss there are serious difficulties in the way of a belief that either could have been the sole exemplar of the other.

In the case of 18d1 there are two substantial uncorrected mechanical omissions in Jl iv 6–7, 14 which could not have been supplied by the copyist of 18g1 without an additional exemplar. There are three non-mechanical omissions and three further errors peculiar to 18d1 which the copyist of 18g1 could hardly have corrected unaided. The most serious of the latter is the substitution of ܒܥܠ for ܒܥܠܐ, ܒܥܠin Jl iv 2.

The two omissions peculiar to 18g1 are less serious, but this Ms does have a number of readings peculiar to itself which the copyist of 18d1 could hardly have corrected unaided. The most serious of these are:

Hs ii 8	ܣܡܐ] ܣܡܠ
Hs vii 4	ܐܪܙ] ܐܪܙܝ
Hs xii 5	ܐܪܡܝ ܒܪ] ܐܪܡܝ ܒܪ, pr
Am iii 11	ܐܘܒܕ] ܐܘܒܕܬ
Hb i 3	ܘܕܝܢܐ] ܘܕܝܢܐ
Hb i 16	ܠܕܝܢܗ] ܠܕܝܢܐ
Sa ii 12	ܢܗܘܝ¹°] om beth

These facts seem to preclude the possibility of either 18d1 or 18g1 having been the sole exemplar of the other. But there remains the possibility that one of them might have been used by the scribe of the other along with one or more other exemplars.

There is one passage which at first sight suggested dependence of 18g1 on 18d1. At Ml i 14 for ܒܪܝܬܗ the scribe of 18d1 wrote originally *stat emph*. This was corrected by attaching a *he* to the final 'alaph, thus producing the hybrid ܒܪܝܬܗ, which actually appears as the reading of 18g1. This suggested the use of the corrected 18d1 by the scribe of 18g1, who had failed to appreciate the true intention of the correction. But further examination revealed two other instances in 18g1 of suffixes attached to nouns in *stat emph* (Na ii 12, Sa xiv 13). The agreement between 18d1[1] and 18g1 at Ml i 14 appears thus to be a coincidence.

On the other hand there is a passage which suggests that 18g1 may have been one of two or more exemplars of 18d1. At Hb iii 10 the scribe of 18d1 began to write ܬܗܘܡܐ but corrected it *cal curr* to ܬܗܘܡܐ, the reading of 18g1. Unless we are to assume that his original intention to write ܬܗܘܡܐ was due simply to misreading his exemplar, it seems as though he must have had access to both readings and deliberately though mistakenly chose ܟܬܒܘܗܝ. This would be consistent with 18g1 having been one of his exemplars but not the only one.

Such a hypothesis might also account for the correction of some readings in 18d1* which agreed with 18g1. The mechanical omission in Jon iv 5 mentioned above seems in fact to have been corrected by a later hand, but there are four readings which required only the addition of a single letter above the word, and this may have been done *cal curr* by the original scribe as he consulted another exemplar. On the other hand the corrections may have been made later, in which case they have no bearing on the question. The passages are:

Jl ii 10	ܐܝܗܘ] ܐܝܘ	
Mi vi 3	ܬܗܒ] *om taw*	
Zf i 11	ܐܘܒܕܐ] *om waw fin*	
Zf ii 3	ܘܒܠܐ] *om waw fin*	

One further passage may be considered. At Ml ii 16 both Mss add after the first ܫܠܝܛ two (18d1 adds three) of the words immediately following the second ܫܠܝܛ before reverting to the true continuation of the text. This is a simple mechanical error, in effect an arrested *homoeoteleuton*, and it occurs also in 19/17d1. In both 18d1 and 18g1 the intruded words have been marked for deletion. In the case of 18g1 this was almost certainly done *cal curr*, since in addition to the deletion mark there is a dash before the text is resumed. In 18d1 however the deletion mark extends beyond the intruded words and may well have been added later. This curious passage admits of more than one possible explanation, but it is difficult to see how either 18d1 or 18g1 can have been directly dependent on the other at this point. It is certainly possible, as the evidence of 19/17d1 shows, that the error occurred independently in the two Mss and was in each case corrected *cal curr* (except for the deletion mark in 18d1). This would account for the fact that 18d1 includes an extra word before reverting to the true text. It is also possible that the two Mss were following a common exemplar in which the *homoeoteleuton* did occur and that the scribes failed to notice the words supplied in the margin or possibly in another exemplar until they had written two or three words respectively.

Certainty is unattainable on this point. On the whole the hypothesis that best fits the facts is that 18d1 and 18g1 were copied from a common exemplar, not at present available to us, which was ultimately derived from an ancestor of 16d1. There is only one passage

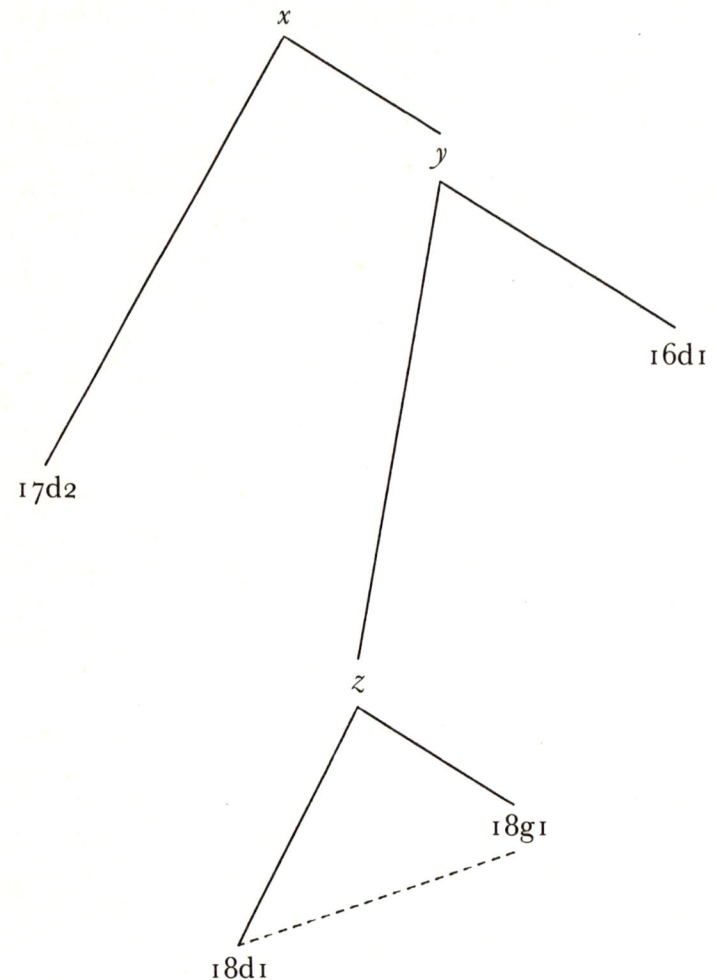

strongly suggesting that the scribe of 18d1 had more than one exemplar, one of which was 18g1, *viz* Hb iii 10.

4. Conclusion

These four Mss have a number of common readings which make it probable that they derive ultimately from a common ancestor. But each of them has a number of peculiar readings, some of which are such as to make it unlikely to have been the sole direct exemplar of any of the others. The only qualification that needs to be made to this conclusion is to note the possibility, suggested by Hb iii 10, that 18g1 was one of two or more exemplars used by the original scribe of 18d1. The four Mss seem then to have belonged to a larger family, and to account for the relationship between them we need to posit at least three other Mss not at present available to us. In the diagram on p. 60 these are designated respectively x, y and z: x denotes the ultimate common ancestor of the whole group, y the common ancestor of 16d1, 18d1 and 18g1, and z the direct common ancestor of 18d1 and 18g1. The dotted line denotes the possibility that 18g1 was one of the exemplars of 18d1.

F. 17d5 18d2 19d1

These three Mss have seven readings in common which occur in no other Ms:

Hs v 9	ܟܬܒܘܡܪܢ] ܟܬܒܡܪܢ
Hs x 13	ܡܢܠ] *pr waw*
Hs xii 3	ܐܪܡܝ¹⁰] *om*
Mi vii 7	ܐܡܪ,] *stat emph*
Hb ii 17	ܐܢܠܗܘܢ] *om dalath*
Zf i 10	ܝܕܥ] ܝܕܝܥ
Zf i 12	ܠܐܝܠܝܗܘܢ] ܠܐܝܠܝܗܘܢ

The most striking of these is Zf i 10, where the substituted reading is an assimilation to the previous phrase.

To these should be added two further readings which occur also in other Mss:

Hs v 15	ܘܒܐܘܠܨܢܗܘܢ] ܘܒܐܘܠܨܢܝ̈ܗܘܢ	(Also in 12d2 17a6.)
Hb ii 13	ܢܠܐ̈ܘܢ] ܢܠܐ̈ܢ	(Also in 12d1 16g6 19g5.7.)

These nine readings are perhaps sufficient to establish an ultimate common ancestry for these three Mss.

There are eight further agreements between 17d5 and the original text of 18d2 which do not occur in 19d1. Four of these are omissions which have been corrected in 18d2. The others are:

Am iii 4	ܐܪܝܐ 2°] *om*	(Also in 14a1*.)
Na ii 6	ܠܫܘܪܐ] *c. sey*	
Sa i 5	ܐܝܟܐ] ܐܝܟܢܐ	(An error)
Sa i 8	ܒܝܢܬ] ܒܝܬ	(Also in 12a1 16/9a1 17a6 *fam*)

Despite this close relationship between 17d5 and 18d2 there are conclusive objections to regarding 17d5 as the sole or main exemplar of 18d2. Most important are nine uncorrected omissions in 17d5, two of them substantial, which could not have been supplied by the scribe of 18d2 without recourse to another exemplar. Moreover 17d5 has a number of readings peculiar to itself, some of which are virtually the substitution of synonyms for the usual readings. These again the scribe of 18d2 could hardly have corrected unaided. The most significant of these are:

Hs vii 3	ܘܒܕܓܠܘܬܗܘܢ] ܘܒܟܕܒܘܬܗܘܢ
Hs vii 4	ܕܢܦܘ] ܕܚܡܥܬ ܟܪ
Am v 5	ܬܥܠܘܢ] ܬܐܙܠܘܢ
Am v 23	ܘܙܡܝܪܬܐ] ܘܩܠܐ
Mi v 4	ܪ̈ܘܪܒܢܐ] ܡܕܒ̈ܪܢܐ
Na ii 13	ܬܒܪܐ] ܟܪܐ
Zf i 18	ܘܒܢܘܪܐ] ܘܒܪܘܓܙܐ
Sa iii 1	ܩܕܡ ܡܚܝܢܗ] ܡܩܕܡܘܗܝ
Sa vi 15	ܫܠܝܬܢܐ] *add* ܐܠܗܟܘܢ
Sa ix 15	ܘܢܟܒܫܘܢ] *add* ܠܗܘܢ
Sa x 11	ܘܢܗܦܟ ܒܢܚܐ ܬܠܠܐ] ܘܢܒܙ ܒܗܦܟܝܐ ܬܠܠܘܗܝ
Ml i 10	ܬܪܥܐ] *pr* ܒܐܦ
Ml ii 12	ܠܡܪܝܐ 2°] ܠܚܡܐ ܡܕܡ ܡܪܝܐ
Ml iii 22	ܦܘܩܕܢܐ] ܢܡܘܣܐ

Finally there are a number of other readings, not peculiar to 17d5, which the scribe of 18d2 could hardly have corrected unaided:

Hs v 10	ܘܢܦܫܬܐ ,ܘܩܢܝ]	tr
Hs xiii 15	ܡܚܕܝܢ]	pr ܡܢ
Hb i 3	ܘܪܝܚܐ ܡܗܠ] ܘܪܝܚܬܐ ܡܗܠ	
Sa ix 9	ܢܩܝܦܐ ܘܡܪܬܐ]	tr
Ml i 13	ܒܗܘܢ] ܒܗܡ	
Ml ii 17	ܥܒܕ] add ܗܡ	
Ml iii 13	ܡܪܝܐ] add ܣܠܝܛܐ	

The last four of these readings incidentally are attested also in some of the ancient Mss, a fact which suggests that 17d5 itself was derived from more than one exemplar, one of them not belonging to this group at all.

The cumulative effect of this evidence is to make it impossible that 17d5 was the sole or main exemplar of 18d2, and improbable that it was an exemplar of 18d2 at all. The agreements between 17d5 and the uncorrected 18d2 are however substantial and make it necessary to posit a common ancestor.

The case of 19d1 is more complex. Any direct dependence on 17d5 is excluded by the facts that the agreements between 17d5 and 19d1 are fewer than those between 17d5 and 18d2 and that there are no exclusive agreements at all between 17d5 and 19d1, as well as by the uncorrected omissions and peculiar readings which have already been noted in 17d5. The relationship between 18d2 and 19d1 is less clear. In the first place there are two passages in 19d1 where a variant reading has been recorded in the margin, possibly by the original scribe but more probably by a later annotator. At Hs v 9 the text of 19d1 has the reading which occurs elsewhere only in 17d5 and 18d2 (*v. supra*), but the usual reading is recorded in the margin as that of another codex. At Hs ii 24 the text of 19d1 has the usual reading ܢܣܒ; the variant reading noted in the margin under a similar rubric is ܢܣܠ, found elsewhere only in 18d2. These two are the only variant readings recorded in the margin of 19d1.

In addition to the nine readings common to the three Mss there are two exclusive agreements between 18d2 and 19d1:

Hs xiii 7	ܐܢܫ¹°] om	(This has been corrected in 19d1.)
Sa vi 13	ܘܡܠܟܐ] ܘܡܠܟܐ	(This diacritic point is erroneous in this context.)

On the other hand there are eight passages where 19d1 differs from 18d2:

(a) the four passages already noted where 17d5 and 18d2 agree against 19d1,
(b) the passage already noted in Hs ii 24, where the reading otherwise peculiar to 18d2 is noted as a variant in the margin of 19d1, and
(c) three further readings in 18d2:

Hs v 1	ܟܠܗ] c. sey	(Also in 19d3.)	
Hb i 4	ܒܐܘܪܚܐ] ܒܐܘܪܚܐ	(Also in 6h9 16d1* 18d1 18g1 19g5.7.)	
Sa viii 19	ܡܢ] om	(Peculiar to 18d2.)	

We may note in passing the possibility raised by the reading of 18d2 at Hb i 4 that like 17d5 this Ms was derived partly from an exemplar outside the group. This reading however is more likely to be a simple corruption in 18d2, and its agreement with a genuine variant in other Mss to be fortuitous.

Most of these eight disagreements between 18d2 and 19d1 are such that an intelligent copyist might have adjusted them without recourse to another exemplar. It is difficult however to account for the readings of 19d1 at Hs ii 24 or Hb i 4 on the hypothesis that the Ms was copied directly from 18d2. On the other hand the two exclusive agreements between 18d2 and 19d1 suggest a link between them.

There can be little doubt that these three Mss ultimately descend from a common ancestor and that there is a closer link between 17d5 and 18d2. 18d2 however cannot derive directly from 17d5, and it is difficult to see how 19d1 can derive directly from 18d2. It is perhaps most probable that 19d1 is a more distant relative, and that its exclusive agreements with 18d2 are a cross-connection within the tradition. In all probability however the marginal variant in 19d1 at Hs ii 24 derives directly from 18d2.

3
Distinctive Readings of the Oldest Manuscripts

1. The oldest manuscripts and the standard text

In the Peshiṭta of the Dodekapropheton, as of some other Books of the Old Testament, the great majority of Mss attest a remarkably homogeneous tradition, from which the oldest Mss diverge in a significant number of readings.

The rules in force at the time when the EDITION of the Dodekapropheton was prepared required the printing of the text of 7a1 as the basic text except (a) where it is manifestly erroneous, and (b) where it lacks the support of at least two of the older Mss, the older Mss being defined for this purpose as those belonging to the twelfth century or earlier. Apart therefore from the exclusion of erroneous readings in 7a1 the distribution of alternative readings between text and apparatus in the EDITION was determined by purely arithmetical considerations, and did not represent a critical judgement between the alternative readings. It is the purpose of the present chapter to attempt such a critical assessment, and to suggest a more convenient way in which the material may be considered.

The first requirement is a more objective standard of comparison than the basic text printed in the EDITION. There is much to be said for adopting for this purpose what we may call the standard text, designated Textus Receptus by Koster, which represents the homogeneous tradition of all but the oldest Mss. Apart from variants of an orthographic nature and those concerning differences in the spelling of proper names, which tend to follow a division between eastern and western Mss, there is only one reading in the Dodekapropheton where the identity of this standard text is in any doubt. This occurs at Jon ii 3 and concerns merely the prefixing of *waw* to the word ܡܢ; in this one passage both the oldest and the later Mss are almost equally divided. Apart from this one uncertain reading, which is in any case of little significance, the standard text may be obtained from the EDITION by following the omission in Sa iii 4 listed at the top of p. XXV and by substituting the following variants from the Second Apparatus for the corresponding readings in the basic text:

Hs iv 14$^{1°}$, 15, 16, vii 14, xii 12$^{1°}$, xiv 8, 9, Jl iv 14, Am iv 1, 6, vi 2, Na iii 3, 19$^{1°}$, Hb i 5, iii 1$^{1°}$, Zf i 18, Hg 1 11, 14$^{1°}$, ii 11$^{1°}$, 18$^{2°}$, Sa i 2, 9, ii 17, v 1, 8, ix 8, 13, xi 4, xiv 9, 10$^{1°}$, 21$^{1°}$. (Note—Each of these variants is accompanied by a list of sigla ending in an arrow; where more than one such variant occurs in a verse the relevant one is indicated by $^{1°}$ or $^{2°}$.)

This standard text rather than the basic text printed in the EDITION will be used as the basis of comparison in the present chapter. It should be noted that the Inscriptions and Subscriptions, apart from those in Jon ii 2 and Hb iii 1, do not constitute part of this standard text and will be left out of account here.

The next requirement is to determine which of the Biblical Mss belonging to the twelfth century or earlier are to be regarded as the "oldest Mss" in the significant sense that they represent a textual tradition distinct from that of the standard text. There is no doubt that 6h9, 7a1, 8a1 and 9a1 must be included in this category. On the other hand the 'd' Mss (9d1 10d1 11d1 12d1–3) all seem to attest the standard text, and their distinctive readings are best understood as deviations from that text. The sole reading found only in these Mss with any claim to originality is the addition of *seyāmē* to ܐܠܗܝܗ in Sa xiv 10 in 12d2.3 where the Hebrew, Syrohexapla and other versions also read a plural. This is however much more likely to be an inner-Syriac development than a survival of an older textual tradition. Of the seven fragmentary Mss 7k7 may be ignored both because it contains no significant variants itself and because the passage it contains is one in which there are no variants agreed by two or more of the oldest Mss against the standard text. 7pj2 is legible only for isolated words, but it does agree in one reading (Zf i 18) with 6h9 against the standard text. The other five fragmentary Mss (7k8 7k10 8j1 10j2 11k4) all agree at least once with one or more of the oldest Mss against the standard text.

12a1 is the most difficult of these Mss to assess. It has a considerable number of readings peculiar to itself and its immediate descendants, and in a majority of cases where it is legible it agrees with the standard text against most or all of the oldest Mss. It does however agree with one or more of the oldest Mss against the standard text in nine readings. 12a1 then seems to belong essentially to the standard textual tradition, but it does retain a few readings in common with one or more of the oldest Mss.

The oldest Mss therefore, in the sense of those representing a textual tradition distinct from that of the standard text, may be listed as follows: 6h9 7a1 7k8 7k10 7pj2 8a1 8j1 9a1 10j2 11k4 (12a1).

It should be noted that the distribution of the oldest Mss is very uneven, 7a1 being the only one present and legible virtually throughout the Dodekapropheton, and being effectively the only one extant for Jl i 10–Am ii 9, except where 8j1 (in Jl iv 2–Am ii 4) and 12a1 are legible. There are a number of other passages where only one other of the oldest Mss is available to offer potential support to readings of 7a1. It will be convenient then to examine the readings of the oldest Mss in three categories: (a) where they all (except in many cases 12a1) agree against the standard text, (b) where one or more agree with the standard text but two or more agree against it, and (c) where the reading is attested in only one of the oldest Mss.

2. Agreed readings of the oldest manuscripts

In view of the varied distribution of these readings between text and apparatus in the EDITION it will be convenient to print them here in the form of variants from the standard text, assigning to each a serial number for ease of subsequent reference. No details will be given here of the occurrence of some of these readings in Mss other than the "oldest Mss". The thirty-six readings in this section may be set out under five sub-headings according to the degree of attestation among the oldest Mss:

(a) Readings in all the oldest Mss, including 12a1:

1. Hs xii 12	ܘܟܦܪ] *om waw*	7a1 8a1 9a1 12a1
2. Hs xiv 8	ܘܢܬܒܠܐ] *om waw*	7a1 8a1 12a1
3. Hs xiv 9	ܐܟܪܐ̈] ܐܟܪܐ̈ܝܢ	7a1 8a1 12a1
4. Am ii 8	ܚܬܝܒܐ] ܚܒܘܠܐ	7a1 (*s. sey*) 12a1

(b) Readings in all the oldest Mss, except 12a1 which agrees with the standard text (probably in the case of nos. 9, 16 and 17):

5. Hs iv 16	ܒܝܬ ܐܘܢܐ] ܒܝܬ ܐܘܢܐ	7a1 8a1* 9a1
6. Am iv 6	ܘܟܦܪ] *om waw*	7a1 7k10 8a1
7. Am vi 2	ܘܓܠܒܐ] *om* ܗܘ	7a1 7k10 8a1
8. Jon i 16	ܟܣܘܡ] *om* ܟܣܘܡ	7a1 8a1*
9. Mi iii 1	ܗܘܠܐ] *om*	7a1 8a1*
10. Mi vii 12	ܫܒܬܐ ܗܘ] *om* ܗܘ	7a1 8a1

11. Na iii 19	ܘܠܝܬ] *om waw*		6h9 7a1 8a1
12. Hb i 5	ܡܫܬܥܐ] ܫܬܥܐ		6h9 7a1 8a1
13. Hg i 11	ܕܐܝ̈ܕܝܗܘܢ] ܕܐܝ̈ܕܝܟܘܢ		6h9 7a1 8a1
14. Hg i 14	ܫܪܟܐ] ܫܪܟܗ		6h9 7a1 8a1
15. Hg ii 18	ܫܠܝܬܐ ܠܬܚܬܝܢ] *om*		6h9 7a1 8a1*
16. Sa i 2	ܪܒܐ] *om*		6h9 7a1 8a1
17. Sa iii 4	ܐܝ̈ܟ] *add* ܐܝ̈ܟ ܡܐܢ̈ܐ ܡܢܗ ܘܐܟܒܪ		6h9 7a1 8a1*
18. Sa ix 8	ܬܘܒ ܥܠܗܘܢ] *tr*		6h9 7a1 8a1* (*vid*)
19. Sa ix 13	ܕܝܘ̈ܢܝܐ] *c. sey*		6h9 7a1 8a1 (*vid*)
20. Sa xi 4	ܐܡܪ ܠܝ] *om* ܠܝ		6h9 7a1 8a1*
21. Sa xii 3	ܒܗ] *om*		6h9 7a1
22. Sa xii 4	ܪ̈ܟܫܗ] *stat emph*		6h9 7a1
23. Sa xiv 21	ܕܒܐܘܪܫܠܡ ܘܒܝܗܘܕܐ] ܕܒܝܗܘܕܐ ܘܒܐܘܪܫܠܡ		6h9 7a1 7k8
24. Ml i 13	ܫܠܝܬܐ 2°] *om*		6h9 7a1

(c) Readings in all the oldest Mss, except 12a1 which is illegible:

25. Jon ii 5	ܗܝܟܠܟ] *pr lamadh*		7a1 8a1
26. Mi vii 15	ܐܝܘܡܐ] *pr waw*		7a1 8a1
27. Mi vii 17	ܘܢܠܚܟܘܢ] *om waw init*		7a1 8a1
28. Na iii 3	ܘܦܪ̈ܫܐ] *om waw*		6h9 7a1 8a1
29. Hg ii 11	ܫܠܝܬܐ] *om*		6h9 7a1 8a1*
30. Sa v 1	ܘܗܦܟܬ ܐܪܝܡܬ] ܘܐܪܝܡܬ		6h9 7a1 8a1*
31. Sa xii 10	ܒܟܘܪܝܗ] *pr* ܥܠܗܘܢ		6h9 7a1
32. Sa xiv 10	ܡܢ 1°] *pr dalath*		6h9 7a1 7k8

(d) Reading in all the oldest Mss, except 8a1 and 12a1 which are illegible:

33. Zf iii 1	ܡܕܝܢܬܗ] *stat emph*		6h9 7a1

(e) Readings in all the oldest Mss, except 12a1 which agrees with the standard text and one other Ms which is illegible:

34. Na ii 2	ܒܣܝܐ] *c. sey*		6h9 7a1 (*l.n.* 8a1)
35. Hb iii 1	ܕܚܒܩܘܩ] *add* ܢܒܝܐ		6h9 7a1 8a1 (*l.n.* 7k10)
36. Sa v 8	ܟܟܪܐ] ܟܐܦܐ		6h9 7a1 11k4 (*l.n.* 8a1*)

These thirty-six readings must now be examined from three points of view. First they must be classified according to type. Next it must be determined where possible which reading is closer to the Hebrew. Finally an attempt must be made where possible to establish which reading is more likely to be a corruption of the other.

The thirty-six readings under consideration may be classified broadly into three groups. Half of them concern minor changes of a grammatical or stylistic nature: seven (1, 2, 6, 11, 26, 27, 28) concern *waw*, six (3, 4, 13, 14, 22, 33) concern suffixes, two (25, 32) concern prepositions, two (19, 34) concern *seyāmē*, and one (12) concerns a variation between a participle and an imperfect. Sixteen concern omissions, additions or metatheses: ten (7, 8, 9, 10, 16, 20, 21, 24, 29, 30) concern the omission and two (31, 35) the addition of single words, one (15) the omission of two words, one (17) the addition of four words, and two (18, 23) the metathesis of adjacent words. The remaining two (5, 36) are more substantial changes.

In almost half of these passages (1, 2, 5, 9, 11, 12, 15, 16, 18, 20, 22, 24, 27, 28, 34, 35, 36) the reading of the oldest Mss is closer to the Hebrew, though in no. 24 the reading of the standard text agrees with that of a few Hebrew Mss. In ten passages (4, 6, 10, 17, 19, 23, 26, 29, 30, 31) the reading of the standard text is closer to the Hebrew. In the remaining nine passages (3, 7, 8, 13, 14, 21, 25, 32, 33) the difference is such as not to admit of resolution by reference to the Hebrew.

It is often difficult to determine which of the two readings is likely to be original. This difficulty may be illustrated by five of the passages under consideration:

14. As this concerns an anticipatory suffix the difference is purely stylistic. Consistency with v. 12 is an argument in favour of the originality of the reading of the oldest Mss, but this could equally have been a motive for modifying the standard text.
33. This also concerns an anticipatory suffix. The following *dalath* shows that in both readings of the Peshitta the noun is regarded as dependent on the following word. The occurrence of the same noun in *stat emph* earlier in the verse might suggest that the reading of the oldest Mss is an assimilation to it. Alternatively the suffix in the standard text could be a stylistic modification.
24. This is an interesting case, because the reading of the standard text agrees with that of a few Hebrew Mss, while that of the oldest Mss agrees with that of the majority of Hebrew Mss. The priority here cannot be determined without a prior judgement about the identity of the Hebrew *Vorlage*. It is also possible however that the "omission" in the oldest Mss is purely accidental.
30. This too is an interesting case. The reading of the standard text is a literal rendering of the Hebrew, and recurs in Sa vi 1. This might

lead to the conclusion either that the standard text is an assimilation to vi 1, or that its consistency with vi 1 is evidence of its originality.

17. This is a very problematic case. The four words, if original in the oldest Mss, could easily have been omitted in the standard text by *homoeoteleuton*. On the other hand these words are peculiar to the Peshitta, and the shorter standard text agrees with the Hebrew and other versions. The additional words could therefore be an expansion in the oldest Mss. It is also possible however that the Hebrew *Vorlage* of the Peshitta itself contained this additional clause, which has been lost in the rest of the tradition.

These five examples illustrate how evenly balanced the arguments for originality may be. Three other passages (21, 25, 32) are equally hard to resolve, but not sufficiently significant to merit discussion.

Fortunately however it is possible in a number of cases to come to a more positive, if not absolutely certain, conclusion. There are four passages where the standard text seems to be original, and an additional passage (26) where the balance of probability also seems to be in favour of the standard text. The four passages are:

4. The 1 sg suffix may easily have arisen through a misreading of the final upstroke of *ḥeth*. Suspicion is aroused by the absence of *seyāmē* in 7a1, giving rise to a solecism (a plural being required after the preceding ܠ), and confirmed by the absence of any basis for the suffix in the Hebrew or other versions.

10. Here the pronoun ܗܘ corresponds to the Hebrew and the other versions. It may have been misunderstood as an enclitic rather than as a demonstrative, and hence mistakenly regarded as dispensable.

31. The additional word in the oldest Mss is peculiar to the Peshitta, but it is a natural amplification, and it is not easy to see why it should have been omitted in the standard text if it were original.

29. The additional divine title in the standard text conforms with the Hebrew and the other versions, and its omission in the oldest Mss is readily explicable as a *homoeoteleuton*.

In the remaining twenty-three passages the balance of probability, in varying degrees, is in favour of the reading of the oldest Mss. Three particular passages will be considered first:

36. The reading of the oldest Mss is a literal rendering of the Hebrew, while that of the standard text is an assimilation (found also in LXX^L) to the previous verse, and may be regarded as a natural

"improvement".

3. The feminine suffix of the oldest Mss represents the persistence of the image of Ephraim as the wife of Yahweh, and is much more likely to have been corrected to a masculine than *vice versa*.

23. The word order in the standard text agrees with the Hebrew, but there is a certain tendency in the Peshitta to reverse the order of paired words in the Hebrew (*cf* Sa ii 6), and there seems little reason why the order of the standard text should have been modified if it were original.

Other passages may be considered more briefly. There is perhaps a greater probability of the loss than of the addition of *seyāmē* in the process of transmission (19, 34). In several passages where the standard text has an additional word or words these additions are plausibly seen as inner-Syriac developments; it is difficult to see why they should have been omitted if original (5, 7, 8, 9, 15, 16, 20; in the case of no. 15 assimilation to Sa viii 9 may have been a factor). Assimilation to the immediate context probably accounts for three readings in the standard text (12, 13, 22). The change of word order in no. 18 may have been deliberate, in order to bring ܒܗ closer to the verb and its negative. The omission of the title in no. 35 may have been due to a desire to abbreviate the Inscription, and possibly also to assimilation to Jon ii 2. In the six remaining cases (1, 2, 6, 11, 27, 28) the difference merely concerns *waw*; in five of them the oldest Mss agree with the Hebrew, while in the remaining one (6) the parallel in the following verse suggests the originality of the reading of the oldest Mss. Allowance must always be made for purely accidental causes, but it may reasonably be claimed that in a majority of these thirty-six passages there is a balance of probability in favour of the readings of the oldest Mss where they diverge from the standard text.

3. Agreed readings of two or more of the oldest manuscripts

It will again be convenient to print these readings in the form of variants from the standard text, this time in a single sequence with serial numbers successive to those in the previous section. After the *lemma* from the standard text and before the *lemma* bracket those of the oldest Mss agreeing with the standard text will be indicated in parentheses. Any of the oldest Mss which are illegible for a particular variant will be indicated in parentheses after the variant. The fifty-three readings in this category are:

37. Hs i 2 ܐܡܪ (8a1 12a1)] *pr waw* 7a1 9a1
38. Hs iv 6 ܐܦ (9a1(*vid*) 12a1(*vid*))] *pr waw* 7a1 8a1
39. Hs iv 14 ܢܦܩܬ (8a1)] *c. sey* 7a1 9a1 12a1
40. Hs iv 15 ܬܐܡܪܘܢ (9a1 12a1)] ܬܐܡܢܘܢ 7a1 8a1
41. Hs v 14 ܐܬܒܪ (8a1 9a1 12a1)] ܐܕܒܪ 7a1 8j1
42. Hs vi 5 ܢܦܘܩ (8a1 12a1(*vid*))] ܢܦܩ 7a1 9a1 (*l.n.* 8j1)
43. Hs vii 14 ܥܠ (8j1)] ܒ 7a1 8a1* 9a1 (*l.n.* 12a1)
44. Hs vii 15 ܪܕܝܬ (8a1 8j1)] ܐܪܕܝܬ 7a1 9a1 (*l.n.* 12a1)
45. Hs viii 4 ܡܬܒܪܐ (7a1 9a1)] *c. sey* 8a1 8j1 (*l.n.* 12a1)
46. Hs ix 15 ܐܘܣܦ (9a1 12a1)] *add* ܬܘܒ 7a1 8a1
47. Hs xiv 3 ܬ̈ܠܐ (8a1 12a1)] *s. sey* 7a1 9a1
48. Am iv 1 ܕܥܨܝܢ (7k10 8a1)] *c. sey* 7a1 12a1
49. Am v 20 ܚܫܘܟܐ ܗܘ (7k10 12a1(*vid*))] *om* ܗܘ 7a1 8a1*
50. Am v 22 ܐܦ (7k10 12a1(*vid*))] *pr waw* 7a1 8a1
51. Am vii 8 ܠ ܡܪܝܐ (7k10 12a1)] *om* 7a1 8a1*
52. Am ix 11 ܕܢܦܠ (7k10 12a1(*vid*))] *pr* ܐܝܟ 7a1 8a1*(*vid*)
53. Ob 16 ܘܢܬܬܪܘܢ (7k10 12a1)] *om* 7a1 8a1*
54. Mi i 8 ܐܪܩܕ ܘܐܝܠܠ ܘܗܠܟ (8a1)] ܐܪܩܕܘ ܘܐܝܠܠܘ ܘܗܠܟܘ 7a1 12a1 (ܐܪܩܕܘ *l.n.*)
55. Mi vi 8 ܐܠܗܟ (8a1 12a1)] *pr* ܡܪܝܐ 7a1 10j2
56. Na i 4 ܒܥܐ (7a1)] ܒܥܝܐ 6h9 8a1 (*l.n.* 12a1)
57. Na i 14 ܠܬ̈ܩܦܐ ܘܬ̈ܫܡܫܬܐ (8a1)] ܠܬ̈ܩܦܝܢ ܘܢܫ̈ܡܫܝܢ 6h9 *7a1* (*l.n.* 12a1)

(Note: ܘܢܫ̈ܡܫܢ in 7a1 is an obvious error for ܘܢܫ̈ܡܫܝܢ.)

58. Na ii 1 ܡܦܘܣ (6h9)] ܢܦܘܣ 7a1 8a1 (*l.n.* 12a1)
59. Na ii 3 ܐܢܐ (8a1 12a1)] ܡܪܝܐ 6h9 7a1
60. Hb i 14 ܕܒܝܡܐ (12a1)] *om beth* 6h9 7a1

(Note: ܒܝܡܐ in 8a1* is probably a corruption of the standard text.)

61. Hb iii 1 (12a1)] *add post finem* ܥܠ ܕܫܠܝܐ 6h9 7a1: ܥܠ ܕܫܘܠܐ 7pj2 (*v. infra*) (*l.n.* 7k10: *rasura* 8a1)
62. Hb iii 17 ܥܒܕܬܐ (7k10 8a1)] ܥܒ̈ܕܐ 6h9 7a1 (*l.n.* 12a1)
63. Hb iii 19 ܒܬܫ̈ܒܘܚܬܗ (7k10 8a1)] *om praep* 6h9 7a1 (*l.n.* 12a1)
64. Zf i 1 ܒܝ̈ܘܡܬܗ (8a1*(*vid*) 12a1)] ܒܝ̈ܘܡܘܗܝ 6h9 7a1 (*l.n.* 7k10)
65. Zf i 18 ܘܕܗܒܗܘܢ ܘܣܐܡܗܘܢ (6h9)] *tr* 7a1 8a1 (*om waw init* 8a1) (*l.n.* 12a1)
66. Zf i 18 ܒܢܘܪ (6h9 8a1)] *add* ܡܪܝܐ 7a1 7pj2 (*l.n.* 12a1)
67. Zf i 18 ܥܠ (7a1 8a1 12a1)] ܥܡ 6h9 7pj2
68. Zf ii 5 ܕܪ̈ܘܫܠܐ (8a1 12a1)] *s. sey* 6h9 7a1

69. Zf ii 9 ܡܠܚܐ (8a1 (*vid*))] *pr lamadh* 6h9 7a1[1] (*l.n.* 12a1)
70. Zf ii 12 ܚܪܒܐ (8a1)] *add* ܐܢܬܘܢ 6h9 7a1 (*l.n.* 12a1)
71. Hg ii 16 ܐܢܬܘܢ (6h9 12a1 (*vid*))] ܗܘܝܬܘܢ 7a1 8a1
72. Hg ii 20 ܠܚܓܝ / ܒܥܣܪܝܢ ܘܐܪܒܥܐ (8a1 12a1 (*vid*))] *tr* 6h9 7a1
73. Sa i 4 ܡܪܝܐ 2° (8a1 12a1 (*vid*))] *add* ܚܝܠܬܢܐ 6h9 7a1
74. Sa i 9 ܘܒܢܐ (8a1 (*vid*))] *om waw* 6h9 7a1 7k8 (*l.n.* 12a1)
75. Sa ii 17 ܡܪܘܡܐ (*6h9* 12a1 (*vid*))] ܡܥܡܪܐ 7a1 7k8 8a1
(Note: 6h9 in fact seems to read ܡܪܘܕܘܐ, but this is probably a corruption of the standard text rather than of the variant.)
76. Sa iii 7 ܚܝܠܬܢܐ (6h9)] *om* 7a1 8a1* (*l.n.* 12a1)
77. Sa iv 12 ܥܢܝܬ (6h9)] *pr waw* 7a1 8a1 (*l.n.* 12a1)
78. Sa viii 6 ܐܦ (6h9 8a1)] *pr waw* 7a1 12a1
79. Sa viii 10 ܘܐܦ (8a1)] *om waw* 6h9 7a1 (*l.n.* 12a1)
80. Sa viii 15 ܘܠܕܒܝܬ (8a1 12a1 (*vid*))] *om dalath* 6h9 7a1
81. Sa xi 2 ܕܢܦܠ 2° (7a1 8a1)] *pr* ܡܛܠ 6h9 12a1
82. Sa xiv 9 ܒܝܘܡܐ (6h9 12a1 (*vid*))] *pr* ܒܗ 7a1 7k8
83. Sa xiv 16 ܟܠ (6h9 12a1)] *add* ܡܢ 7a1 7k8
84. Sa xiv 18 ܐܦ (7a1)] *pr waw* 6h9 7k8 (*l.n.* 12a1)
85. Ml i 4 ܡܪܝܐ 1° (6h9 12a1)] *add* ܚܝܠܬܢܐ 7a1 7k8
86. Ml ii 9 ܐܦ (8a1 12a1)] *pr waw* 6h9 7a1
87. Ml ii 16 ܚܝܠܬܢܐ 1° (7a1 12a1 (*vid*))] *om* 6h9 8a1*
88. Ml ii 17 ܥܒܕ (8a1 12a1 (*vid*))] *add* ܗܘ 6h9 7a1
89. Ml iii 13 ܡܪܝܐ (7a1)] *add* ܚܝܠܬܢܐ 6h9 8a1 (*l.n.* 12a1)

These fifty-three readings must similarly be classified according to type, closeness to the Hebrew, and probable originality. It will also be necessary to make some observations on the relation of each of the oldest Mss to the standard text in these readings.

Twenty-five of these readings concern minor changes of a grammatical or stylistic nature: nine (37, 38, 50, 74, 77, 78, 79, 84, 86) concern *waw*, five (39, 45, 47, 48, 68) concern *seyāmē* and one other (62) a variation between singular and plural, four (60, 63, 69, 80) concern prepositions, two (42, 58) concern variation between imperfect and participle and one (44) that between Pe'al and Aph'el, while one (71) concerns a difference in participial construction involving strictly a change of tense. Yet another (56) concerns the difference between the active and passive participles of a stative verb, where the meaning is hardly affected. One (57) concerns suffixes. Twenty concern omissions, additions or metatheses: four (49, 53, 76, 87) concern the omission and twelve (46, 52, 55, 66, 70, 73, 81, 82, 83,

85, 88, 89) the addition of single words, one (51) the omission and one (61) the addition of two words, and two concern the metathesis of adjacent words (65) or pairs of words (72). The remaining eight (40, 41, 43, 54, 59, 64, 67, 75) are more substantial changes, though the alternative readings in one (64) are synonyms.

In eighteen of these passages (37, 41, 42, 46, 47, 48, 51, 55, 57, 63, 66, 68, 73, 74, 76, 78, 83, 89) the reading of the standard text is closer to the Hebrew, and in seventeen (39, 40, 43, 45, 58, 59, 60, 61, 62, 65, 67, 72, 75, 77, 85, 86, 87) the variant reading is closer to the Hebrew. In the remaining eighteen passages (38, 44, 49, 50, 52, 53, 54, 56, 64, 69, 70, 71, 79, 80, 81, 82, 84, 88) the difference is not such as to admit of resolution by reference to the Hebrew.

In thirteen of these passages (41, 46, 47, 51, 53, 54, 63, 64, 71, 73, 76, 78, 81) it is most natural to regard the standard text as original and the variant as a corruption or amplification of it. The balance of probability, though finer, is also in favour of the standard text in ten other passages (48, 52, 55, 57, 59, 77, 83, 84, 87, 88). In nine passages (39, 40, 60, 61, 62, 72, 74, 75, 85) the variant is more likely to be original than the standard text, while in a further five (45, 49, 67, 70, 80) the balance of probability is also in favour of the variant. In the remaining sixteen passages (37, 38, 42, 43, 44, 50, 56, 58, 65, 66, 68, 69, 79, 82, 86, 89) it is difficult to determine which of the two readings is more likely to be original. Eight of these passages may be examined in more detail by way of illustration:

40. Here the distinctive reading of 7a1 and 8a1 agrees with the Hebrew. The weaker reading of the standard text is readily explicable as a corruption of it, and is without support in the other versions.

43. The variant could be explained as assimilation to the previous verse and the standard text as assimilation to the following verse. The variant is closer to the Hebrew, but the standard text to usual Syriac usage with this verb. The arguments seem thus to be evenly balanced.

48. The variant fails to recognize a place-name and treats the word as an adjective, an interpretation found also in Symmachus, Targum and Vulgate. Loss of *seyāmē* could easily be a corruption, but the *dalath* suggests that the Peshitta translators did interpret the word as a place-name. The variant is therefore most probably an inner-Syriac corruption due to misinterpretation. The name 'Bashan' is rendered ܕܒܝܫܢ in Mi vii 14 and Na i 4, but ܒܝܫܢ in Sa xi 2.

54. The 2 *f. sg* of the standard text is peculiar to the Peshiṭta, the Hebrew being in 1 *sg*. Only 12a1 is consistent in using the plural; 7a1 itself has 2 *f. sg* in the next verb ܘܟܣܝ. This, together with the greater probability of modification to the plural than *vice versa*, tilts the balance in favour of the standard text.

59. The pronoun of the standard text is peculiar to the Peshiṭta, while the variant agrees with the Hebrew and the other versions. It is much easier to see why the standard text should be changed to the variant than *vice versa*. *Cf* p. 148 *infra*.

68. The omission of *seyāmē* could easily be a corruption, but the name might equally have been intended by the original translators as that of the country rather than as that of its inhabitants. The arguments are again evenly balanced.

71. The variant here is probably to be explained as assimilation to the previous clause. It is also possible that it is due to the influence of the Syrohexapla.

89. The additional title in the variant finds some support in LXX^L and *may* therefore derive from the Hebrew *Vorlage* of the Peshiṭta. It may equally well be explained as accommodation to common usage. If original, its omission in the standard text could be a simple case of *homoeoteleuton*.

The fact that in all but four (38, 40, 46, 61) of these passages the standard text is attested as early as the eighth century, while in no less than twenty-six (45, 48, 49, 50, 51, 52, 53, 56, 58, 62, 63, 65, 66, 67, 71, 75, 76, 77, 78, 81, 82, 83, 84, 85, 87, 89) it is attested in the seventh century or earlier, robs the variants in this section of the weight of those in the preceding section, where the testimony of the oldest Mss is unanimous. It is significant that barely over a quarter of these variants can be regarded with any probability as representing the original reading.

Finally some assessment must be made of the relation of each of the oldest Mss to the standard text in these readings. It will be convenient to set this out in the form of a table, in which the five columns give respectively the Ms, the number of readings in which it is extant, the number in which it is illegible or uncertain, the number in which it agrees with the standard text and the number in which it differs from it. 11k4 is not included, because it is not extant for any of the readings in this section.

6h9	34	1	10	23
7a1	53	–	6	47
7k8	6	–	–	6
7k10	10	2	8	–
7pj2	2	–	–	2
8a1	49	6	25	18
8j1	5	1	2	2
9a1	11	1	4	6
10j2	1	–	–	1
12a1	53	31	17	5

4. Readings peculiar to each of the oldest manuscripts

It is neither necessary nor practicable to give detailed consideration to all the unique readings of the oldest Mss, though it must be remembered that in a number of passages only one other of the oldest Mss is extant and legible, and that in a few 7a1 is effectively the only witness available from the oldest Mss. The most convenient procedure in this section will be to consider each of the oldest Mss separately. After listing the unique readings of the Ms by reference to the Second Apparatus (or the First Apparatus in the case of 7a1), some assessment of the character of the Ms will be attempted, taking into account also the errors peculiar to the Ms as described in the Introduction to the EDITION. Finally some consideration will be devoted to those readings, if any, considered to have some claim to being original. These will be given serial numbers successive to those in the preceding section.

6h9

This Ms, though extant for slightly less than half of the Dodekapropheton, has no less than fifty-four readings peculiar to itself among the oldest Mss. These may be found in the Second Apparatus at Na iii 15, Hb i 4, 13, iii 8, Zf i 11, 14, ii 1, 6, 11, 12, 13, iii 7, 8, 11, Hg ii 6, 16, 18, 19, Sa ii 12, 15, 16, iii 5, iv 6, 9, v 4, 6, 11, vi 5, 11, 13, vii 13, viii 5, 10, ix 1, 8, 11, 12, 16, x 4bis, xi 1, 2bis, xii 3, xiv 10, 12, 17, Ml i 5, 10, ii 17, iii 1, 2, 3, 20. Nine of these readings must be considered below, but none of the remaining forty-five are at all likely to be original.

Two categories among these forty-five readings are of special interest. Six of them are explicable as assimilations to adjacent (Hb i 13, Sa ii 15, 16, xiv 10) or remoter (Sa iv 9, vii 13) passages, and two are substitutions of synonyms for the words used in the standard text (Sa v 4, Ml iii 2); the former adopts the word used in the Syrohexapla. There is a metathesis of two words in Na iii 15. The remainder are either improbable omissions (eight) or additions (three) of single words, or minor variants concerning *waw*, *dalath*, *seyāmē* (added six times) and the like. This is consistent with the kind of error noted in the Introduction to the EDITION. One can hardly avoid the conclusion that this is not a very accurate Ms, and its peculiar readings deserve serious consideration only when they possess some inherent textual probability.

The nine readings worthy of consideration fall into two groups:

(a) Those which are probably to be preferred to the standard text:

90. Zf ii 11. The reading of 6h9 agrees with the Hebrew, while *'e* may have been corrupted into *yudh* in the standard text.
91. Sa iv 6. The suffix is in agreement with the Hebrew, but may have been misread as the final upstroke of the preceding *ḥeth* and so lost in the standard text.
92. Sa ix 12. The singular suffix agrees with the Hebrew, while the plural suffix of the standard text seems to be a natural assimilation to the context.
93. Sa xiv 17. The additional word in the standard text is not in the Hebrew, and may have arisen through assimilation to the previous verse.

(b) Those where the arguments are more finely balanced:

94. Hb i 4. On this reading *cf* p. 56 *supra*.
95. Hb iii 8. The plural is closer to the Hebrew, but the singular of the standard text could be a natural assimilation to the context.

96. Sa ix 8. If the plural is taken in the sense 'garrison', this is a possible interpretation of the Hebrew; the singular of the standard text yields another possible interpretation, perhaps identical with that of LXX.

97. Sa ix 11. The *waw* of the standard text is not in the Hebrew.

98. Sa x 4 2°. The *waw* of the standard text is not in the Hebrew.

Despite numerous idiosyncratic readings this Ms preserves a number of readings with a high claim to originality, mostly in company with one or more of the other oldest Mss, but sometimes alone. The high expectations with which one approaches what may be the oldest extant Ms of the Dodekapropheton (*cf* pp 102f. *infra*) are not disappointed.

7a1

This Ms is of peculiar interest as the oldest Ms with a virtually complete and legible text of the Dodekapropheton. The patch containing Hb iii 4–7 and Zf ii 9–10, described by Ceriani as "antiquitus ... suppleta" (*cf* Introduction to the EDITION, p. IX), is shown indeed to contain an ancient text by the agreement with 6h9 at Zf ii 9 (no. 69 above). The Ms however has a relatively large number of readings peculiar to itself among the oldest Mss, though in a few of these passages (Jl ii 20, 27, Am ii 4) it is the only one of the oldest Mss extant and legible. Sixty-three of these readings may be found in the First Apparatus at Hs i 7, ii 1, 18, 19, v 1, 8, vii 3, 12, x 6, xiii 5, xiv 4, Jl i 4, 15, 20, ii 10, 20, 27, Am i 14, ii 4, iii 1, 15, v 6, 17, viii 10, ix 11 2°, Jon iii 4, Mi i 8 2°, ii 4, iii 2, iv 2, 3^{quater}, v 6, 13, vi 7, 11bis, 13, vii 12 2°, 20, Na i 14 1°, iii 10, Hb ii 19, iii 9, Zf i 8bis, 11, 12, 15, ii 6, Hg ii 13, 16 1°, Sa iii 8, ix 15, xi 7, xii 2, 9, xiii 9, Ml i 12, 13 1°, iii 11. No less than fifteen of these readings merit serious consideration.

> One further reading should be mentioned since it is one where the standard text differs from the Basic Text printed in the EDITION. This occurs at Jl iv 14, where 7a1 is the only one of the oldest Mss to read ܪܘܚܐ ܝܢ with *seyāmē*; of the other oldest Mss extant for this passage 8j1 is illegible and 12a1 agrees with the standard text. This variant is regarded as orthographic (*collectivum cum/sine seyāmē*) and of no real importance. The reading of 7a1 was printed as the Basic Text because of its possible or probable support in 10d1 12d1 (14a1).

Nearly half of the remaining forty-eight of these readings concern *waw*, *dalath* or *seyāmē*. Six (Hs ii 19, vii 12, Am v 17, Mi v 13, Hb iii 9,

READINGS PECULIAR TO EACH OF THE OLDEST MSS   79

Zf i 15) are most probably to be regarded as inner-Syriac corruptions, several of them involving confusion of *dalath* and *rish*. Assimilation to other passages, near or far, seems to be a factor in at least ten readings (Hs v 8, Jl i 4, Am ii 4, viii 10, Mi iv 2, 3$^{1°}$ *et* $^{2°}$, Hb ii 19, Hg ii 16, Sa xi 7). The majority of the unique errors in this Ms consist of the omission or alteration of single letters, or the misuse of *seyāmē* or diacritical points, and this tendency to inaccuracy in detail reduces the value of this Ms. It does none the less preserve a number of valuable readings either in isolation or in conjunction with one or more of the other oldest Mss.

The fifteen readings to be considered fall into two groups:

(a) Those which are probably to be preferred to the standard text:

99. Am i 14. The reading of 7a1 is in agreement with the Hebrew and consistent with the rendering of the same Hebrew phrase in vv. 7 and 10. The standard text is probably a corruption.

100. Mi iv 3$^{3°}$. In Mi iv 2, 3$^{1°}$ *et* $^{2°}$ 7a1 seems to reflect assimilation to the parallel passage in Is ii 3f. Here and in the following reading it is the standard text which seems to be assimilated to Is ii 4 and, in the present case, Jl iv 10.

101. Mi iv 3$^{4°}$. In addition to what has been said under the preceding reading, it should be noted that 7a1 here is closer to the Hebrew.

102. Sa iii 8. The reading of 7a1 is in agreement with the Hebrew, while that of the standard text is probably an assimilation to the end of the previous verse.

(b) Those where the arguments are more finely balanced:

103. Hs ii 18. The word-order of 7a1 is closer to the Hebrew, while that of the standard text may be due to a desire to bring ܬܘܒ closer to the negative.

104. Hs vii 3. The singular of 7a1 is closer to the Hebrew. It is *possible* that *seyāmē* have been added later in 8a1 and 8j1, but existing *seyāmē* may simply have been touched up.

105. Jl i 15. The reading of 7a1 is closer to the Hebrew. In this and the following reading 7a1 is the only one of the oldest Mss extant, except for 12a1 which agrees with the standard text.

106. Jl ii 10. The reading of 7a1 here is closer to the Hebrew, though in iv 15 where the same Hebrew clause occurs it is rendered in 7a1 in the same way as in the standard text in both passages.

107. Jl ii 27. The reading of 7a1 is closer to the Hebrew. 12a1, the only other of the oldest Mss extant for this passage, is illegible.

108. Mi v 6. The plural of 7a1 is closer to the Hebrew, and *seyāmē*

could easily have been lost in the standard text. The prosthetic *'alaph* in 7a1 is a distinct orthographic variant.
109. Mi vi 13. The reading of 7a1 is closer to the Hebrew.
110. Mi vii 20. The rendering of 7a1 is more literal.
111. Zf i 11. The passive participle of 7a1 is closer to the Hebrew and more likely to have been changed to the active than *vice versa*.
112. Sa xii 2. The reading of 7a1 is closer to the Hebrew.
113. Ml iii 11. The reading of 7a1 is closer to the Hebrew, and confusion between *dalath* and *waw* is a fairly common corruption which may account for the standard text.

7k8

There are no readings or errors peculiar to this Ms, which suggests that it is a much more accurate copy than 6h9 or 7a1. Its consistent agreement with the oldest Mss against the standard text in all eight of the passages 1–89 for which it is extant is thus highly significant. Were more of this Ms extant it would be of the utmost interest and importance.

7k10

Out of the thirteen of the passages 1–89 for which this Ms is extant it is illegible in three, agrees with the standard text in eight and with the oldest Mss in two. Its chief importance therefore is as an early witness to the standard text. The eight errors described in the Introduction to the EDITION suggest that the ten readings peculiar to this Ms among the oldest Mss are not likely to be of great value. They may be found in the Second Apparatus at Am iii 9, iv 5bis, 9, v 16, 27, viii 3, ix 6, Ob 13, Hb iii 10. Three of these consist of the omission of one in a series of divine titles and three of the omission of *waw fin* in imperative verbs; one is a metathesis of two adjacent words and one the addition of *seyāmē*. Two however have some inherent plausibility, and in view of the two agreements of this Ms with the other oldest Mss against the standard text (nos. 6 and 7) they must be given some consideration, though in each case the balance of probability remains with the standard text:
114. Am ix 6. This is another instance of the omission of one in a series of divine titles and should probably be regarded as a case of *homoeoteleuton*. It differs from the other instances in yielding a text corresponding exactly to the Hebrew, while the additional title in the standard text finds support in the LXX.

READINGS PECULIAR TO EACH OF THE OLDEST MSS   81

115. Hb iii 10. The omission of the copula yields a text closer to the Hebrew.

7pj2

Only fragments of this Ms are legible, but these contain no less than three readings unique among the oldest Mss:

116. Hb iii 1. See no. 61 above. The reading of 7pj2 is synonymous with that of 6h9 and 7a1 and just possibly a corruption of it. The main importance of this reading is its support for the fuller rendering of the Hebrew of this verse in the Peshitta.
117. Hb iii 6. The addition of the copula yields a text closer to the Hebrew. The support however of 6h9 7a1 7k10 and 8a1 for the standard text lessens the probability of this reading being original.
118. Sa ix 9. The metathesis yields a text less close to the Hebrew than that of the standard text, which is supported by 6h9 7a1 8a1 and 12a1.

It seems unlikely then that any of these three readings is to be preferred to that of the standard text.

8a1

This Ms has twenty-four readings peculiar to itself among the oldest Mss, and these may be found in the Second Apparatus at Hs iv 2, v 8, Am ii 9, iii 14, vi 14, ix 14, Ob 19, 20, Jon iv 5, Mi ii 9, iii 3, vi 16, Hb i 14 (*cf* no. 60 *supra*), 15, Zf i 12, 18 (*cf* no. 65 *supra*), ii 9, 14, Hg ii 11, 18, Sa viii 17, x 6, Ml ii 15, iii 11. Most of these readings are probably corruptions or merely stylistic variants. *Seyāmē* are added five times, and anticipatory suffixes introduced twice. Am iii 14 is probably a case of assimilation to the following clause, and Zf i 12 may be due to Syrohexaplaric influence. When it is recalled that in the preceding section this Ms was found to agree with the standard text more often than not (though this must be balanced against the passages where it agrees with all the oldest Mss against the standard text), the expectation of the survival of primitive readings in this Ms alone is reduced. In fact only four of its readings deserve serious consideration, and none of these is sufficiently significant to be preferred to the standard text. The four readings are:

119. Am vi 14. The omission of the copula yields a text closer to the Hebrew.
120. Jon iv 5. The metathesis yields the word-order of the Hebrew and the other versions.

121. Hg ii 11. The singular imperative agrees with the Hebrew and the other versions.

122. Sa viii 17. The singular agrees literally with the Hebrew and the other versions, though the plural of the standard text is a natural interpretation of the generic singular.

8j1

We have seen in the previous section that this Ms agrees twice and disagrees twice with the standard text in the four passages where some of the oldest Mss diverge from the standard text and this Ms is legible. None of the three readings peculiar to itself among the oldest Mss is likely to be original. The addition of the copula at Hs vii 16 yields a text less close to the Hebrew than the standard text. The omission at Am i 12, itself uncertain, is probably due to assimilation to v. 10. The variant in Am ii 1, also uncertain, is most probably an inner-Syriac corruption (*rish* for *dalath*).

9a1

This Ms, which is extant only for Hs i 1–xiv 6, agrees with some or all of the oldest Mss against the standard text eight times, but with the standard text against some of the oldest Mss four times. One reading where 9a1 is uncertain (iv 6) and one where it is itself illegible (x 6) have been left out of account; the latter has been reckoned in this chapter among the readings peculiar to 7a1 among the oldest Mss. There remain altogether forty-two readings where 9a1 certainly or probably disagrees with the standard text apart from the other oldest Mss. One (xii 3) is absolutely peculiar to this Ms, and twenty-three occur otherwise only in its descendants. Two (ix 9, xiii 15) occur in later Mss which are not dependent on 9a1. In nine 9a1 itself is illegible and in seven its reading is only probable; in these sixteen readings together with that in x 6 the main evidence for the reading of 9a1 is that of its descendants in 9a1 *fam* (cf. chapter 2, section A 1). It is unfortunate that three of the only four of these readings with some intrinsic probability fall among these sixteen, and the last two are among those where no indirect help may be gained from 17a8^{mg}. Since the forty-two readings in question form the greater part of the Second Apparatus for Hosea it is hardly necessary to print a list of passages here. The four readings worthy of consideration are:

123. iv 3. The omission of *beth* yields a text closer to the Hebrew, but could also be due to Syrohexaplaric influence. The standard text

on the other hand is a natural expansion (cf. 7a1 at ii 1).

124. iv 14. The addition of the copula again yields a text closer to the Hebrew and in agreement with the Syrohexapla. It is however perhaps easier to envisage the addition of the copula than its omission if original.

125. vii 16. The omission of *dalath* again yields a text closer to the Hebrew and in agreement with the Syrohexapla. The standard text may be regarded as a natural expansion. Unfortunately 8j1, which is extant for this passage, is illegible for this variant.

126. xi 11. Here the variant agrees with the Hebrew and the other versions including the Syrohexapla (which is not however literally identical). The standard text seems to be inferior and may readily be explained as an inner-Syriac corruption. Despite the illegibility of 9a1 itself this reading should probably be preferred to that of the standard text. Some hesitation however may be felt in view of the fact that in xi 10, where 9a1 shares the reading of the standard text ܢܒܠ, which is probably an inner-Syriac corruption of ܢܒܠ, 17a6 *fam* does read ܢܒܠ. One must allow for the possibility of deliberate correction of the standard text by Sergius Risius or one of his sources other than 9a1.

The other thirty-eight readings are for various reasons improbable. Nearly half of them seem to be merely stylistic variants. Eight are additions of *waw*. At least four (v 15, viii 1, xi 8$^{2°}$, xii 3) are probably corruptions. Several readings are in fact less close to the Hebrew than the standard text, and a few (ix 6, x 15$^{1°}$, xii 14$^{2°}$) seem most readily explicable as assimilations to the LXX or Syrohexapla.

10j2

The only reading peculiar to this Ms is the omission of *seyāmē* in ܟܠܒܐ in Mi vi 7, where the plural is attested in the rest of the tradition, and 7a1 and 8a1 support the standard text. This reading is thus in all probability an inner-Syriac corruption.

11k4

In the only reading where more than one of the oldest Mss agree against the standard text for which this Ms is extant (no. 36 above) it agrees with the other oldest Mss. In the Introduction to the EDITION it has been noted that there are no less than six errors in this fragment of less than twenty-three verses. It is not surprising that the six readings peculiar to this Ms among the oldest Mss (Sa v 3, 6, vi 1bis, 6, 12) should prove to be improbable in varying degress, the second and fourth being probably due to assimilation to nearby clauses.

12a1

In the eighty-nine passages reviewed in the two preceding sections 12a1 was found to agree with some or all of the other oldest Mss against the standard text in nine readings, and with the standard text against some or all of the other oldest Mss in thirty-seven readings. In the remaining forty-three readings 12a1 is uncertain or illegible. Against this background must now be considered the thirteen readings peculiar to 12a1, the fifty-five readings in which it is supported only by its descendants or other Mss related to it (see chapter 2, sections A and C), and the thirty-two other readings where 12a1 lacks the support of any of the other oldest Mss. These hundred readings may be found in the Second Apparatus at Hs iv 6, 14, v 11, vii 1, 3, 6, viii 12bis, ix 13, 15, 17, xi 7, xii 13, xiii 1, 10, 14, xiv 7, 9, 10, Jl i 14bis, 18, ii 3, 16, 22, iv 13, Am i 6, iv 2, 13, v 25, 27, vi 1, 8, vii 1, 12, viii 5, ix 1, Ob 5, 9, 11, 13, Jon i 2, 5, 6, 7bis, 8, ii 10bis, iv 2, 8bis, Mi i 6, 8$^{2°}$, 14, ii 9, 13, iii 1, 5, 8bis, iv 10, 13bis, v 1, 7, Na ii 11, 13, iii 14, 19$^{2°}$, Hb ii 5, 6, iii 9, 11, Zf i 7, Hg i 14$^{2°}$, ii 2, 18$^{1°}$, Sa i 6, 8, vii 5bis, viii 13, 18, ix 9, 10bis, x 10, 11, xii 6bis, xiv 10, 21$^{2°}$, Ml i 13, 14bis, ii 3, 5, 9, iii 2.

Seven of these readings are worthy of consideration:

127. Hs vii 6. The omission of the copula is in agreement with the Hebrew and the other versions.
128. Hs xiii 10. The plural of 12a1 is in agreement with the Hebrew, but the Peshiṭta's unanimous rendering of ושרים in the singular may favour the standard text here.
129. Hs xiii 14. ܘܡܚܐ may be a stylistic addition in the standard text, and its omission in 12a1 is in agreement with the Hebrew.
130. Ob 5. ܐܢ in the standard text agrees with the LXX, while the ܘܐܢ of 12a1 is closer to the Hebrew, which however lacks the copula.
131. Ob 13. The reading of 12a1 agrees with the Hebrew and the other versions and should probably be preferred to that of the standard text, which may well be a corruption of it.
132. Hb iii 11. The singular agrees literally with the Hebrew, but the Peshiṭta's unanimous rendering of the following חנית in the plural may favour the standard text here.
133. Ml iii 2. The addition of the copula is in agreement with the Hebrew and the other versions.

Of the other ninety-three readings twenty-six concern *waw, seyāmē* or the reading of a plural for a singular (Sa ix 10$^{2°}$), three concern the substitution of *stat emph* for suffixes (Hs iv 6, ix 17, Hg ii 2), and seventeen are abbreviations (e.g. Hs xii 13, Sa xiv 10) or omissions, usually of single words and particularly of one of a series of divine titles (e.g. Am iv 13). Twenty-two seem to be attempts to improve the sense (e.g. Hs viii 12 *bis*) or the style (e.g. Hs xiii 1, Sa ix 9), and five are substitutions of synonyms for the words used in the standard text (Hs v 11, vii 3, ix 15, Jl ii 3, Jon i 2). The remaining twenty are either inner-Syriac corruptions (e.g. Hs xi 7, Am vii 1, Mi iv 10, Na iii 19$^{2°}$, Sa x 11) or minor variations of an improbable nature.

It has become clear that each of the major Mss considered in this section (6h9 7a1 8a1 9a1 12a1) has a substantial number of readings peculiar to itself among the oldest Mss, only a minority of which are worthy of serious consideration as possible original Peshitta readings. Of the forty-four readings surveyed here only ten (90–93, 99–102, 126 and 131) are judged clearly preferable to the standard text. 6h9 and 7a1 each have four of these preferred readings, while 9a1 and 12a1 each have one. While 8a1 has by far the fewest readings peculiar to itself among the oldest Mss, none of them appears to be superior to the standard text. In the case of the six fragmentary Mss only five readings were found worthy of consideration, and none of these proved demonstrably superior to the standard text. It should however be remembered that 7k8 has no readings peculiar to itself. This Ms emerges as the best of the oldest Mss of the Dodekapropheton, and it is a matter for great regret that it is extant for less than eighty-six verses out of the thousand and fifty of the whole Dodekapropheton.

5. Some general considerations

In completing this chapter it will be well to give some consideration to the larger issues that arise from a study of the distinctive readings of the oldest Mss. First however it is desirable for the sake of completeness to record the evidence of the oldest Mss for the one passage where the identity of the standard text is uncertain:

134. Jon ii 3   ܒ 7a1 8a1] *pr waw* 12a1

Neither the Hebrew nor the other versions have the copula here, and it seems most probable that its addition should be regarded as an inner-Syriac development. The agreed reading of the two oldest Ms extant for this passage is thus most likely to be the original Peshiṭta text.

The great majority of the hundred and thirty-four variant readings considered in this chapter are of a relatively minor nature. Many concern such matters as the presence or absence of the copula, an enclitic pronoun or an anticipatory suffix, or the differences between singular and plural, the persons of a verb or alternative prepositions. Some (43, 64, 110, 116) concern variation between virtually synonymous expressions. The majority of the omissions and additions either concern the presence or absence of one in a series of divine titles or are of a relatively minor and in some cases essentially stylistic nature. Only twenty-five readings appear to be truly significant: four omissions (9, 15, 16, 53), three additions (17, 66, 70) and eighteen substantial differences (5, 36, 40, 41, 59, 75, 90, 91, 94, 96, 99, 100, 101, 102, 106, 126, 130 and 131). It is of interest to note that on textual grounds fifteen (5, 9, 15, 16, 36, 40, 75, 90, 91, 99, 100, 101, 102, 126 and 131) and probably one other (70) of these variants were found to be preferable to the standard text, while in two (41 and 53) and probably one other (59) the standard text was found to be preferable to the variant. It proved impossible to reach a decision in the remaining six cases (17, 66, 94, 96, 106 and 130).

In a majority of cases either the standard text or the variant was found to be closer to the Hebrew, and in general the reading closer to the Hebrew has been thought more likely to be original. Out of twenty-nine passages where the standard text agrees with the Hebrew it is thought to represent the original text in eighteen; in four however (6, 19, 23 and 74) the reading of the oldest Mss was preferred, and in seven the priority was unresolved. Out of seventy-two passages where the oldest Mss agree with the Hebrew their reading is thought to be original in thirty-six; in three (59, 77 and 87) the reading of the standard text was preferred, and in thirty-three the priority was unresolved.

A question which has not so far been raised is whether any of the readings which are closer to the Hebrew should be regarded as deliberate revisions to conform to the Hebrew. This is at least a theoretical possibility in the case of nineteen readings of the standard text (17, 23, 30, 31, 37, 42, 46, 51, 55, 57, 63, 66, 68, 73, 74, 76, 78, 83 and 89) and sixty-one readings of the oldest Mss (5, 7–9, 15, 16, 18, 20, 43, 45, 58–62, 65, 67, 72, 77, 85–87, 90–93, 95, 97–99, 101–115, 117, 119–129, and 131–134). The chief objection to this hypothesis is

SOME GENERAL CONSIDERATIONS 87

that neither in the standard text nor in any individual Ms is such a revision to agree with the Hebrew carried through consistently. HAYMAN (p. 267) goes so far as to affirm: 'The "revision according to the M.T." hypothesis may be firmly laid to rest.' It may however be suggested that this is too sweeping a dismissal of the hypothesis, and that, while there is no evidence in either the standard text or any individual one of the oldest Mss of a consistent attempt at revision to conform with the Hebrew, such an intention may have been present intermittently, and may be the best way of accounting for a few of the variants, which are hard to explain on the hypothesis that the reading closest to the Hebrew is original.

It may be of interest to observe how the twenty-five most significant readings appear from this point of view. In six (53, 70, 94, 96, 100 and 130) the difference is not such as to admit of resolution by reference to the Hebrew. In sixteen (5, 9, 15, 16, 36, 40, 59, 75, 90, 91, 99, 101, 102, 106, 126 and 131) the reading of the oldest Mss is closer to the Hebrew, and in fourteen of these it is the preferred reading. In one (106) the priority of reading is unresolved, and in one (59) the standard text was thought more likely to be original. This last is a case where it is difficult to account for the standard text if the variant were held to be original, while the variant itself could be explained as a deliberate revision to conform to the Hebrew. In three passages the standard text is closer to the Hebrew; in one (41) it is thought to be original, while in the other two (17 and 66) the priority of reading is unresolved. It is reasonable to conclude that in general terms the oldest Mss preserve a text closer to the original Peshitta than the standard text, and that the text of the oldest Mss is closer to the Hebrew than the standard text. There are however sufficient instances which go against both these trends to make it necessary to consider each variant on its merits.

One of the puzzling features of the transmission of the Peshitta is the almost universal diffusion of the standard text from about the ninth century. Apart from the relatively small number of older readings preserved in 12a1 and, as we shall see, some older readings preserved in even later Mss, 9a1 is the latest Ms to present a text essentially different from the standard text. How old is the standard text? We saw that in all but four of the fifty-three readings surveyed in section 3 of this chapter it is attested by the eighth century, and that in twenty-six readings it is attested in the seventh century or even the sixth. On the other hand there is no extant evidence for its existence before 9d1 (where extant) or 10d1 in the case of the thirty-six readings surveyed in section 2. As far as the forty-four readings surveyed in section 4 are concerned, in all but the fifteen peculiar to 7a1 the standard text is attested in 7a1 and hence by the seventh century. For the fifteen passages where 7a1 has a peculiar reading the standard text is attested in four by the sixth century, in five (and probably another three) by the eighth century, and in all by the ninth century. In at least eighty-seven passages then the standard text is attested by the eighth century or earlier.

It is hardly conceivable that there was an official revision of the Peshitta as late as even the sixth century which could have won almost universal diffusion throughout the Syriac-speaking churches. It is much more likely that the standard text, or something very like it, was in existence at the time when the oldest extant Mss were written. It is at this point that the relative paucity of the ancient biblical Mss of the Dodekapropheton is so restricting. The ten passages where 6h9 already attests the standard text against the combined evidence of two or more of the other oldest Mss and the four where it attests the standard text against 7a1 suggest that were 6h9 extant for the earlier part of the Dodekapropheton or were more fifth or sixth century Mss extant the standard text would be seen to be indeed as old as the oldest Mss that are extant. This would not alter the fact that the standard text is on the whole an inferior text to that of the oldest Mss, but it would allow for the subsequent general diffusion of the standard text. In terms of general probabilities, and we are here reduced to surmise by the paucity of the evidence available to us, it would seem likely that the standard text antedates the divisions of the fifth century (though it is known that these did not preclude access to biblical texts across these boundaries), that the oldest Mss on the whole represent an earlier and better text-form than that of the standard text, though this itself is a corrupted form of the original Peshitta (*cf* chapter 4), and that in a minority of readings the standard text seems to preserve the original Peshitta text against the oldest extant Mss.

What then are we to make of the oldest Mss? Do they constitute a particular textual tradition which is both older than and superior to the standard text? It is clear that no one of the oldest Mss may be regarded as the direct exemplar of any other, for this is precluded by the omissions and readings peculiar to each of those of which a sufficient portion is both extant and legible to permit the investigation of any such possibility. It may however be of some use to note the extent of agreements and disagreements between the most significant of the oldest Mss (6h9, 7a1, 7k8, 8a1 and 9a1) within the variants considered in section 3 above, excluding cases where these Mss agree in reading the standard text.

Let us consider first the pattern of relationships between 6h9 7a1 7k8 and 8a1 over the part of the Dodekapropheton where 6h9 is extant (from Na i 4); 7k8 is extant only for part of Hg i 1–Ml i 4, while 8a1 is not extant for Sa xi 6–Ml ii 8. 6h9 agrees with 7a1 against 8a1 in sixteen readings (57, 59, 60, 62–64, 68–70, 72–74, 79, 80, 86 and 88), in one of which (74) the reading of 6h9 and 7a1 is shared by 7k8. 7a1 agrees with 8a1 against 6h9 in six readings (58, 65, 71 and 75–77), in one of which (75) the reading of 7a1 and 8a1 is shared by 7k8. 6h9 agrees with 8a1 against 7a1 in three readings (56, 87 and 89). 7k8 figures in four readings (82–85) where 8a1 is not extant; in three it agrees with 7a1 against 6h9, while in one (84) it agrees with 6h9 against 7a1. It may also be worth noting that 7pj2 agrees once (66) with 7a1 against 6h9 and 8a1, and once (67) with 6h9 against 7a1 and 8a1.

Next let us consider the pattern of relationships between 7a1 8a1 and 9a1 over the part of the Dodekapropheton where 9a1 is extant (to Hs xiv 6). 7a1 agrees with 9a1 against 8a1 in five readings (37, 39, 42, 44 and 47), in one of which (44) 8j1 agrees with 8a1. 7a1 agrees with 8a1 against 9a1 in two readings (40 and 46) and probably also in a third (38). 8j1 figures in three further readings: in 41 it agrees with 7a1 against 8a1 and 9a1, in 45 it agrees with 8a1 against 7a1 and 9a1, while in 43 it agrees with the standard text against an agreed reading of 7a1 8a1* and 9a1.

When these figures are considered alongside the table on p. 76 it becomes clear that the surviving oldest Mss are at best fairly distant relatives within a distinct family tradition, and that all of them to varying degrees have been "contaminated" by the standard text. 7k8 might appear to be an exception to this conclusion since in none of the readings for which it is extant in section 3 does it agree with the standard text against an agreed reading of two or more of the oldest Mss. 7k8 is extant however for one of the readings considered in section 4 (93), where the shorter text of 6h9 was thought probably to represent the original Peshitta text. In this passage 7k8 agrees with the standard text. If then 6h9 does represent the original Peshitta reading in this passage, 7k8 like the other extant oldest Mss must be regarded as having suffered some "contamination" by the standard text. If one were to regard the distinctive readings of the oldest Mss as constituting an earlier and purer tradition of the Peshiṭta than the standard text, one would have to posit that the extant oldest Mss all present a "mixed" text containing readings characteristic both of this putative earlier tradition and of the standard text.

When the readings considered in section 2 and 4 are added to the picture, they do not seriously modify this conclusion. It appears that the standard text was in circulation and exercising a strong influence already at the time when the oldest extant Mss of the Dodekapropheton were being written, and that the earlier tradition has survived only in part. In the next chapter we shall see reason to believe that a few early readings have survived almost miraculously in later Mss, though not appearing in any of the oldest extant Mss. We shall also see reason to believe that the original Peshiṭta text suffered a number of inner-Syriac corruptions so early in the course of its tranmission that they have been perpetuated throughout the whole course of the subsequent transmission and appear in all extant Mss. Once again we are led to lament the relative paucity of ancient Mss of the Peshiṭta, particularly in the case of the Dodekapropheton.

It may be worth while to draw attention to the fact that 9a1, which in some Books of the Old Testament appears to represent a very early text-form (*cf* WEITZMAN, p. 298), is disappointing in this respect in the Dodekapropheton. It agrees with the standard text against a shared reading of more than one of the other oldest Mss half as often as *vice versa*, and in one of these passages (40) 9a1 appears manifestly to follow the inferior reading.

Finally it is to be noted that nearly half of the readings of the oldest Mss considered in this chapter are to be found also in some later Mss. A number of readings found in only one of the oldest Mss and not considered in detail in section 4 also occur in later Mss. A number of these later attestations are due to the dependence of such Mss as 16/9a1 and 17a6 *fam* on 9a1 and 12a1. Others are certainly to be regarded as coincidental, such as the seven (1, 3, 21, 49, 112, 118 and 128) which occur in 17a3, which we have seen good reason to believe to have been copied from 14a1, which does not contain these readings. A few of these later attestations however are probably genuine survivals of ancient readings, and indicate that some of the later Mss contain ancient and sometimes significant readings. We proceed to note those later Mss with significant incidence of readings of the oldest Mss; many of these readings are in themselves, as we have seen, of

SOME GENERAL CONSIDERATIONS 91

little significance, and their only importance is their cumulative evidence that the Ms in question preserves some ancient readings. Readings significant for this purpose are indicated by italics.

Seven (20, 25, 34, *41*, 42, 68 and 82) occur in 13a1. Five (34, 35, 54, 108 and 121) occur in 13d1, which also has a slightly different version of 61 (ܕܚ ܛܠܐ). Five (*3*, 14, *61*, 84 and 129) occur in 15d2 and the Mss related to it. Five (45, 48, 94, 104 and 122) occur in 16d1 and in some cases also in Mss related to it; two more (*3* and *4*) occur in 18d1 alone within this group. One each occurs in 17a7^{mg} (84) and 17a8^{1} (62). Three (*4*, *89* and 118) occur in 16g6, 19g5.7; two (108 and 128) occur in 16g6 and 19g5, and nine (21, 22, 32, 46, 48, 49, 82, *94* and 112) in 19g5.7. Three (39, 45 and *81*) occur in 16g6 only, three (71, *91* and 95) in 19g5 only and two (*17* and 35) in 19g7 only.

These statistics are sufficient to encourage the expectation that occasionally, especially in those parts of the Dodekapropheton where few of the oldest Mss are both extant and legible, valuable ancient readings may have survived only in later Mss. One may draw attention to two particularly striking cases among those listed in the previous paragraph. The fuller text at Sa iii 4 (17) attested in all the oldest Mss except 12a1 is found otherwise only in 19g7 and in part in 19g5^{1}. The reading of 6h9 at Sa iv 6 (91) is found otherwise only in 19g5, the latest of the biblical Mss! If this reading had occurred in the part of the Dodekapropheton for which 6h9 is not extant, this reading would have been attested only in 19g5. Yet it is a reading which has been thought preferable to that of the standard text! A few readings of varying degrees of intrinsic probability which are attested only in later Mss will accordingly be considered in the next chapter.

4
Towards the Original Peshiṭta

1. The Text of the EDITION

Our first task now must be to summarize the results of the previous chapter and relate them to the Basic Text and the variants printed in the First and Second Apparatus of the EDITION. We began the previous chapter by listing thirty-two places where the standard text differs from the Basic Text of the EDITION. It has become clear that in only two of these (Am iv 1 and Hg ii 11$^{1°}$, respectively numbers 48 and 29 in the previous chapter) is the standard text clearly preferable to the Basic Text. To these must be added the variant at Jl iv 14, discussed on p. 78 above, which was considered to be orthographic, but where the *seyāmē* of 7a1 receive only limited and uncertain support from other biblical Mss. In the case of the one reading (134, Jon ii 3) where it was impossible to determine the reading of the standard text we found that the Basic Text was most likely to preserve the original reading of the Peshiṭta. There were seven passages (14, 17, 30, 32, 43, 66 and 82) where it proved impossible to reach a decision whether the reading of the standard text or that of the oldest Mss was original. In the remaining twenty-two passages where the Basic Text differs from the standard text the reading of the oldest Mss, which is printed in the Basic Text, was judged superior. There are then only three of the thirty-two places where the standard text differs from the Basic Text in which the reading printed in the Second Apparatus is clearly preferable to that of the Basic Text (Jl iv 14, Am iv 1 and Hg ii 11$^{1°}$).

We must next present a list of those readings of the oldest Mss which were also judged to be superior to those of the standard text, and which appear in the EDITION only in the First or Second Apparatus. If we include those passages where the balance of probability is in favour of the oldest Mss there are twenty-five in all: 99–102 appear in the First Apparatus, while the other twenty-one (8, 9, 22, 27, 34, 45, 49, 60–62, 67, 70, 72, 80, 85, 90–93, 126 and 131) appear in the Second Apparatus. Ten of these readings (9, 70, 90, 91, 99–102, 126 and 131) are among the twenty-five passages where the difference of readings is considered significant. Of the remaining fifteen of these significant passages, the six where the reading of the oldest Mss and the three where that of the standard text was judged to be superior are all cases where the reading judged to be superior is in fact printed in the Basic Text.

It remains to consider the possibility that one or more readings which are not attested in the oldest Mss may in fact be original. Two such readings appear in the Second Apparatus of the EDITION. The first is the reading uniquely attested by the lectionary Ms 9l6 at Sa vii 2 (where however the absence of *seyāmē* is erroneous, as is clear from the suffix). This is the only significant reading to be attested solely in a lectionary Ms. The reading of the standard text, shared by the extant oldest Mss and all the later biblical Mss (except 14d1, which is illegible at this point) is best explained as an inner-Syriac corruption of the reading of 9l6 (with *seyāmē* added), which agrees with the Hebrew and the other versions. The second reading in this category is the attestation of *seyāmē* in 12d2.3 in the last variant recorded for Sa xiv 10. The general character of 12d2.3 does not lead us to expect the preservation of original readings in these Mss alone, and the presence of *seyāmē* in this word in these two Mss may well be accidental or even possibly due to assimilation to the Syrohexapla (*cf* p. 66). The plural however is in agreement with the Hebrew and the other versions, and is probably to be regarded as representing the original text of the Peshiṭta.

This leaves us with the following list of thirty readings which are probably to be preferred to the Basic Text printed in the EDITION: Am i 14, Mi iv 3$^{3° \ et \ 4°}$ and Sa iii 8 in the First Apparatus, and Hs viii 4, xi 11, Jl iv 14, Am iv 1, v 20, Ob 13$^{2°}$, Jon i 16$^{1°}$, Mi iii 1$^{1°}$, vii 17, Na ii 2$^{1°}$, Hb i 14$^{1°}$, iii 1$^{2°}$, iii 17$^{3°}$, Zf i 18$^{3°}$, ii 11, ii 12$^{2°}$, Hg ii 11$^{1°}$, ii 20, Sa iv 6, vii 2 (*c. sey*), viii 15$^{1°}$, ix 12$^{2°}$, xii 4, xiv 10^{ult}, xiv 17 and Ml i 4 in the Second Apparatus.

2. Some readings not printed in the EDITION

We now consider some sixteen passages where there is a strong probability that the standard text represents an inner-Syriac corruption of a reading which is in fact attested in one or more of the later biblical Mss (in one case only indirectly through Ishoʻdad). Some of these later attestations are probably coincidental, but there is good ground in the case of the first ten for regarding them as genuine survivals of older readings. In each case the oldest Mss have been reexamined, and in all cases where they are legible they clearly read the standard text. It will be convenient to examine these sixteen readings according to their attestation, affixing serial numbers for ease of reference.

The first six are attested in the work of Sergius Risius:

1. Hs xi 10   ܥܠܘ] ܥܠܘ   17a6 *fam*
2. Am v 10   ܐܠܡܣܟܢ] ܐܠܡܣܟܢ   17a6 *fam*
3. Am vi 13   ܩܪܢ] ܩܪܢܬ   17a6 *fam*
4. Hb iii 4   ܒܩܪܢܬ] ܒܩܪܢܬ   17a6 *fam*
5. Jon ii 5   ܕܐܬܕܟܪܬ] ܕܐܬܕܟܪܬ   17a7mg.8mg
6. Na ii 1   ܐܠܨܬܢ] ܐܠܨܬܢ   17a7mg

We have already seen evidence of Sergius Risius' careful evaluation of the divergent readings of his sources (chapter 2, section A). Two of the variants recorded in 17a7mg.8mg which are not derived from either 16/9a1 or 16d1 are readings found also in one or more of the oldest Mss (Mi i 8³° and Sa xiv 18, the latter in 17a7mg alone), and several variants recorded in 17a7mg.8mg are not otherwise attested in the biblical Mss. It is reasonable then to presume that at least some of these six readings are recorded by Risius from one or other of his sources.

In the case of the first, third and fourth of these passages the reading of the standard text appears in 17a7mg.8mg and in (16/)9a1, while there is no other attestation of the reading of 17a6 *fam*. (In Hb iii 4 17d4 appears to read *nun* instead of *yudh*, but as it lacks *seyāmē* and as its exemplar 15d2 reads the standard text this reading of 17d4 must be dismissed as a miscopying of the standard text rather than as evidence for the reading of 17a6 *fam*). In the case of the second reading no variant is noted in the margins of 17a7.8, though 16/9a1 clearly reads the standard text. In this case we must allow for the possibility that the metathesis of *semkath* and *caph* was accidental in Risius' original copying of 17a8; it is also possible that he thought the reading of the standard text attested in 16/9a1 and 16d1 to be a corruption and deliberately declined to record it in the margin of 17a8. In the case of the fifth passage the reading of the standard text is found in 17a6 *fam*, while the reading of 17a7mg.8mg is found otherwise only in 17d1 (*vid*). In the case of the sixth passage the reading of 17a7mg is unique among the biblical Mss. It may be added that the second, third, fifth and sixth of these readings are in agreement with the Syrohexapla, a fact which will be considered in Section 4 below. For the present it seems

SOME READINGS NOT PRINTED IN THE EDITION   95

reasonable to conclude that Risius found all of these readings, with the possible exception of the second, in one or more of his exemplars.

The intrinsic probability of all six of these readings is clear from a comparison with the Hebrew. In the first passage the variant corresponds exactly with the Hebrew, while the standard text can easily be understood as a corruption of it (reading *'e* for *yudh*), the more natural since it yields an intelligble sense. In the second passage the standard text may well be an inner-Syriac corruption of the variant, which corresponds to the Hebrew; it is a case of metathesis of *semkath* and *caph*, and the corruption may have been provoked by the occurrence of ܟܣܡܐ in the following verse. This corruption was suspected already by SEBÖK. The third and fourth passages belong together: in each case the variant again agrees with the Hebrew, while the standard text could easily be a corruption of it (reading *yudh* for *nun*) and offers an intelligible sense at least in the third passage. The corruption may have been facilitated by unfamiliarity on the part of the copyists with the Hebrew idiom underlying the variant. Against the originality of the variant in the fourth passage it may be argued that the rendering of חביון by ܒܩܘܠܬܐ ("in a suburb"), which is without support in the rest of the tradition, suggests that ܩܪܢܬܐ was the original rendering of קרנים. On the other hand it may be argued that ܩܪܢܬܐ is a much more probable rendering of קרנים, and that the corruption to ܩܪܝܬܐ may have been assisted by the proximity of ܠܩܘܠܬܐ. The fifth passage concerns simply the difference between *dalath* and *rish*, and the variant is closer to the Hebrew (גרש is in fact rendered by ܪܓܫ in Am viii 8). The sixth passage again concerns the difference between *dalath* and *rish*, and the variant is again closer to the Hebrew. The fact that it occurs in 17a7^{mg} only might suggest the possibility that Risius offered it as a hypothetical emendation of the text, but there is nothing to suggest that he made a practice of doing this, and it is more likely that he came across the reading in a Ms which was not accessible to him when he copied 17a8. In view of the intrinsic superiority of all these six variants over the standard text, and the probability that most of them at least derive from one or other of the exemplars used by Risius, we have little hesitation in concluding that they represent the original Peshitta text.

The next four variants may also be accepted with some confidence. They are:

7. Hs xiv 8   ܬܟܒܘܢ] ܬܦܒܘܢ   15d2 *fam* 19d4

8. Jl iv 13	ܢܘܼܪܒ	] ܢܘܼܪܦ	19g5.7
9. Mi iii 4	ܒܛܥܢܐ	] ܣܥܢܐ	19g5.7
10. Sa xi 4, 7	ܦܘܠܛܐ	] ܦܠܝܛܐ	codd vett (v. infra)

The first of these involves only the difference between *beth* and *pe* and the variant is an exact rendering of the Hebrew, while the standard text lacks any support in the rest of the tradition and is difficult to understand in the context. We must however allow also for the possibility of Syrohexaplaric influence. The second is yet another instance of the difference between *dalath* and *rish*; the variant is again an exact rendering of the Hebrew, while the standard text would represent an easy corruption and yields an intelligible sense. (The occurrence of this reading also in 17a11 is probably to be discounted as a coincidence, arising from miscopying of 17a9, cf. chapter 2, section A5). It is worth recalling that 19g5.7 have a number of readings in common with one or more of the oldest Mss (cf. chapter 3, section 5). In some cases (e.g. Hb i 13, Sa xi 7 and xii 4) they are the only other biblical Mss to attest readings of one or more of the oldest Mss. The third variant, likewise attested only in 19g5.7, is a more exact rendering of the Hebrew than the standard text, which could easily have arisen as a corruption of it (reading *gamal* for *qoph*). The fourth variant does not occur in any of the extant biblical Mss, but is attested by Ishoʿdad as being the reading of some old Mss, and corresponds closely to the Hebrew. The standard text could easily have arisen through a shortening of the *lamadh*, and again yields an intelligible sense.

The attestation of the remaining six variants to be considered in this section is much less strong, but they deserve consideration in any case on their own merits. The first four concern either *seyāmē* or the distinction between *dalath* and *rish*.

11. Jl ii 20	ܐܝܘܒܐ¹°	] ܐܝܘܒܐ	(ܐܝܘܒܐ 17a10)
12. Na ii 12	ܐܪܝܘܬܐ¹°	] *c. sey*	17a6.11
13. Na iii 11	ܬܘܪܝ	] ܬܘܪܝ	17a11
14. Hb i 13	ܒܩܫܐ	] *s. sey*	14d1 16g6 17a11

The first of these, if substantiated, would yield an almost exact agreement with the Hebrew (strictly the Paʿel or Aphʿel would be required). The corruption could have been facilitated by the occurrence of ܢܚܬ only two words later. The evaluation of the points in 17a10 is difficult: the point above might be verbal, and that below might belong to the *rish* of ܐܪܝܐ in the line below (though there is another point which may serve this purpose). Alternatively the copyist may deliberately preserve a double reading, offering both *dalath* and *rish* as alternatives. One would hardly in any case look with confidence to 17a10 for the survival of an older reading, but there is some intrinsic probability that the original Peshitta rendering of this word used ܪܘܚ rather than ܕܘܚ. The second of these variants represents agreement with the plural of the Hebrew, and the loss of *seyāmē*, particularly over *rish*, would have been an easy corruption in the standard text. The actual occurrence of *seyāmē* in 17a6.11 is however likely to be coincidental, and probably a spontaneous correction in each case by the copyist rather than a survival of the original reading from an older Ms (*cf* chapter 2, section A5 *ad fin*). The third variant also represents agreement with the Hebrew, and the standard text could easily have arisen as a corruption of it. Its presence in 17a11 could be accidental, a deliberate correction by the copyist, or an assimilation to the Syrohexapla. It is unlikely however to derive directly from an older Ms (*cf ibidem*). The fourth variant is significant only if the word is interpreted in the abstract "evil" rather than the personal "evil-doer", and this is precluded in the case of 14d1 and 17a11 by the retention of the diacritic point above the word. The absence of *seyāmē* in these Mss is thus to be regarded in all probability as a mere error. The vocalization in 16g6 however suggests that the word was understood as the abstract noun in distinction from the ܥܒܕܐ later in the verse which is vocalized as the *nomen agentis*. The abstract noun would correspond exactly with the Hebrew. It is possible that this is a genuine survival of an old, indeed an original, reading, though the fact that 12a1 clearly agrees with the standard text in this passage precludes the possibility of its derivation through that channel.

The attestation of the last two variants may almost certainly be set aside as deliberate corrections of 17a5 to conform with the Hebrew in preparation for its use in the preparation of the Paris Polyglot (*cf* EMERTON, p. xxii). They too however are worthy of consideration in their own right.

15. Na ii 5   ܘܡܒܙܐ] ܘܡܒܘܙܐ   17a5$^{(1)}$
16. Sa xii 13 ܕܒܗ] *add* ܕܒܗ ܪܡܝܘܬܐ ܐܝܟܐ ܘܡܫܒܚ ܐܝܟܐ, ܠܐ
                                                                                                         17a5^1

The first of these is undoubtedly closer to the Hebrew, and the standard text could have arisen as a corruption of it (reading *mim* for *waw* and *qoph*). The word has been touched up in the Ms and it is certainly possible that 17a5* read the standard text. The interpretation of יתהוללו as though it were יתהללו may well have facilitated the corruption. The second variant is clearly the correction of a *homoeoteleuton* that has occurred throughout the extant Mss of the Peshiṭta, but the correction is certainly made by a later hand in the margin, and is almost certainly a deliberate correction to conform with the Hebrew.

Of these last six variants only the fourth (14) can claim any plausible attestation, and then in the case of 16g6 only. 12, 13 and 16 however have a strong claim to represent the original Peshiṭta on the grounds of intrinsic probability, while 11 (at least in the form ܐܝܢܘ) and 15 are also deserving of consideration on grounds of intrinsic probability.

3. Inner-Syriac Corruptions

The previous section has prepared us for the possibility that there are a number of inner-Syriac corruptions in the earliest extant text of the Peshiṭta. The relative paucity of ancient Mss, particularly for the Dodekapropheton, obliges us to resort at this stage to conjecture. The probable survival of a few original readings only in late Mss in passages where the standard text seems to have suffered inner-Syriac corruptions does however give some encouragement to proceed in an area where conjecture is at present the only course open to us. It is always to be hoped that further ancient Mss may be discovered or that some conjectures may be vindicated by quotations in the Syriac fathers. For the present however the only argument that can be offered on their behalf is that of intrinsic probability. This naturally varies considerably in degree from instance to instance. We begin with the most convincing examples, adding in brackets where appropriate the name of the earliest scholar known to us to have made the suggestion of each particular inner-Syriac corruption. The material is listed in the form of *lemmata* from the Basic Text followed, after the *lemma* bracket, by the suggested original readings of which they are thought to be corruptions.

Jl i 17   ܕܢܒܚ] ܘܒܚܥ
Jl iv 17   ܒܚܕܪܘܗܝ] ܒܚܕܪܘܗܝ   = Syh (Sebök)
Am vi 2   ܠܚܠܬ] ܚܠܬܐ   (Rudolph)
Am vi 11   ܪܒܐ] ܪܒܐ

Mi i 10 ܬܚܕܘܢ] ܬܚܘܘܢ *cf* Targum (SEBÖK)
Mi ii 12 ܕܡܟܠܝܢ] ܕܡܟܠܠ (Barhebraeus uses ܟܠܐ in his comment) (SEBÖK)
Mi v 5 ܘܢܐܪܥܘܢ] ܘܢܪܥܘܢ (SEBÖK)
Mi v 7 ܕܥܢ̈ܐ 1°] ܕܥܒܐ (SEBÖK)
Mi vi 7 ܕܚܝܠܐ ܕܡܫ̈ܚܐ] ܕܢ̈ܚܠܐ ܕܡܫܚܐ (Roorda, cit. RYSSEL)
Mi vii 14 ܥܢ̈ܐ] ܥܒܐ *cf* v 7 *supra* (SEBÖK)
Na ii 2 ܡܕܒܪܢܐ] ܡܒܕܪܢܐ (SEBÖK)
Na iii 14 ܡܘܠܒܢܐ] ܡܠܒܢܐ *cf* Jeremiah xliii 9 (Bernstein, cit. SEBÖK)
Hb i 8 ܢܫܪ̈ܐ] ܢܡܪ̈ܐ *cf* ܢܫܪ̈ܐ later in the verse; also possible assimilation to 2 Samuel i 23, Jeremiah iv 13 (RUDOLPH)
Hb i 12 ܢܡܘܣ] ܢܡܘܬ (SEBÖK)
Zf ii 14 ܒܟܘܗ̇ 2°] ܒܒܘܗ̇ *cf* Targum (GERLEMAN)
Zf ii 14 ܕܒܘܪܗ̇] ܕܒܪܘܬܗ̇ *cf* Ezekiel xvii 3 (Bernstein, cit. SEBÖK)
Zf iii 6 ܕܘܝܬܐ] ܙܘ̈ܝܬܐ (SEBÖK)
Sa i 17 ܘܢܒܢܐ] ܘܢܓܒܐ (SEBÖK)
Sa iv 10 ܘܢܚܘܪܘܢ] ܘܢܚܙܘܢ (SEBÖK)
Sa viii 16 ܒܬܪ̈ܥܝܬܟܘܢ] ܒܬܪ̈ܥܝܟܘܢ *cf* possible assimilation to ܒܠܒܟܘܢ in the next verse
Sa xi 14 ܐܘܝܘܬܐ] ܐܚܘܬܐ

These twenty-one putative corruptions are all of such a kind as to involve only the change, addition or metathesis of single letters, and the proposed original readings are natural renderings of the Hebrew. To these may be added six further instances where the supposed corruption consists either of the loss of *seyāmē* or of confusion between *dalath* and *rish*, and where the proposed original readings also offer a closer rendering of the Hebrew.

Hs v 9 ܒܚܪܒܬܐ] *c. sey*
Mi i 11 ܥܒܕܝ] ܥܒܪܝ (RYSSEL and SEBÖK)
Na i 8 ܥܒܕ . . . ܢܥܒܪ] ܥܒܪ . . . ܢܥܒܕ (Rosenäcker, *cit* SEBÖK)
Hb ii 18 ܦܬܟܪܐ ܣܪܝܩܐ] *c. sey* (*bis*)
Hb iii 7 ܡܫܟܢܐ] *c. sey*
Sa xiv 10 ܕܙܘܝܬܐ] *c. sey*

We now add some twenty further possible instances where, however, either the corruption presupposed is less likely to have occurred mechanically or the Peshiṭta text might reasonably be regarded as the original rendering of the Hebrew, though the suggested alternative original reading would have been a more literal rendering.

Hs iii 5	] vel	(Sebök)
Hs vi 2	] add	(presupposing a *homoeoteleuton*)
Hs ix 12	] vel	(Sebök)
Hs x 4	]	(Sebök)
Hs xi 8	]	(Sebök, but he also allows the possibility that the text is original in view of the following clause)
Hs xii 5	] vel add	(presupposing a *homoeoteleuton*, cf Rudolph)
Jl ii 14	]	cf ii 3
Am vi 1	]	
Am vi 11	]	
Am vii 16	]	(Sebök, but he also allows the possibility that the text is original)
Jon ii 10	]	(Sebök)
Mi ii 13	]	cf masc suffix (Rudolph)
Mi iv 14	]	
Mi vii 4	]	(Sebök)
Na ii 7	]	(Bernstein, cit Sebök)
Hb iii 2	]	
Hb iii 6	]	(Bernstein, cit Payne Smith)
Zf i 1	]	(Gerleman)
Sa xiii 9	]	
Ml iii 16	]	cf Targum

Many more examples could be given, but we have tried to restrict the list to those which seem worthy of serious consideration. In the absence of objective evidence they are very much a matter for individual judgement. Studies of the translation technique of the Peshiṭta translators, as yet in their infancy, will also assist a more objective assessment of suggestions such as these. It would however be surprising if none of the instances presented in this section proved to be the original Peshiṭta text. It is worth adding that several of Sebök's conjectural emendations, to mention no others, have been vindicated by their appearance in biblical Mss, and have accordingly been considered in the previous section or the previous chapter.

4. Syrohexaplaric Influence

All the variants in the biblical Mss have been compared with the text of the Syrohexapla. It is not surprising that many agreements have been discovered, and the great majority are probably of no significance at all since they represent merely slight differences in the rendering of what is ultimately the same original text into Syriac. One example is the preference of 17a1 for *stat emph* + ܠܗ to pronominal suffixes, which is also a characteristic of the Syrohexapla. Syrohexaplaric influence on Peshitta Mss may reasonably be suspected only in cases where distinctive readings are concerned, or where there are a number of instances in a particular Ms. Attention will however be paid to all possible cases of Syrohexaplaric readings among those considered in section 2 above.

It will be convenient to consider first seventeen readings which have already been discussed. Brief comments will now be added with respect to the question of possible Syrohexaplaric influence.

(a) Readings discussed in chapter 3:
16. Sa i 2. The additional word in the standard text could have arisen through assimilation to Syh, but could also be explained as assimilation to Sa i 15 or vii 12.
55. Mi vi 8. The additional word in 7a1 10j2 results in a text less close to the Hebrew than the standard text, and may well be due to assimilation to Syh or LXX.
59. Na ii 3. The reading of 6h9 7a1 is closer to the Hebrew than the standard text, but might again be explained alternatively as assimilation to Syh. If so, this would have implications for the dating of 6h9, and this will be considered below.
71. Hg ii 16. The reading of 7a1 8a1 19g5 is most naturally explained as assimilation to the first half of the verse and the agreement with Syh is coincidental.
87. Ml ii 16. The shorter text of 6h9 8a1* is closer to the Hebrew, but could also be explained as assimilation to Syh.
90. Zf ii 11. The reading of 6h9 was thought to be original, in which case the agreement with Syh is coincidental.
130. Ob 5. It proved impossible to determine whether this variant or the standard text was original. Assimilation to Syh is one possible explanation of the variant.

(b) Reading discussed in chapter 4, section 1:
Sa vii 2. Syh also has ܐܪܥܐ rather than ܐܪܥܗ, but as it uses ܕܗܘ rather than a pronominal suffix the possibility of assimilation to

Syh as the cause of the reading of 9l6 is remote.

(c) Readings discussed in chapter 4, section 2:

2. Am v 10. The reading of 17a6 *fam* was seen to be patient of several possible explanations, to which assimilation to Syh must be added.

3. Am vi 13. The reading of 17a6 *fam* was thought to have a high probability of being original; assimilation to Syh would be another possible explanation.

5. Jon ii 5. The derivation of this reading in 17a7^{mg}.8^{mg} from Syh is a possibility; it would only be likely if there were evidence of a substantial number of Syh readings in Risius' apparatus. The probable occurrence of this reading also in 17d1 suggests that it is a genuine Peshitta variant.

6. Na ii 1. The same general considerations apply as in the last instance.

7. Hs xiv 8. The reading of 15d2 *fam* and 19d4 was seen to be closer to the Hebrew than the standard text, which might well be a corruption of it. Assimilation to Syh would be another possible but less likely explanation.

8. Jl iv 13. Assimilation to Syh is certainly a possible explanation of the reading of 19g5.7, but we have seen reason to believe that it may represent the original Peshitta text.

9. Mi iii 4. The same general considerations apply as in the last instance. Aural confusion is another possible factor in this case.

12. Na ii 12. The agreement with Syh is most probably coincidental.

13. Na iii 11. The agreement with Syh is again most probably coincidental.

In only one of these seventeen readings (Mi vi 8) can assimilation to Syh be said to be a probable explanation. In six (Am v 10, vi 13, Ob 5, Na ii 3, Sa i 2 and Ml ii 16) it is a possible explanation to be weighed against others. In the remaining ten passages it has been thought to be a less probable explanation of the origin of the reading than others.

Eight further readings fall to be considered in this section, and it will be convenient to group them according to their attestation. The first two concern readings in the oldest Mss. The reading peculiar to 6h9 at Sa v 4 (the substitution of a synonym for the word in the standard text) is most naturally in itself explained as an assimilation to Syh. This however immediately raises a question about the date of 6h9, as we have already seen in the case of Na ii 3 considered above. If 6h9 does in fact contain one or two readings derived from the

Syrohexapla it must itself have been copied at a date subsequent to the making of the Syrohexapla translation in A.D. 617-8. The sixth century date ascribed to the Ms in its *siglum* derives presumably from WRIGHT's description, "The writing is a fine, regular Estrangĕlā of the vi[th] cent.", but the evidence suggestive of "contamination" from the Syrohexaplaric text may perhaps be allowed to bring the date of this Ms down to the first half of the seventh century. Alternative explanations, such as pure coincidence, or the existence of some otherwise unknown independent Syriac version which influenced both 6h9 and Syh, are of course possible, but it seems simpler to revise the putative date of 6h9 and admit that it has been subject to Syrohexaplaric influence. The reading of 8a1 12d1 and 14d1 at Zf i 12 is also most naturally explained as assimilation to Syh or LXX.

There next fall to be considered three readings peculiar to 13a1:

Hs iii 3   ܙܟܠ] add (.) ܐܝܪ
Am vii 8   ܣܠܝܗ] ܐܠܗ ܣܠܝܗ
Sa iii 5   ܩܪܡ] add ܗܘܐ

The first of these readings is an interpretative addition found also in LXX[Mss]. The second could be explained as assimilation to the Hebrew, and the third as assimilation to v. 1 in the same chapter. On the other hand all three could be explained as due to Syrohexaplaric influence, and the incidence of three such readings in a single Ms is at least suggestive.

The reading (ܝܢܣܝ for ܝܣܘܣܗ) at Hs x 2 peculiar to 17a6 *fam*, where the reading of the standard text is recorded as a variant in 17a7[mg].8[mg], could also be explained as assimilation to Syh, and if this proved to be the right explanation it would modify the provisional judgement on the readings in Jon ii 5 and Na ii 1 on p. 102 above. A more plausible explanation however lies to hand in the fact that this word is omitted in 9a1*, where a correction has been made in the margin which is illegible but could well be the reading of 17a6 *fam*. This would mean that Risius adopted the reading in the margin of 9a1 for his text and relegated the reading of 16d1 (i.e. the standard text) to the margins of 17a7 and 17a8, a procedure consistent with his practice elsewhere. It is of course quite possible, perhaps even probable, that the supplement in the margin of 9a1 was derived from Syh, but this would not carry with it any implication that Risius himself drew directly on Syh for any of his readings.

This leaves only two further readings to be considered, both of which occur in 16g6:

Am viii 4   ܣܚܕܬ] ܗܠܝܢ   16g6*
Jon ii 4 ܣܘܝܢ ܡܢܘܬܐ] ܘܡܢܘܬܗ ܣܘܝܢ 16g6 19g5.7

It is of interest to note that in both of these passages the standard text is closer to the Hebrew, and that it is read by 12a1 certainly in the first and probably in the second. In the first Syh has both words (those of the standard text and the variant), and it may be thought that if the reading of 16g6* were derived from Syh both words would likewise be found in the Ms. An alternative explanation is that the copyist of 16g6 wrote originally the word he expected (*cf* e.g. Mi iii 9), which was subsequently corrected to the standard text. Assimilation to Syh is certainly a possible explanation of the plural in Jon ii 4.

As we have seen Syrohexaplaric influence is always difficult to prove, even where it may be strongly suspected. In many of the twenty-five readings considered in this section other explanations are possible; in all but four (Hs x 2, Ob 5, Na ii 1 and Sa v 4) assimilation to LXX is an alternative possibility, though it may be thought that this is unlikely at least in the later stages of the transmission of the Peshitta. Assimilation to Syh seems however to be the most probable explanation of six of these readings (Hs iii 3, x 2, Jon ii 4, Mi vi 8, Zf i 12 and Sa v 4) and it is interesting to note that the last three of these are readings attested in one or more of the oldest Mss, two of them indeed only in Mss of this group. Assimilation to Syh was thought to be a possible explanation of eight further readings (Am v 10, vi 13, vii 8, Ob 5, Na ii 3, Sa i 2, iii 5 and Ml ii 16); two of these (Na ii 3 and Ml ii 16) are also attested only in the oldest Mss. It seems reasonable then to conclude that there was probably some Syrohexaplaric influence in the tradition from which the oldest Mss stem, and possibly also in 13a1 and the group 16g6 19g5.7. Assimilation to the Syrohexapla appears not however to have been a major factor in the transmission of the Peshitta.

5. Conclusion

The title of the present chapter indicates that a definitive text of the Peshitta of the Dodekapropheton at present eludes us. In Part Two we shall see reason to believe that the Peshitta version of these Books originated at a time when the Masoretic Text of the Hebrew Bible was

CONCLUSION   105

not finally determined. If we are right in tracing Syrohexaplaric influence behind 6h9, with the corollary that this Ms must be redated in the seventh century, this means that there is a gap of hardly less than five centuries between the original translation of the Dodekapropheton in the Peshitta version and the copying of the oldest extant Ms of that version, a Ms which itself seems to have suffered some "contamination" by the Syrohexapla. Within those five centuries almost certainly, and very probably before the major division between East and West Syrians in the fifth century, emerged what we have called the standard text, which from the ninth century at least dominated the Peshitta tradition. At the same time we have found reason to believe that a number of older and superior readings have persisted in the tradition alongside the standard text, particularly in one or more of the oldest Mss though also occasionally only in later Mss. We have also found reason to believe that a number of inner-Syriac corruptions occurred in the earliest period of the transmission of the Peshitta and have been perpetuated throughout the extant Mss. It remains now only to draw together in summary form the results of our investigations into the transmission of the Peshitta text, and to indicate in which directions further research in this area may proceed.

While there is inevitably considerable scope for individual differences of judgement about the originality of particular readings, we have listed on p. 93 *supra* thirty readings in the Apparatus of the EDITION which are considered to be probably superior to the Basic Text. We also saw good reason to suppose that most of the sixteen variants attested only in later Mss which were considered in Section 2 of this chapter represent the original Peshitta text. The suggested inner-Syriac corruptions considered in Section 3 are necessarily material of a more hypothetical nature and inevitably offer greater scope for variations of subjective judgement. It is quite possible too that additional convincing examples will occur to future scholars. However meagre may appear this harvest of variant readings with some claim to originality, it serves indirectly to confirm the high degree of homogeneity in the transmission of the Peshitta of the Dodekapropheton. Leaving aside the hypothetical inner-Syriac corruptions, we have found only forty-six passages where the Basic Text of the EDITION appears clearly inferior to other readings actually attested in the Mss, and in only twenty-five of these is the difference of reading substantial. These readings are: Am i 14, Mi iv $3^{3°\ et\ 4°}$ and Sa iii 8 in the First Apparatus, Hs xi 11, Ob 13$^{2°}$, Mi iii 1$^{1°}$, Zf ii 11, ii 12$^{2°}$, Sa iv 6 and vii 2 (*c. sey*) in the Second Apparatus, and readings 1–10 and 13–16 of those listed in Section 2 of this chapter. Six further substantially different readings are deserving of serious consideration: Jl ii 10$^{2°}$, Ob 5, Hb i 4, Zf i 18$^{2°}$ and Sa ix 8$^{1°}$ in the Second Apparatus and the omission at Sa iii 4 listed at the top of p. XXV in the Introduction to the EDITION.

What lines are open for future research? The discovery of additional, particularly older, Mss would of course be invaluable. Failing that, there is perhaps some harvest to be gained from a painstaking study of massoretic Mss, lectionary Mss, and citations in the Syriac Fathers, though in the last two of these sources allowance has to be made respectively for minor variations due to adaptation for liturgical purposes and for imprecise allusions or citations from memory; assimilation to other passages is also to be expected in this material. Probably the greatest advance is to be expected when detailed studies of the present kind have been completed for a wider selection of Books of the Old Testament Peshitta, preferably indeed of the whole, and when comparative studies of the translation technique of the Peshitta translators are facilitated by the provision of such tools as a Peshitta concordance. For the immediate future the greatest need is to extend the present kind of investigation into other Books of the Old Testament Peshitta. Only then will widely-based judgements be possible.

Appended Note to Chapter Four

Part I of this monograph was already complete when that of R.J. Owens, *The Genesis and Exodus Citations of Aphrahat the Persian Sage* (Leiden, 1983) appeared. Reference may be made to the present writer's review of this work in *JSS* XXIX, 2 (1984), pp 303–5.

While it is clear that a thorough analysis of the citations of the Dodekapropheton in Aphrahat and Ephrem would be a substantial study which cannot be undertaken here, it has been felt worthwhile to take a few preliminary soundings, the results of which are presented in this Note. The citations of Aphrahat were examined in the edition of

J. Parisot[1] and those of Ephrem in the commentaries on Jon, Na, Hb, Zf and Hg in that of T.J. Lamy.[2] It should be noted that the authorship of the latter is disputed.[3]

All citations from the Dodekapropheton listed in Parisot's index were examined, but only seven unambiguous citations were found to occur in passages where either there are variants in one or more of the oldest Mss (listed below by the serial numbers used in chapter 3) or primitive inner-Syriac corruptions (listed in chapter 4, section 3) have been suspected. In view of Owens' conclusion that the citations of Aphrahat are of mainly corroborative value passages of these kinds seemed the most potentially fruitful. A rather larger number (23) of such passages was found in Ephrem, to which must be added five others where variants attested only in later biblical Mss come into question. No single quotation of either kind of passage occurred in both Aphrahat and Ephrem, the seven passages in Aphrahat coming from Hs, Am, Mi and Sa.

The first impression gained from this brief examination is that both fathers were familiar with the standard text. In particular the standard text is corroborated by the patristic citations in all eleven passages where primitive inner-Syriac corruptions have been suspected (Am vii 16, Mi vi 7, Na i 8, ii 7, iii 14, Hb i 12, iii 6, 7, Zf i 1, ii 14$^{1°}$, Sa i 17). In a further eleven passages where there are variants in one or more of the oldest Mss (nos. 28, 47, 55, 56, 59, 64, 91, 94, 95, 111, 132) the patristic citations support the standard text. To these may be added three from those listed in chapter 4, section 2 (nos. 4, 12, 13). On the other hand there are eight passages in which the patristic citation agrees with a reading in one or more of the oldest Mss against the standard text (nos. 25, 46, 57, 62, 63, 66, 68, 70). Two further readings attested only in later Mss (listed in the second apparatus of the EDITION at Hb ii 13 and iii 14, and regarded hitherto as probably simply inner-Syriac corruptions) appear in Ephrem's citations. In one passage (no. 67) Ephrem offers a reading different from both the standard text and the variant (ܠܟܘܡܗ).

No conclusions can be drawn from a few further citations. Four concern the presence or absence of initial *waw* (nos. 50, 86, 115, 117), but since in each case the citation begins with the word in question it

---

1. *Patrologia Syriaca*, Paris, vols. i and ii (1894, 1907).
2. *Sancti Ephraem Syri Hymni et Sermones*, Mechelen, vol. ii (1886), cols. 229–310.
3. *Cf* R. Murray, *Symbols of Church and Kingdom*, Cambridge, 1975, pp. 366f.

cannot be determined whether *waw* was present in the biblical text known to the patristic writer. Two other citations are too imprecise to admit of any conclusions concerning variants 13 or 133, while Aphrahat's citation potentially relevant to variants 100 and 101 proves to be not from Mi but from the parallel passage in Isaiah.

An analysis of the nineteen readings listed above where there are variants in one or more of the oldest Mss may be of interest. Eight (25, 56, *66*, 68, *94*, 95, 111, 132) are among those where it proved impossible to determine which reading was more likely to be original. Of the other eleven readings the patristic citations agree with two of those of the oldest Mss considered superior (62, *70*) and with three considered inferior (46, 57, 63). They agree with four readings of the standard text considered superior (47, 55, *59*, 64) and with two considered inferior (28, *91*). The five italicized numbers indicate readings belonging to the group of twenty-five where the variants are considered to be significant. These statistics indicate that the patristic citations agree almost equally with the standard text and with variant readings of the oldest Mss, while the citations are also almost equally divided between those readings considered original or secondary on intrinsic grounds. Clearly it would be unwise to draw any far-reaching conclusions from such slender and evenly balanced data.

PART II
THE PESHIṬTA AS A VERSION

5
The Hebrew Text behind the Peshitta

1. Introduction

The primary significance of the Peshitta for the majority of Old Testament scholars consists in the evidence it affords for the reconstruction of the Hebrew text of the Old Testament. Retroversion of an ancient translation into Hebrew is however far from conclusive evidence that such a Hebrew text once existed and was the *Vorlage* of the ancient version concerned. Many differences between a version and its *Vorlage* are best explained in terms of the different idiomatic usages of the two languages concerned, the stylistic characteristics of the translator, and deliberate attempts to interpret a text which the translator himself may have found difficult to understand. Even conjectural emendations may not have been beyond the scope of ancient translators, whose primary purpose was usually less to preserve the exact meaning of the original than to produce a readable and intelligible rendering in their own language of the Hebrew scriptures still used by their own community in public worship. Intelligibility was often a more important objective than minute and literal accuracy. The scientific evaluation of the Peshitta as evidence for its Hebrew *Vorlage* requires therefore a careful study of the style and translation technique of the Syriac translator(s), a study which needs to be much more broadly based than is possible in the present work. In the next chapter a few preliminary observations will be made on this aspect of the question.

In the present chapter however it will be of some value to set out the specific evidence which does suggest that the *Vorlage* of the Peshitta was not identical with the Masoretic Text (hereafter MT). Three main lines of investigation immediately suggest themselves. The most important of these is an examination of passages where Hebrew readings exist which are divergent from those of MT. Of prime importance are the variants attested directly or indirectly in the manuscripts discovered in the region of the Dead Sea, but it will be convenient also to consider a number of variants attested in later Mss within the Masoretic tradition, including some *Qre* and *Kthibh* variants. The question we need to ask in relation to these variants within the Hebrew tradition itself is whether in any particular case the *Vorlage* presupposed by the Peshitta is more likely to be the reading of MT or that of the variant. A second line of investigation based on MT itself is concerned with passages in which the Peshitta seems to presuppose a different vocalization or even a different word-division of the same Hebrew consonantal text as MT.

The third line of investigation is based on the less direct evidence of the other ancient versions. When for instance the Peshitta agrees with one or more of the other ancient versions in a rendering which is readily explicable as deriving from a common Hebrew *Vorlage* different from MT this may be felt to constitute *prima facie* evidence for the existence of such a *Vorlage*. Evidence of this kind however needs to be carefully sifted, for an alternative explanation can be sought in the influence of the versions themselves on one another, or sometimes in a common exegetical tradition. The relation of the Peshitta to the Septuagint (hereafter LXX) and to Targum Jonathan will be examined more specifically in chapters 7 and 8. The most plausible instances of agreement of the Peshitta with either or both of these versions suggesting derivation from a common Hebrew *Vorlage* distinct from MT will however be included in the present chapter. Exclusive agreements between the Peshitta and the Vulgate will also be examined here. There is scarcely any likelihood of direct influence of the Peshitta on the Vulgate, and the Peshitta is certainly older than the Vulgate, which excludes the possibility of any influence in the reverse direction. The possibility that exclusive agreements between these two versions are due to derivation from a common Hebrew *Vorlage* distinct from MT is therefore one that has to be taken seriously.

The necessarily limited studies inspired by these three lines of investigation will at least make possible a preliminary answer to the question whether the Hebrew *Vorlage* presupposed by the Peshitta is essentially identical with MT or not. If the answer is negative, the way will be open to consider the possibility that other passages where the Peshitta differs substantially from MT may not also depend on a distinctive Hebrew *Vorlage*.

2. Non-Masoretic Readings

There is not a great deal of material from Qumran or its neighbourhood available for the text of the Dodekapropheton, and the significance of what there is is reduced when it is realized that much of it presents a text or (in the case of the famous Greek scroll which will also be considered here) presupposes a Hebrew *Vorlage* very similar to that of MT at least in its consonantal form. All the published manuscript evidence listed in J.A. Fitzmyer, *The Dead Sea Scrolls— Major Publications and Tools for Study* (1975), pp. 167–170, has been carefully examined and compared with the Peshitta. There are in fact a number of variant readings in the Hebrew which cannot be detected with any certainty in the Syriac, such as the presence or absence of the article. A more striking example may be given in passing: the difference between M.T. ידי and 4QpNah יורו in Na iii 10 cannot be detected behind the Peshitta's ܐܝܕܘܗܝ. What follows is an examination of the Peshitta for traces of a Hebrew *Vorlage* distinct from MT attested in these Mss.

The only Hebrew manuscript of the Dodekapropheton to have survived in any considerable extent is Mur 88. This Ms, apart from orthographic variants and a few patent errors, exhibits a text very similar to that of MT. Only five passages have been found where the Peshitta agrees with divergent readings of Mur 88:

Am vii 15	על] אל
Ob 17	מורישיהם] מורשיהם
Mi vii 5	אל²°] *pr waw*
Zf iii 9	על העמים] אל עמים
Zf iii 15	איביך] איבך

In the fourth of these readings it must be noted that the agreement between Mur 88 and the Peshitta is clear only with respect to the preposition; the use of the emphatic ܥܡܡܐ does not necessarily presuppose the article of Mur 88.

It is important however to note that there are some distinctive readings of Mur 88 which are not reflected in the Peshitta. In Hb iii 10 Mur 88 reads the first three words of Psalm lxxvii 18 in place of the clause זרם מים עבר, and in doing so may preserve the original reading; the Peshitta here however agrees with MT. Five further readings of Mur 88 which are not reflected in the Peshitta may be noted:

Am vii 16	תטיף [	עוד *add*
Am ix 5	ואבלו ... יושבי [	*sing*
Jon iii 8	אל [	על
Mi vii 12	יום [	ב *pr*
Hg ii 1	ביד [	אל

In two readings (שערו in Ob 11 and פרזו in Hb iii 14) Mur 88 agrees with the *Kthibh* of MT while the Peshitta agrees with the *Qre*, and in Mi i 10 where Mur 88 agree with the *Qre* (התפלשי) the Peshitta is different from both *Kthbih* and *Qre*.

The five agreements of the Peshitta with Mur 88 are all explicable in terms of either the presence or absence of vocalic letters in the Hebrew or the translator's licence of interpretation rather than as constituting evidence for a *Vorlage* distinct from MT. It is interesing that when Mur 88 has truly distinctive readings the Peshitta is found to be in agreement with MT. In the same way none of the distinctive readings of the meagre remaining Hebrew biblical Mss from Qumran (4QXII^d, 4QXII(?) which comprises fragments of Hs xiii 15–xiv 6, and 5QAmos) are reflected in the Peshitta.

The next class of material requiring examination is that of the Qumran Pesher texts, of which the most substantial and the most important is 1QpHab. A distinction must be made here between the direct quotations of the text and passages in the commentary which may suggest variant readings. For instance the striking reading in ii 16 of והרעל for והערל (MT) is slightly offset by the Pesher, which introduces the idea of circumcision of the heart, thus showing awareness of the reading of MT. In this passage the Peshitta agrees with the variant reading in the text quotation of 1QpHab, which is also presupposed in LXX, Aquila and the Vulgate. In his monograph, *The Text of Habakkuk in the Ancient Commentary from Qumran* (JBL Monograph Series, Vol. XI, 1959), W.H. BROWNLEE listed this on p. 119 with four other "dual readings" (one of which he eliminated on pp. 121f.); in each of these other cases the Peshitta agrees with MT. In one passage (i 5) where the text quotation is not extant but a variant reading (בוגדים for the בגוים of MT) is implied in the Pesher, this variant reading is also reflected by the Peshitta in company with LXX, the other versions agreeing with MT.

Other agreements between the Peshitta and the text quotations of 1QpHab are slight. They consist of the addition of the copula in three places (i 13, 15, ii 3), its omission in one (ii 13) and its transfer from

תמיד to לא in i 17, the addition of a plural ending to ויאמר (ii 6), the reading יעלה for העלה in i 15, the omission of interrogative *he* at the beginning of i 17, and the addition of a 3 *m. sing* suffix to להוכיח (i 12), where however the Peshitta presupposes the infinitive of MT rather than the participle of 1QpHab. All of these are readily explicable in terms of the translator's licence of interpretation rather than as evidence for a *Vorlage* distinct from MT.

There are however a number of passages where the Peshitta presupposes MT rather than a variant text quoted in 1QpHab. Most of the differences are quite minor, but two significant readings of 1QpHab which are not presupposed in the Peshitta are למשל for לא משל (MT) in i 14, and חרבו for חרמו (MT) in i 17, the latter being reflected by 8HevXII gr (μάχαιραν αὐτοῦ). A list of further variants in 1QpHab which are not reflected in the Peshitta follows (in BROWNLEE's enumeration): 11, 52, 69, 70, 73, 76, 82, 86, 93, 96, 106, 114 and 127.

The next Pesher text to be examined is 4QpNah. Here again the evidence is divided, the Peshitta agreeing sometimes with MT and sometimes (though never in its distinctive readings) with the variant text quoted in the Pesher. Six agreements with the variant text have been noted, of which two (iii 8, 11) consist of the addition of the copula, one (iii 8) of that of a suffix, one (iii 10) of the substitution of the preposition *beth* for *lamedh*, and the remaining two (iii 7, 9) of *plene* vocalizations distinct from those of MT. Against these must be set eight variant readings in the Pesher text which are not reflected in the Peshitta, of which two consist of additional words (טרף in ii 13 and בעיר in iii 11), one (iii 6) is the substititon of כאורה for כראי (MT), and the remaining five (iii 3, 5 *bis*, 8 *bis*) are minor variants affecting single letters.

The Peshitta agrees with one variant in 4QpHos[b] (היה for יהיה (MT) in viii 6; LXX reads ἦν), but disagrees with two others (כי חכה for וכחכי (MT) at vi 9 and the omission of the copula in וסופתה in viii 7). It also disagrees with a variant of 1QpMic at i 2 (יהוה אדני יהיה for ויהי אדני יהוה (MT)).

We must also consider six of the citations from the Dodekapropheton in the Damascus Document, which include readings distinct from MT. Five of these variants are not reflected in the Peshitta; the citations concerned are those of Hs v 10 at CD xix 15-16, Mi vii 2 at CD xvi 15, Na i 2 at CD ix 5, Sa xiii 7 at CD xix 7-9 and Ml i 10 at CD vi 13-14 (in the last case the variant in question is the reading of דלתו for דלתים (MT); the omission of גם, though common to the Peshitta, being less easy to evaluate). The sixth variant however, which is the addition of כן before סרר in Hs iv 16 quoted at CD i 13-14, has its counterpart in the Peshitta which reads ܗܟܢܐ and the Targum which reads כין.

The last Ms from the Dead Sea region to be considered is the famous Greek scroll of the Dodekapropheton (8HevXII gr), which was the subject of a meticulous study by D. BARTHÉLEMY (*Les Devanciers d'Aquila, VTS* X, 1963). From a detailed study of the nine best preserved verses he concluded that this Ms is a copy of a recension of LXX, corrected to conform more exactly to the Hebrew text (*cf* the restoration of עם in Zf ii 10, omitted in all but Lucianic Mss of LXX, and the literal rendering of איש as ἀνήρ rather than the idiomatic ἕκαστος of LXX in Mi iv 4). The Hebrew text used by the corrector was almost identical with MT, only three small divergences being detected in the nine verses analysed in detail by Barthélemy (*op. cit.*, p. 198, 3 (f)). It is of some interest that in the two of these divergences which are confined to matters of vocalization and word-division (the pointing וְיָשְׁבוּ in Mi v 3 and the reading of עב טיט thus as two words in Hb ii 6) the Peshitta reads the Hebrew in the same way as 8HevXII gr (though in the latter case they interpret עב differently). In the third case, where there is a difference in the consonantal text (the reading of a 1 *pl* in place of a 1 *sing* suffix in להפיצנו in Hb iii 14), the Peshitta has a quite different reading, whose affinity is with the Barberini Ms of the LXX. A few more substantial differences from MT are explained as LXX readings which the corrector failed to emend (BARTHÉLEMY, *ibid*); some of these may derive ultimately from a Hebrew *Vorlage* distinct from MT, while others simply reflect a different vocalization of the same consonantal Hebrew.

When the fragments are examined in their entirety only two passages are found where 8HevXII gr and the Peshitta agree in presupposing a common distinctive Hebrew consonantal text. The first is Hb ii 17, where יחיתך rather than יחיתן (MT) is presupposed by 8HevXII gr and the Peshitta in common with LXX, Targum and some Mss of the Vulgate. The other is Zf iii 7, where in place of מעונה (MT) the consonantal text מעינה is presupposed by 8HevXII gr, LXX and the Peshitta; the vocalization presupposed by 8HevXII gr (מֶעְיְנָה) however differs from that presupposed in common by LXX and the Peshitta (מַעְיָנָה). In none of the following instances where 8HevXII gr seems to presuppose a Hebrew *Vorlage* distinct from the consonantal

MT is this variant reading reflected in the Peshitta:

Mi i 1	מֶלֶךְ] מלכי	
Mi ii 8	יְקוֹמְמוּ] יקומם	(*cf* Targum)
Mi v 5	בְּפִתְחָהּ] בפתחיה	(*cf* Aquila and Vulgate)
Na iii 16	כְּכוֹכְבֵי] מכוכבי	(*cf* LXX^{Mss})
Hb i 8	וּפָשׁוּ] ופשו	
Hb i 17	חֶרְמוֹ] חרמו	(as in 1QpHab)
Hb ii 3	וְיָפֵחַ] ויפח	(*cf* LXX and Vulgate)
Hb ii 8	ישלוך] *pr waw*	
Hb ii 18	מַרְאֶה] מורה	(so LXX)
Hb iii 9	תָעִיר] תעור	(*cf* LXX and Vulgate)
Hb iii 9	אָמַר] אמר *et add* יהוה	(so LXX)
Zf iii 7	לָכֵן] אכן	(*cf* Targum)

One interesting passage is Na ii 6, where in place of וְהֵכַן (MT) the Peshitta presupposes וְהֵכִינוּ in common with LXX and Targum; 8HevXII gr retains the transitive interpretation of the verb, but corrects to the singular as in MT, thus presupposing the vocalization וְהֵכִין.

Where 8HevXII gr merely presupposes a non-Masoretic vocalization of the same consonantal Hebrew text, agreement with the Peshitta is more common. Three instances have been noted in addition to those at Mi v 3 and Hb ii 6 already mentioned. In Na iii 8 where MT vocalizes מִיָּם, 8HevXII gr and the Peshitta presuppose the vocalization מַיִם in common with LXX and Vulgate, while the Targum has a conflate reading (מי ימא). In Na iii 9 where MT vocalizes עָצְמָה, 8HevXII gr and the Peshitta presuppose the vocalization עֲצֻמָה in common with LXX. In Na ii 6 where MT vocalizes חוֹמֹתֶהָ, LXX and 8HevXII gr presuppose the vocalization חוֹמֹתָה; here the Peshitta agrees with LXX and 8HevXII gr in understanding the *he* as a *he locale* rather than as a suffix, but with MT in reading the noun as a singular, thus presupposing the vocalization חוֹמָתָה (as in a few Hebrew Mss). In Na ii 8 where LXX and 8HevXII gr presuppose the vocalization of מנהגות as a Pu'al, the Peshitta appears to recognize a different root.

Apart from the two distinctive readings in Hb ii 17 and Zf iii 7, neither of which is exclusive to 8HevXII gr and the Peshitta, the agreements between them are most naturally explained as the result of dependence on common traditions of vocalization and interpretation. An example of the latter is the interpretation of ערב in Hb i 8 as "evening" with Aquila, Targum and Vulgate rather than "Arabia" with LXX. There are no exclusive agreements between 8HevXII gr and the Peshitta, and there is thus no reason to suppose any direct link between them. On the other hand there is every reason to suppose that their agreement in presupposing a distinctive consonantal Hebrew text in Hb ii 17 and Zf iii 7 is the result of common dependence on a Hebrew *Vorlage* distinct from MT.

The result of this investigation is clear. Out of even the small number of significant variants that have survived in the non-Masoretic Mss only a very few are reflected in the Peshitta. The only substantial ones are the addition of כן in Hs iv 16 and the readings בוגדים (Hb i 5), והרעל (Hb ii 16), יחיתך (Hb ii 17) and מעינה (Zf iii 7). In each of these cases an alternative explanation could be found for the reading of the Peshitta with reference to one or more of the other ancient versions. It is hard to avoid the conclusion that the Hebrew *Vorlage* of the Peshitta was very nearly identical with MT, though it seems probable that the translation was made at a date when some variant readings were still in circulation.

3. Variants within the Masoretic tradition

In this section we shall consider first variants which are explicitly attested within the Masoretic tradition, *viz.* the *Tiqqune sopherim* and the *Kthibh/Qre* variants. Next we shall consider variant readings contained in later Hebrew Mss, notably a few in Mss from the Cairo Geniza. Finally we shall consider a fairly large number of passages where the Peshitta presupposes a different vocalization of the same consonantal Hebrew text as MT, including those where the difference concerns the presence, absence or alteration of *matres lectionis* and can be explained on the hypothesis that the text was at one stage written in *scriptio defectiva*. In two of these cases the difference extends to word-division as well as vocalization. This last category of variants thus presupposes not a different consonantal *Vorlage* from MT, but a different tradition of vocalization and interpretation. Where this tradition is reflected in other ancient versions this is noted. No attempt is made here to evaluate these traditions over against MT; opinions will in any case sometimes differ, although some of these vocalizations are manifestly inferior to those of MT. The more significant cases are discussed in the commentaries. Our present purpose is simply to determine so far as possible the Hebrew *Vorlage* of the Peshitta.

Readings and vocalizations already noted in the previous section are not repeated here.

There are four passages in the Dodekapropheton where the Masoretic tradition records *Tiqqune sopherim*. In Hs iv 7 where כבודם ... אמיר is held to be a correction of כְּבוֹדִי ... הֵמִירוּ the Peshitta and Targum reflect the 3 *pl* verb but not the 1 *sing* suffix to the noun. In Sa ii 12 where עינו is held to be a correction of עיני (attested only in LXX^W) the Peshitta agrees with MT. In Ml i 13 where אותו is held to be a corretion of אותי the Peshitta reads ܒܗܘܢ. This again presupposes MT, the suffix being plural because the Peshitta has rendered the word taken to be the antecedent (אכלו at the end of v. 12) in the plural (so LXX). The most interesting passage however is Hb i 12 where נמות is held to be a correction of תמות. Here the Peshitta's unintelligible ܢܡܘܬ is an evident inner-Syriac corruption of ܢܡܘܬܐ. At first sight this seems to represent agreement with MT, but in Syriac the 1 *pl* imperfect is identical in form with the 3 *m. sing* imperfect, and the structure of the sentence in the Peshitta indicates that this is indeed to be taken as a 3 *m. sing*, whose subject is ܐܠܗܐ 1°. In place of the two stops within this verse there should be one only, following ܢܡܘܬܐ. The relative clause ܕܠܐ ܢܡܘܬܐ thus follows the previous description of ܐܠܗܐ as ܩܕܝܫܐ, ܐܠܗܝ—"my holy immortal God". This may well be the translation of a Hebrew *Vorlage* **אלהי קָדְשִׁי לא תמות** (the supposed 'original' text, at least in its consonants). The third person of the Syriac verb is due to its place within the relative clause (*cf* Nöldeke 350B), which is made explicit in the Syriac. It appears then that the Peshitta presupposes an 'uncorrected' *Vorlage* in Hb i 12, and in respect of the verb (but not the suffix to the noun) in Hs iv 7.

In the remaining lists of readings in this chapter the following abbreviations will be used to denote the agreement of other versions with the Peshitta: A = Aquila, S = Symmachus, Th = Theodotion, T = Targum Jonathan and V = the Vulgate.

Two passages have already been noted in the previous section where the Peshitta follows the *Qre* rather than the *Kthibh*: Ob 11 (LXX V) and Hb iii 14 (8HevXII gr LXX V). There are seven further passages where the Peshitta follows the *Qre*:

Hs viii 12	רבי	(S)
Hs x 10	עונתם	(Hebrew Mss LXX V T)
Am viii 8	ונשקעה	(Hebrew Mss LXX S Th V T)

Zf ii 7	שביתם	(LXX V T)
Zf ii 9	גויי	(LXX V)
Sa iv 2	וָאֹמַר	(Cairo Geniza and other Hebrew Mss LXX^Mss V T)
Sa xiv 6	וקפאון	(LXX S V T)

One passage where the Peshiṭta agrees with the *Kthibh* (with 8ḤevXII gr and V) is Na ii 6 (בהליכותם).

There are three further passages where the Peshiṭta agrees with a variant recorded in a Ms from the Cairo Geniza:

Zf iii 8	לְקַבֵּץ	(LXX T)
Sa iv 9	וידעתם	(Hebrew Mss LXX^Mss V T)
Sa xiv 10	וממגדל	(Hebrew Mss V T^Ms)

Forty-six further readings in later Hebrew Mss are reflected in the Peshiṭta:

Hs iv 8	נפשם] נפשו	(LXX S Th V T)
Hs iv 12	התעם] התעה	(V T)
Hs vii 5	הֶחֱלוּ] הֵחֵלוּ	(LXX V T)
Hs vii 14	יתגודדו] יתגוררו	(LXX T?)
Hs viii 10	שרים] *pr waw*	(LXX A V T^Mss)
Hs ix 2	בם] בה	(LXX V T)
Hs x 9	עֲוֹלָה] עלוה	(LXX V)
Hs xi 3	זרועתי] זרועתיו	(LXX V)
Jl ii 23	יורה] מורה	(LXX V T)
Jl ii 23	כראשון] בראשון	(LXX V^Mss)
Am ii 2	בקול] *pr waw*	(LXX)
Am iii 11	וְהוֹרַד] וְהוֹרִד	(V T)
Am viii 8	כַּיְאֹר] כאר	(LXX V T)
Am viii 11	דבר] דברי	(LXX V T)
Mi i 15	אבי] אביא	(LXX S Th V T)
Mi ii 4	אמר] *pr waw*	
Mi vii 19	חטאתם] חטאתנו	(LXX V)
Na iii 7	לה] לך	(LXX^A V)
Na iii 16	הרבית] הרביתי	
Zf i 1	חזקיה] חלקיה	
Zf i 4	את 2°] *pr waw*	(LXX V T^Mss)
Zf iii 15	תיראי] תראי	(LXX)
Zf iii 20	שבותיכם] שבותכם	(LXX V)
Hg i 11	אשר] *pr* כל	(T)

VARIANTS WITHIN THE MASORETIC TRADITION 121

Hg i 12	אֲלֵיהֶם 2°] add אליהם	(LXX^{Mss} V T^{Ms})
*Sa i 4	וּמִמַּעֲלִילֵיכֶם] וּמעלליכם	(LXX)
Sa i 16	יהוה 1°] add צבאות	(LXX ^A)
Sa ii 12	אל] על	(T)
Sa iv 2	וגלה] וּגְלָה	(LXX T)
Sa v 6	עינם] עֵוֹנָם	(LXX)
Sa vi 11	עטרות] עֲטֶרֶת	(LXX^{Mss} T)
Sa vii 4	צבאות] om	(LXX^{Mss} T^{Mss})
Sa viii 17	אשר] om	(LXX)
Sa x 1	להם] לכם	
Sa xi 5	ורעיהם] ורעיהן	
Sa xi 13 bis	היוצר] הָאוֹצָר	
Sa xii 7	ישב] יֹשְׁבֵי	(LXX V T)
Sa xii 10	יושב] יֹשְׁבֵי	(LXX V T)
Sa xii 13	בית] pr השמעי	(LXX ^{Mss} T)
Sa xiii 8	pr waw [יגועו	(LXX V T ^{Mss})
Sa xiv 5	pr waw [כל	(LXX V T ^{Mss})
Sa xiv 5	עמך] עמו	(LXX V T)
Sa xiv 18	לא] om ולא עליהם	(LXX)
Ml i 13	וּאת 1°] om waw	(V)
†Ml i 13	יהוה 2°] add צבאות	(LXX)
Ml iii 19	עשה] עֹשֵׂי	(LXX V T)

Two further passages should be mentioned here. In Sa vi 12 and vii 9 לאמר is omitted in a few Hebrew Mss, but the fact that it is not represented in the Peshitta does not necessarily or even probably suggest that it was absent from the *Vorlage*, since it was not uncommon for the translator to omit it (*cf* Jon iii 7, Sa ii 4 and the other occurrence of the word in Sa vi 12!). It may be added that some of the other agreements listed above between the Peshitta and the readings of later Hebrew Mss may also be coincidental.

Turning to passages where the Peshitta clearly vocalizes the

---

* The first *yodh* is omitted in the *Qre*, but the real variant here is the additional *mem* after the initial *waw*.

† It will be recalled that while the standard text of the Peshitta reflects this additional word it is absent from 6h9 and 7a1 (see chapter 3, reading 24, with comment on p. 69). It still seems impossible to resolve the question whether the word belongs to the original text of the Peshitta. The additional divine title could equally well be an addition in assimilation to common usage or an accidental omission; it is also possible that it was deliberately excised in the recension to which 6h9 and 7a1 belong in order to bring the version into conformity with a current Hebrew text in which it was absent. There can be no certainty amidst so many possibilities.

consonantal MT differently from the traditional Masoretic vocalization, we must note first the two passages (additional to Hb ii 6 mentioned in the previous section) where the difference affects the division between words:

| Hs vi 5 | וּמִשְׁפָּטֶי כָאוֹר] וּמשפטיך אור | (LXX T) |
| Na ii 10 | כְּבֵדִים כָּל] כבד מכל | |

A further instance presupposed in LXX is only partly reflected in the Peshiṭta: this is the division of מפניהם in Hs xi 2 into מִפָּנַי הֵם, where the Peshiṭta translates מִפָּנַי but ignores the הֵם, except in so far as it is represented in the plural verb ܘܟܒܢܘ.

Next we list thirty-eight passages where the vocalization presupposed by the Peshiṭta differs from the traditional Masoretic vocalization only in matters concerning the addition, omission or alteration of *matres lectionis*:

Hs vii 1	וְרָעַת] ורעות	(LXX V T)
Hs vii 12	לְעֵדוּתָם] לעדתם	(S Th)
Hs vii 14	יָסֹרוּ] יסורו	(T)
Hs viii 4	יִכָּרֵתוּ] יכרת	(LXX V T)
Hs xi 11	וַהֲשִׁיבֹתִים] והושבתים	(LXX T)
Hs xii 2	יוֹבִילוּ] יובל	(T)
Hs xiii 9	שִׁחַתִּיךָ] שחתך	
Hs xiii 13	עַתָּה] עת	(LXX^Mss V T)
Hs xiii 15	בֵּין] בן	(LXX V)
Hs xiv 8	(וְ)יֵשְׁבוּ] ישבי	(LXX T)
Am iii 11	יְסוֹבֵב] וסביב	
Am v 9	יָבִיא] יבוא	(LXX S V)
Am v 26	סִכַּת] סכות	(LXX S V)
Am vii 1	יֵצֶר] יוצר	(LXX T)
Am vii 2.5	יָקוּם] יקום	(LXX V)
Am viii 1.2	קֵץ] קיץ	(*v. infra* p. 144)
Am viii 3	הִשְׁלַךְ] השליך	(V)
Mi i 9	מַכֹּתָהּ] מכותיה	(LXX V T)
Mi ii 6	כְּלִמּוֹת] כלמות	(S V)
Mi ii 8	מַעֲבִירִים] מעברים	(LXX)
Mi iv 12	מַחְשְׁבַת] מחשבות	(LXX)
Mi v 1	וּמוֹצָאֹתָיו] ומוצאתיו	
Mi vi 5	צִדְקֹת] צדקות	(LXX)
Mi vi 13	הֶחֱלוֹתִי] החליתי	(LXX A Th V)
Na i 10	מָלְאוּ] מלא	

VARIANTS WITHIN THE MASORETIC TRADITION

Na i 12	וְעָבְרוּ	ועבר	(T)
Na ii 5	יִתְהוֹלְלוּ	יתהוללו	
Na ii 12	לָבוֹא	לביא	(LXX V)
Hb i 7	יוֹצִיא	יצא	
Hb iii 2	פָּעָלְךָ	פעלך	(LXX T)
Hb iii 2	תּוֹדִיעַ	תודיע	(LXX)
Hb iii 5	לְרַגְלָיו	לרגליו	
Zf ii 11	נִרְאָה	נורא	(LXX)
Zf iii 5	מִשְׁפָּטָיו	משפטו	
Sa iii 9	פְּתָחֶיהָ	פתחה	(A)
Sa ix 10	וְהִכְרִית	והכרתי	(LXX)
Sa ix 12	שָׁבוּ	שובו	(LXX)
Sa x 6	וַהֲשִׁיבוֹתִים	והושבותים	(V)

Finally in this section we list sixty-six passages where the vocalization presupposed by the Peshiṭta differs from the Masoretic vocalization without affecting the consonantal text:

Hs i 2	דִּבֶּר	דבר	(LXX T)
Hs iii 1	אֹהֶבֶת	אהבת	(LXX)
Hs iii 1	רֵעַ	רע	(LXX)
Hs v 1	לְמִצְפֶּה	למצפה	
Hs v 5	וְעָנָה	וענה	(LXX T)
*Hs vi 9	(וּ)כְחַכֵּי	וכחכי	(LXX)
Hs vii 6	אֹפֵהֶם	אפהם	(T)
Hs vii 10	וְעָנָה	וענה	(LXX V T)
Hs viii 10	יִתְנוּ	יתנו	(LXX)
Hs viii 11	לַחֲטֹא 2°	לחטא	(V)
Hs ix 1	אַל	אל	(LXX V T)
Hs x 11	יְשַׂדֶּד	ישדד	
Hs xi 6	וְכָלְתָה	וכלתה	
Hs xii 1	עַד ... עַם bis	עד ... עם	(T)
Hs xii 11	אֲדָמָה	אדמה	(LXX V)
Hs xiii 7	אַשּׁוּר	אשור	(LXX V)
Hs xiii 8	וַאֲכָלֵם	ואכלם	
Hs xiv 8	יְחַיּוּ	יחיו	(LXX V T)
Jl iv 2	פִּזְּרוּ	פזרו	(LXX)
Am i 7	בְּחוֹמֹת	בחומת	(LXX T)

* The Peshiṭta omits the copula.

Am i 15	מַלְכָּם	] מלכם	(LXX^L A S V)
Am ii 1	שָׂרְפוּ	] שרפו	(LXX)
Am ii 8	חֲבָלִים	] חבלים	(LXX)
Am ii 15	יְמַלֵּט	] °1ימלט	(LXX V T)
Am iii 12	מִטָּה	] מטה	(LXX)
Am iv 3	וְהִשְׁלַכְתֶּנָה	] והשלכתנה	(LXX S V)
Am vi 1	נְקֻבֵי	] נקבי	
Am vi 3	שֶׁבֶת	] שבת	(LXX)
Am viii 8	כָּלָה	] כלה	(LXX)
Am viii 11	רָעֵב ... צָמֵא	] רעב ...2° צמא	(cf T)
Am ix 1	וּבְצַעָם	] ובצעם	(V)
Am ix 5	כָּלָה	] כלה	(LXX)
Mi ii 8	שַׂלְמָה	] שלמה	(LXX)
Mi ii 12	בָּצְרָה	] בצרה	(LXX)
Mi iii 1	וָאֹמַר	] ואמר	(LXX)
Mi iv 9	רֵעַ	] רע	(LXX)
Mi vi 10	הַאִשׁ	] האש	(LXX V)
Mi vii 4	טוֹבָם	] טובם	(LXX)
Mi vii 14	שֹׁכְנִי	] שכני	(LXX V T)
Na i 10	אֻכְּלוּ	] אכלו	
Na i 11	יָצָא	] יצא	(LXX V^{Mss})
Na iii 18	רֹעֶיךָ	] רעיך	
Na iii 18	עַמְּךָ	] עמך	
Hb ii 10	קָצוֹת	] קצות	(LXX V T)
Hb ii 13	הִנֵּה	] הנה	(LXX V)
Hb ii 18	יֵצֶר יֹצְרוֹ	] יצר יצרו	(T)
Hb iii 4	וְשָׁם	] ושם	(LXX A S)
Hb iii 9	שְׁבֻעוֹת	] שבעות	(cf LXX^{Barberini})
Zf i 2.3 bis	אָסֵף	] אסף	(V T)*
Zf i 5	בְּמַלְכָּם	] במלכם	(LXX^L V)
Zf ii 14	חֶרֶב	] חרב	(A S?)
Zf iii 7	הִשְׁכִּימוּ הִשְׁחִיתוּ	] השכימו השחיתו	(cf LXX)
Zf iii 8	לָעַד	] לעד	(LXX)
Zf iii 10	מִנְחָתִי	] מנחתי	(LXX T)
Zf iii 19	מְעֻנַּיִךְ	] מעניך	
Hg i 2	בָּא	] בא	(LXX V T)
Hg i 11	חֶרֶב	] חרב	(LXX)

* V and T support this reading only in v. 2.

Sa iii 7	בְּדָרְכִּי] בדרכי	
Sa iii 7	מְהַלְּכִים] מהלכים	(LXX V)
Sa vi 14	וְהָעֲטָרֶת] והעטרת	(LXX)
Sa ix 1	מִנְחָתוֹ] מנחתו	(LXX)
Sa x 9	וְחִיּוּ] וחיו	(LXX)
Sa xi 4.7	הַהֲרָגָה] ההרגה	*
Ml i 13	הִנֵּה] הנה	(LXX)
Ml i 13	מִתְלָאָה] מתלאה	(LXX V T)
Ml iii 16	וַיִּכָּתֵב] ויכתב	(LXX)

The evidence reviewed in this section suggests that the Hebrew *Vorlage* of the Peshitta, while essentially within the Masoretic tradition of the consonantal text, contained a number of variant readings attested in later Hebrew Mss, and a few whose record is preserved in the Masoretic tradition only in the *Tiqqune sopherim* and the *Kthibh/Qre* variants. It is clear also that the translator(s) vocalized the text in a number of passages in a way different from that of the traditional Masoretic vocalization. It is also probable that the *Vorlage* of the Peshitta or its ancestor contained rather less *scriptio plena* than M.T. This does not necessarily suggest that what was to become the traditional vocalization was not yet in existence, though it does suggest that it was not normative at the time when the Peshitta translation was made, at least in the circle of the Peshitta translator(s). Nevertheless it is possible that some of these apparent differences in reading or vocalization may be due to the translator's interpretative licence or to the influence of another ancient version (especially the LXX) rather than to an actual divergence of the *Vorlage* from MT. The extent to which allowance must be made for these factors will become clearer in the light of the following chapters. The general picture of the *Vorlage* which emerges from this section is consistent with the findings of the previous section.

4. Further evidence for a consonantal *Vorlage* distinct from MT

In this section we consider the evidence suggesting that the Hebrew *Vorlage* of the Peshitta differed from the consonantal MT in a number of variants not attested within the extant tradition of the Hebrew text. Since many renderings of the Peshitta which at first sight suggest such

---

* See chapter 4, section 2, no. 10.

a distinct *Vorlage* may find an alternative explanation in the methods of the translator(s) or in the direct influence of another ancient version we shall confine the evidence offered here to the more probable examples. Most of them are corroborated by at least one other ancient version, though a few are included at the end of the section which are attested only in the Peshitta. Agreement of the Vulgate with LXX is noted when it occurs, but it is not in itself significant, since it is likely to be due to the direct influence of LXX on the Vulgate.

First we note three variants presupposed by the Peshitta in common with both LXX and Targum:

*Hs xi 3	קחם] וָאֶקָּחֵם	(V)
†Hs xiii 5	ידעתיך] רְעִיתִיךָ	
Hs xiii 10	אהי] אַיֵּה	(V)

Two further passages may be considered here. In Hb iii 3 הודו is rendered ܘܐܘܕܐ ܘܬܫܒܘܚܬܗ, and a second noun is attested also in LXX^{Barberini} A Th and T. These other versions all point strongly to a *Vorlage* כבודו for this second noun, and the original Hebrew text was probably either הוד כבודו or הודו וכבודו, MT having been corrupted by *homoeoteleuton* (וד). In Sa xi 16 the scarcely intelligible הנער is rendered ܘܗܠܟܢ, and the context certainly suggests a feminine adjective or participle describing sheep which have strayed or been scattered or lost. A similar sense is given by LXX, V and T, though it is possible that the versions independently interpret what they found to be an unintelligible text in the light of the context. If they are dependent on a common distinctive *Vorlage*, the proposals closest to MT are הַנִּזְרָה and הַנָּעָה (*cf.* JANSMA, OTZEN and SAEBØ). No firm conclusion can be reached about this passage.

Next we list nineteen variants presupposed by the Peshitta in common with LXX:

Hs iii 4	מצבה] מִזְבֵּחַ	(V)
Hs iv 19	מזבחותם] מִמִּזְבְּחוֹתָם	(*cf* T)
Hs vii 6	קרבו] קָדַח *vel* קָדְחוּ	
Hs x 5	לעגלות] לְעֵגֶל	(Th)
Hs xiii 9	בי] מִי	
Hs xiii 14 *bis*	אהי] אַיֵּה	(*cf* xiii 10 *supra*)

---

* Only the Peshitta has the copula, but all the versions agree in a 1 *sing* past tense; MT seems to be corrupt.

† The Targum paraphrases, but clearly presupposes the variant rather than MT.

Hs xiv 9	עִנִּיתִי] עניתי	
Am vi 1	הַשָּׁאטִים] השאנוים	
Mi iii 4	וַיַּסֵּר] ויסתר	(cf pp 151f., 171)
Mi vii 12	צוֹר]2° מצור	
Na ii 4	וְהַפְּרֹשִׁים] והברשים	(V)
Na ii 14	רִבֵּךְ vel רִבְכָה] רכבה	
Na iii 9	בְּעֶזְרָתָהּ] בעזרתך	
Hb iii 2	שְׁנֵי חַיִּים] שנים חייהו	(see Rudolph)
Zf ii 11	יְרֻזֶּה] רזה	(V)
Zf iii 17	יְחַדֵּשׁ] יחריש	
Sa i 17	עָרִים] ערי	
Sa viii 9	מִיּוֹם] ביום	
Sa xiv 6	וְקָרוּת] יקרות	(S V)*

One variant is presupposed by the Peshiṭta in common with Aquila alone:

| Sa vi 7 | וְהָאֲדָמִים] והאמצים | |

Two variants are presupposed by the Peshiṭta in common with the Targum alone:

| Hs vi 3 | יְרְוֶה] יורה | |
| †Am viii 4 | הַשָּׁאטִים] השאפים | |

Some of the exclusive agreements between the Peshiṭta and the Vulgate are best explained as coincidental interpretations of MT rather than in terms of dependence on a common distinctive *Vorlage*. Examples of this are the taking of Bethel as the object of the last two verbs in Am v 6 and of Balaam as the subject of the infinitive דעת in Mi vi 5, the rendering of the plural מנחמים in Na iii 7 by a generic singular, the rendering of both חטא in Hs xii 9 and הגיד in Mi vi 8 by a 1 *sing* verb, and the interpretation of וימן in Jon ii 1 in the sense "prepare" (which is a possible meaning also of the Targum's וזמין).

Three of the exclusive agreements between the Peshiṭta and the Vulgate are however more suggestive:

---

* If Rudolph's suggestion that the Targum's עדי is a corruption of עָרִי is correct this version may also be cited in support of the variant. The variant itself is a widely accepted conjectural noun formed from קרר = "be cold" (cf BHS, KBL).

† Cf the similar variant presupposed by the Peshiṭta and LXX at Am vi 1 listed above. In both cases the variant may have arisen from misreading an obscure or damaged exemplar.

Hs viii 10   ויחלו] ܘܫܬܘܩܘܢ, et quiescent.

Sebök suggestst that the *Vorlage* may have been וינוחו.

Hs xiv 9   ואשורנו] ܘܐܬܪܨܝܘܗܝ, et dirigam eum.

Rudolph suggests that both translations derive the Hebrew from a root אשר rather than the root שור, though they differ over which of the two roots אשר they identify as the appropriate one in this context. It is thus reasonable to suppose that both translations derive from a common *Vorlage* ואאשרנו.

Am i 11   ויטרף] ܘܐܚܕ, et tenuerit.

While it is possible that these are independent 'improvements' of MT, they suggest a common derivation from a *Vorlage* which lacked the final *pe* of MT, reading simply ויטר.

Finally we suggest tentatively a few instances where the Peshitta may presuppose a *Vorlage* distinct from MT which is without any firm attestation in either Hebrew Mss or the other ancient versions:

*Hb ii 5	יְרוֶה] יונה	(Sebök)
†Zf iii 19	כֻּלָּם] ¹ºכל	(Sebök)
Sa i 15	הַשְּׁאָגִים] השאננים	(Sebök)
Ml iii 7	שְׁמַעְתֶּם] שמרתם	

* This may find support in S, if we accept Jerome's testimony.
† The *mem* would have been lost in MT by haplography before the following מעניך.

To the third of these suggestions it may be objected that the Peshitta renders שאג consistently by ܢܗܡ in its eight other occurrences in the Dodekapropheton (Hs xi 10 *bis*, Jl iv 16, Am i 2, iii 4, 8, Zf iii 3 and Sa xi 3). The translator may however have felt that while ܢܗܡ is appropriate in passages where it describes the roaring of lions, or by analogy that of God, it was less suited to express the uproar of nations, while Ps ii 1 may readily have suggested the root ܪܓܢ. In the case of the fourth suggestion it is of course possible that the change from *rish* to *ʿe* arose as an inner-Syriac corruption. The Peshitta however generally renders שמר in the Dodekapropheton by the root ܢܛܪ, and only once (in Sa vii 12, where the sense is rather different) by ܫܡܥ. It seems more likely therefore that the change had already occurred in the Hebrew *Vorlage* of the Peshitta.

To these four suggested readings we may add the additional clause in the middle of Sa iii 4: ܘܠܐܚܕܝܢ ܡܢܗ ܛܠܐ, which is peculiar to the Peshitta, but as we have seen (see chapter 3, section 2, esp. p. 70) is not certainly part of the original Peshitta text. The most we can say about this reading is that it may derive from a Hebrew *Vorlage* which contained the extra clause, which was lost by *homoeoteleuton* in MT.

CONCLUSION

Two general observations may be made in concluding this section. In the first place the great majority of the putative variants in the Hebrew text considered here differ from MT only by the addition, omission, alteration or metathesis of single consonants, and some may have arisen simply from misreading an obscure or damaged exemplar. The picture of the Hebrew *Vorlage* of the Peshitta which emerged from the two previous sections, *viz* that it differed little from the consonantal MT, is not brought into serious question by the evidence reviewed in this section. In particular the Peshitta in isolation contributes very little to our knowledge of the Hebrew text of the Dodekapropheton.

In the second place a number of the examples given are patient of more than one interpretation. To revert, for instance, to the reading in Hb iii 3 (*supra*, p. 126), it may reasonably be objected that the Peshitta's ܕܬܫܒܘܚܬܗ is not an obvious rendering of a putative *Vorlage* (ו)כבודו. An alternative explanation is that it is a rendering of סלה earlier in the verse, which is not otherwise translated. In verse 9 סלה is indeed translated by ܬܫܒܘܚܬܐ. On the other hand ܕܬܫܒܘܚܬܗ does not correspond to the position of סלה in verse 3, and in verse 13 סלה is rendered ܠܥܠܡܝܢ. In the light of these considerations it must remain doubtful whether the Peshitta can be regarded as providing evidence for the *Vorlage* presupposed by LXX^{Barberini} A Th and T in verse 3. This example illustrates the hazardous nature of any attempt to reconstruct the Hebrew *Vorlage* of any ancient version, and underlines the tentative nature of the results of this survey.

5. Conclusion

Despite inevitable uncertainties about particular readings a fairly clear general picture has emerged of the Hebrew *Vorlage* of the Peshitta of the Dodekapropheton. It contained only a small number of the non-Masoretic readings known from our relatively scanty extant Hebrew sources to have existed. It contained a fair number of the mostly minor variants known to have existed within the Masoretic tradition, and it was not infrequently vocalized, at least by the Peshitta translator(s), in a way different from that of the Masoretes. In a few cases we may be reasonably sure that it contained a distinctive reading known to us otherwise only from the *Tiqqune sopherim* or one or more of the other ancient versions. In a very few cases we may tentatively claim the Peshitta as witness for an otherwise unknown Hebrew reading. In general, however, it is clear that the Peshitta has little distinctive contribution to offer to the reconstruction of a putative original Hebrew text, at least of the Dodekapropheton, and that when it does appear to presuppose a *Vorlage* distinct from MT it is by no means a straightforward matter to reconstruct it with confidence. The textual critic of the Old Testament is well advised to be cautious in the use he makes of the Peshitta for the reconstruction of the Hebrew text.

6
The Peshitta as a Version of the Hebrew

The reconstruction of the Hebrew *Vorlage* of the Peshitta is at best a hazardous undertaking and must often lack final certainty. Much work needs to be done on the methods and technique of the Syriac translator(s) before any serious attempt can be made to reconstruct the Hebrew *Vorlage*. In the present chapter several aspects of the nature of the Peshitta as a translation are examined in a preliminary and necessarily selective way in order to provide at least a general indication of the degree of freedom the translators allowed themselves, and thus of the degree of probability with which their Hebrew *Vorlage* can be reconstructed from their work.

1. Stylistic modifications

A number of differences between the Hebrew and Syriac texts may be explained as the result of differences in the syntactical structure and idiomatic usages of the two languages. These may be loosely grouped with other deviations from a literal rendering of the Hebrew which are probably not intended to introduce any change in the actual meaning of the text. The distinction between these two kinds of modification is not always easy to draw, and this justifies their inclusion in a single section.

The differences most immediately obvious to anyone who compares the Hebrew and Syriac texts word by word are the cases where a word in the Hebrew has no counterpart in the Syriac, and those where words are introduced into the Syriac which appear to have no basis in the Hebrew. It will be convenient to refer to these as pluses and minuses in respect to MT. A number of these arise from the idiomatic differences between the two languages, and indicate no intention to modify the sense of the original but merely a desire to render it in the idiom of the translators' own language.

We may begin with some characteristic minuses in the Peshitta. One such is the absence of any rendering of לאמר before direct speech in Jon iii 7, Hg i 2, 13, ii 2, 11, 21, Sa ii 4, 8, iii 4, iv 4, 6 *bis*, 13, vi 8, 12 *bis*, vii 3², 5, 9 (though it is rendered in e.g. Sa vii 3¹°); in Am ii 12 it is omitted and the direct speech is changed to indirect speech. Another is the absence of any rendering of והיה in Hs i 5, Jl iv 18, Na iii 7, Sa vi 15, viii 13, xiii 2, 3, 4, xiv 6, 7²°, 8, 13. Infinitive absolutes in Jl i 7, Sa vi 15, xi 17 *bis* have no counterpart in the Syriac. Words repeated within a verse in Sa i 7, v 6, viii 10, 23, xi 7, xiii 3, Ml i 13, ii 2 are rendered only once in the Syriac, although the reverse of this is to be found in the repetition of ܠܚܕܗ in Jon i 3 and of ܡܠܝ ܚܣܕܐ in Sa xiii 6. These modifications are doubtless to be regarded as mere clarifications or simplifications in accordance with the idiom of Syriac.

A slightly less straightforward category is a group of passages where a single Syriac word seems to represent a pair of words in the Hebrew: Hs xi 8 ܐܚܒܟ (אתנך ... אשימך), Jon i 5 ܘܐܪܡܝ (וירדם ... וישכב), Na ii 8 ܬܢܚܬܐ (מנהגות ... מתפפת), Sa iv 6 ܐܡܪ (ויען ... ויאמר), Sa viii 9 ܒܝܬ ܡܩܕܫܐ ܕܐܠܗܐ (בית יהוה ... ההיכל) and Ml iii 10, ܐܘܨܪܐ (בית האוצר). A further probable example of this is to be found in Na ii 5, where if ܒܫܘܩܐ is the original reading (*cf supra*, pp 97f.) it may well be thought to represent בחוצות ... ברחבות in the Hebrew. Possible reasons for this phenomenon may be the relative paucity of Syriac vocabulary and a certain tendency to streamline and simplify sentence structure. An example of the reverse process must also however be noted: in Sa i 9 the Hebrew ויאמר is expanded to ܥܢܐ ... ܘܐܡܪ (*cf* iv 6).

Other categories appear as both pluses and minuses. Personal pronouns in the Hebrew are not represented in the Syriac at Hs viii 4, Mi vi 14, Na i 2, Sa vi 10, vii 6, ix 9 and Ml iii 12, and the same is true of demonstratives at Jon i 10, Mi v 4, Hb i 11 and Sa v 7. On the other hand the following pluses in the Syriac should be noted: ܗܘ ܗܘܐ at Jon i 12 (introduced because of a change in word order involving a *casus pendens*), ܗܘ *bis* at Jon i 10, ܐܝܬ²° at Hb i 12, ܠܗܘܢ at Hg ii 19, ܗܘܝ at Sa iii 8 and iv 12 (the latter perhaps in assimilation to v. 11), ܐܝܬ *bis* at Sa vii 13 and perhaps ܠܗ at Ml ii 13. Ethic datives appear in the Hebrew but not the Syriac at Hs viii 9, Mi v 1, Ml ii 3, iii 11 *bis*, while they appear in the Syriac but not the Hebrew at Jon i 5, iv 2, 5 (ܠܗ¹°) and Sa ix 5. We may note further here the addition in the Syriac of anticipatory objects at Jon iv 5 (ܠܗ³°), Hb i 14 and Sa xi 6, and the addition of *lamadh* with a suffix after a verb of saying at Jon iv 10, Hg ii 13, Sa i 10, iv 14, v 6, 8, vi 7, viii 23. Somewhat similar Syriac pluses are ܥܠܝ at Jon i 11, ܥܠܝ at Sa viii 1, ܠܐ¹° at Sa xi 12, ܠܗ at Sa xiv 14 and the suffix to ܘܪܘܚܝ at Hb ii 3.

There are also a number of pluses and minuses in respect to particles. Particles unrepresented in the Syriac include גם (Jl ii 3, 12, iv 4, Sa iii 7 *bis*, xiii 2, Ml i 10, ii 2; *cf* its replacement with the simple copula at Ml iii 15 *bis*), נא (Jon iv 3, Hg ii 2, Sa i 4, iii 8, Ml iii 10), אך (Hs xii 9, Zf iii 7), כי (Hs xiii 9, Hb iii 8, Sa vii 6²°), כן (Na i 12 *bis*, Sa xi 11), אשר (Sa viii 9, 20, 23), עתה (Hs viii 10, Am vi 7) and שם (Zf i 14). Less consistent are הִנֵּה (untranslated at Jl iv 1, Hb ii 4, Sa i 8, 11, ii 5, 7, iv 2, v 1, but ܗܐ is introduced at Jon i 11), עוד (untranslated at Am viii 14, Hb ii 3, Ml ii 13, but ܬܘܒ is introduced at Mi v 11, vii 8), and כל (untranslated at Hs xiii 2, Hb ii 8, Sa iv 2, Ml iii 10 but ܟܠ is introduced with or without a suffix at Jon ii 9, Mi vii 19, Hb ii 13, Sa v 4, viii 9).

A number of other minuses may reflect the judgement of the translators that not every word of the *Vorlage* needed to be expressly represented in the Syriac version, while yet others may be due simply to oversight. These categories also are difficult to distinguish, but many of the following minuses may be thought to fall into one or other of them:

Hs vii 10	בכל־זאת	
Hs viii 1	אל	
Hs ix 1	דגן	
Hs ix 10	בראשיתה	
Hs x 11	טוב	
Hs xi 8	עלי ... יחד	
Jl ii 6	קבצו	(also in Na ii 11)
Mi vii 2	לדמים	
Mi vii 17	ממך	
Na iii 17	אים	
Hb ii 9	כף	
Hb ii 19	וכסף	
Hg i 1	יום	
Hg i 9	צְבָאוֹת	
Sa vi 8	אתי	
Sa ix 1	משא	
Sa xiv 8	יהיה	
Sa xiv 13	יד¹°	
Ml i 14	נוכל	(*v. infra* p. 165)
Ml ii 2	וגם ארותיה	
Ml ii 15	עשה ... ומה	

Ml ii 16   כי שנא שלח

The absence of any rendering of סביב in Sa ii 9 may be due to the rendering of לה by ܒܓܘܗ under the influence of בתוכה, while the apparent omissions of חק in Mi vii 11 and אמצים in Sa vi 3 perhaps more probably reflect mechanical omissions in the *Vorlage*, and חרב at Sa xi 17 was perhaps damaged in the *Vorlage*.

Similarly a number of pluses in the Syriac may reflect adaptation to the natural idiom of the language, minor enhancement of the style, an attempt to clarify the sense (particularly the identification of Jonah as the speaker in Jon i 9, 12) or assimilation to the wording of similar passages. Most of the following may be thought to fall into one or other of these categories:

Jon ii 7	ܐܡܪܬ	(*cf* V)
Jon iv 1	ܠܗ	
Jon iv 6	ܘܩܡ	
Hg i 13	ܫܠܝܚܐ	(also in Ml ii 11)
Hg ii 3	ܫܒܝܼ	
Hg ii 19	ܐܡܪ ܠܟܘܢ	
Sa iii 4	ܡܠܐܟܐ	
Sa iv 3	ܐܠܗ	
Sa iv 5	ܬܘܒ ܐܡܪ	
Sa vii 5	ܢܒܝܐ	
Sa viii 4	ܘܗܘܐ ܐܡܪ	(*cf* LXX)
Sa xiii 9	ܕܐܠܗܐ ܗܘ	
Sa xiv 4	ܘܗܘܐ ܒܗ	
Sa xiv 6	ܐܠܐ	(*cf* V T)
Ml ii 3	ܕܐܝܪܐ	(*cf* T)
Ml ii 12	ܘܠܐ ܗܘܐ ܠܗ	
Ml ii 15	ܥܒܕ	
Ml ii 15	ܒ	
Ml ii 15	ܐܢܬ	
Ml iii 11	ܐܦ ܠܐ ܬܘܒ	

In the light of this it may now be reasonable to suggest that the four additional words in the middle of Sa iii 4 in the oldest Mss of the Peshiṭta (*cf supra*, pp 70, 128) are more likely to be an expansion *ad sensum* on the part of the Syriac translator(s) than a genuine rendering of a Hebrew *Vorlage* otherwise lost to the tradition, although the latter possibility must remain open.

In the light of the pluses which we have just considered it may seem not unreasonable to attribute the following more substantial pluses, which have no attestation in the tradition outside the Peshiṭta, to the translator(s) rather than to their Hebrew *Vorlage*:

Jl i 9	ܬ̈ܟܠܐ	
Sa iii 2	ܡܠܐܟܗ ܕ	
Sa viii 10	ܡܢ ܩܕܡ ܕܒܢܐ ܗܘ	
Ml iii 5	ܐܢܫܐ ܕܡܬܦܢܐ ܠܘܬܝ	(*v. infra* p. 165)

Before leaving the subject of the pluses and minuses it is convenient to list a few which are found also in one or more of the other ancient versions, but which are also more likely to be due to the translators than derived from a Hebrew *Vorlage* distinct from MT. Pluses in this category are:

Jl ii 27	ܠܒܪ ܡܢ	(LXX) (*v. infra* p. 163)
Hg ii 2	ܟܠܗ	(LXX)
Sa iii 3	ܕܡܪܝܐ	(LXX^{Mss})
Sa viii 17	ܣܠܬܢܐ	(LXX^{Mss})
Sa x 2	ܠܗܘܢ	(V)
Sa x 7	ܡܢ	(LXX^{Mss} V)
Sa xii 7	ܕܒܝܬ	(LXX^{Ms} T)
Sa xiii 2	ܕܓ̈ܠܐ	(LXX T) (*v. infra* p. 153)
Sa xiv 5	ܕܗܘܐ	(T)
Sa xiv 17	ܟܠܗܝܢ	(LXX)
Ml i 13	ܡܢ 2°	(V)
Ml iii 6	ܡܢ ܥܘܠܟܘܢ	(*cf* LXX)

Minuses in this category are:

Na ii 8	קול	(LXX V)
Hb i 13	ממנו	(LXX^{Mss})
Hg ii 6	מעט היא	(LXX)
Ml ii 11	בת	(LXX)

A few further minuses will be discussed in the next section.

Turning now to more specific matters of syntax we may note first a curious occasional tendency to invert the order of words forming a pair. Five clear examples of this are:

Hb i 6	ܡܪܝܪܐ ܘܡܪܗܒܐ
Zf iii 19	ܠܫܡܐ ܘܠܬܫܒܘܚܬܐ

Sa ii 6 ܐܘܪܟܗ̇ . . . ܦܬܝܗ̇
Sa xiv 21 ܕܒܝܗܘܕܐ ܘܒܐܘܪܫܠܡ (*cf supra*, p. 71)
Ml iii 5 ܘܕܝܬܡܐ ܘܕܐܪܡܠܬܐ

Another possible instance is in the last two words of Sa xiii 1, where ܪܘܣܣܐ may be thought to be a more likely rendering of נדה than of חטאת (*cf* also T for this inversion, which may possibly derive from a Hebrew *Vorlage*, *cf* the text cited by Odo as recorded by JANSMA).

Use of the construct state is avoided in e.g. three consecutive verses in Sa x 3–5, and a *casus pendens* is avoided at the beginning of Hs xii 8. A surprising literalism is the rendering ܒܝ rather than ܥܡܝ or ܠܘܬܝ in the phrase ܡܠܐܟܐ ܕܡܡܠܠ ܒܝ which occurs eleven times in Sa i 9–vi 4, particularly in view of the freedom practised elsewhere in the rendering of prepositions (e.g. ܡܢ for על in Sa iv 11 *bis* (*cf* iv 3), ܒ for ל in Sa v 4 and ܡܢ for ב in Ml ii 8). In addition to the omission of some infinitive absolutes already noted we may observe the replacement of an infinitive absolute by a finite verb, e.g. ܘܐܠܒܫܬܟ for והלבש in Sa iii 4 (*cf* V T). An example of the modification of direct into indirect speech in a passage where לאמר does not occur in the Hebrew may be found at the end of Hs x 8.

Modification of tense, number and person are by no means uncommon. A few illustrations will suffice. A Syriac imperfect is used to render a Hebrew perfect in Hs x 9 (ܢܩܦܘܢ), and conversely a Syriac perfect is used to render a Hebrew imperfect in Hs xii 2 (ܦܣܩܘ, *cf* LXX V T); in neither case is there any question of a *waw* consecutive in the Hebrew. Specially characteristic is the use of a Syriac participle to render a Hebrew perfect or imperfect: an example of each may be found in Hs vii 2 (ܐܡܪܝܢ . . . ܥܗܕ, *cf* T), while an example of the opposite change may be found in Hb ii 10 (ܘܐܚܛܝܬ, *cf* LXX V T). A Hebrew infinitive is often rendered by a finite verb in the Syriac, e.g. Am ii 7 (ܢܛܠܦܘܢ, *cf* LXX V), while Hs i 6 (ܠܡܪܚܡܘ, *cf* LXX V T) affords a rare instance of the opposite change. Two Hebrew infinitives are rendered by Syriac participles in Ml ii 13 (ܡܬܦܢܝܐ . . . ܡܩܒܠ). In Hs vi 9 a noun in the Hebrew is rendered by a verb in the Syriac (ܐܫܬܘܬܦܘ, *cf* LXX T); other examples of this are ܘܡܪܡܪ at Hs xii 15 (*cf* LXX) and ܐܘܬܪܢ at Ml iii 14.

Changes of number are found in both nouns and verbs, though the most frequent category is that of singular nouns in the Hebrew which may be regarded as collective or generic and are rendered in the plural in the Syriac, e.g. Hg ii 22 (ܡ̈ܪܟܒܬܐ, *cf* LXX T). A double example of the opposite change may be found in Hs ii 19 (ܫܡܗܐ ܕܒܥܠܐ, *cf* T for the first word). Examples of modification in the number of verbs may be seen in Am iv 2 (ܘܢܫܩܠܘܢܟܝܢ, *cf* LXX V T) and Sa vi 10 (ܕܐܬܐ, *cf* LXX). A particularly interesting double change from 2 *fem sg* to 2 *masc pl* may be found in Zf iii 7 (. . . ܬܕܚܠܘܢ ܬܩܒܠܘܢ, *cf* LXX T), where the *fem sg* of the Hebrew is a personification of Jerusalem.

Changes of person also are by no means uncommon. A 1 *sg* in the Hebrew appears as a 3 *masc sg* (Sa ii 15 ܘܒܥܐ, *cf* LXX), or a 3 *masc pl* (Mi vi 11 ܢܙܕܕܩܘܢ, *cf* LXX T) in the Syriac, a 2 *masc sg* as a 3 *masc sg* (Hs v 3 ܝܕܥ, *cf* LXX V T), a 3 *masc sg* as a 1 *sg* (Mi vi 8 ܚܘܝܬܟ, *cf* V), and a 3 *pl* as a 2 *masc pl* (Hs xii 12 ܕܒܚܬܘܢ).

There are a number of similar changes in both nominal and verbal suffixes. An example of a change from 2 *fem sg* to 3 *fem sg* in a nominal suffix may be found in Na iii 9 (ܒܥܘܕܪܢܗ̇, *cf* LXX), while a change from 2 *fem sg* to 2 *fem pl* in a verbal suffix may be found in Zf ii 5 (ܘܐܘܒܕܟܝܢ, *cf* LXX T). Not all such changes are necessarily deliberate; the improbable ܠܝ for לו in Hs i 6, peculiar to the Peshiṭta, is more probably to be explained as due to a damaged or indistinct Hebrew *Vorlage*. Not infrequently suffixes present in the Hebrew are unrepresented in the Syriac, e.g. כזביהם in Am ii 4 and באמונתו in Hb ii 4, while in other passages they are introduced in the Syriac where they have no counterpart in the Hebrew, e.g. ܫ̈ܘܪܝ in Hs xii 11 and ܘܐܥܒܕܝܘܗܝ in Na i 14.

In Ml i 11 the construction involving the passive participle מגש is modified by the recasting of the clause in a transitive sense, using the active participle ܡܩܪܒܝܢ (*cf* LXX T). Another passive avoided by recasting in the active is רטשה in Hs x 14 (*cf* LXX), while an example of the reverse modification may be found in the rendering of תבקע in Hb iii 9 (*cf* LXX 8ḤevXII gr).

One characteristic of the Peshiṭta translator(s), noted briefly by Sebök (p. 73, n. 3), is a tendency to avoid questions, particularly of a rhetorical nature. The negative interrogative particle הלוא is omitted at Ob 8, Mi i 5 *bis*, Hb ii 6, 13, Sa i 6, iii 2, vii 7, though the clause may still sometimes be interpreted as a question. It is replaced by the positive particle ܗܐ at Jl i 16, Am ix 7, Mi ii 7, iii 11, Hb ii 7, by ܗܟܢܐ ܗܘ at Am v 20 and by ܡܛܠ ܕ at Hb i 12. On the other hand the negative is preserved, and presumably in an interrogative sense, at Ob 5 2°, Jon iv 2, Mi iii 1, Hg ii 3, Sa iv 5, 13, vii 6, while הלוא is rendered by ܕܠܡܐ ܠܐ at Am vi 13, Ml i 2, ii 10. Curiously however ܕܠܡܐ ܠܐ is also used to render the straightforward negative particle אֵין at Ml i 8 *bis* and the particle לֹא at Ml ii 15 (which is also interpreted as a question in V and T). Positive questions introduced by the particle הֲ are rendered by negative statements at Mi vi 7, Hg ii 19, Ml i 9, 13. The negative question עַל־מִי לֹא at Na iii 19 is rendered by the positive ܠܐ ܥܠ ܡܢ. A disjunctive question is avoided at Hb iii 8, being replaced by a straightforward positive statement. Once again we note a prevailing tendency to modify a particular syntactical pattern, with a few exceptions to the rule and one or two instances where the pattern usually modified is actually introduced in a context where it is not present in the Hebrew.

Finally we return to modifications in word order. A number of changes may be attributed to the desire to improve the flow of the sentence. A good example of this is the coupling together of ܟܣܦܐ ܘܕܗܒܐ in Hs ii 10, making it clear that the following clauses refer to both the precious metals. Similarly the coupling together of ܠܟܘܫ ܘܡܨܪܝܢ before the predicate ܚܝܠܬܐ in Na iii 9 results in a neater syntax than the Hebrew. The deceptively simple transfer of the copula from וְהוּא to ܘܗܘܐ in Hs viii 6, resulting in a considerable syntactical modification, may also have been intended to effect a simplification and clarification of the sense. It is less easy to discern a motive for the interchange of יוֹצֵר הָרִים and בֹּרֵא רוּחַ in Am iv 13. The rearrangement of the first three words of Na i 3 is probably to be regarded as an adjustment to the idiom of Syriac, *cf* the similar rendering of the same idiom at Jl ii 13 and Jon iv 2. The insertion of ܕܗܘܐ before ܢܕܝܕܐ in Na iii 17 serves to bring out the sense of the copula before נוֹדֵד in the Hebrew (*cf* T).

While many of the examples reviewed in this section are relatively minor modifications, their cumulative significance is a clear demonstration that the Peshiṭta is in no sense a slavish translation of the Hebrew *Vorlage*. The translators exercised considerable freedom in modifying the syntax and sometimes the actual wording of the text in their attempt to provide an idiomatic Syriac translation. This means that retroversion into the putative Hebrew *Vorlage* underlying the Peshiṭta must always be carried out with considerable caution, and that it can probably approximate certainty only in respect to specific details. The other interesting feature to emerge is that while there is often a prevailing tendency to make a particular modification, there is often also the occasional instance of its opposite! The translators could on occasion be literal to a fault, and were by no means consistent in their translation methods. This may suggest that more than one translator was at work.

2. Lexical equivalents

In this section we shall take a few preliminary soundings in the vocabulary used by the Peshiṭta translators. Any thorough investigation of this subject will be possible only when the critical EDITION is complete and a Syriac concordance to the whole of the Old Testament Peshiṭta is available. The Dodekapropheton however affords sufficient material to enable us to formulate some preliminary answers to certain questions which immediately arise. How consistent were the translators in rendering the same Hebrew word by the same Syriac equivalent? How extensive and how accurate was their knowledge of biblical Hebrew? How often did they confuse or mistake homonymous roots in the Hebrew? What did they do when confronted by Hebrew words of whose meaning they were ignorant or uncertain? To what extent can we look to them to provide accurate information about the meaning of Hebrew words of which we ourselves are ignorant or uncertain?

The extent of lexical overlap between Syriac and biblical Hebrew is not as great as might be expected. BARR (pp. 162f., 305–7) concludes from an analysis of Syriac verbs beginning with *beth* that only about 40% have closely corresponding cognates in Hebrew, while a slightly higher proportion have no cognate at all in Hebrew. The alleged paucity of Syriac vocabulary is also relative: there are lexical areas in which Syriac is quite rich. These factors obviously have a bearing on the question of consistency both in the rendering of a particular Hebrew word and in the use of a particular Syriac word.

First we must note a few passages where the Peshiṭta uses two different words to render the same Hebrew word or at least words which are cognate in the Hebrew. In Na ii 1 the force of the cognate accusative in the Hebrew חגי ... חגיך is lost in the Syriac ... ܚܓܐ ܚܓܝܟܝ, *cf* Sa xiv 16–19. The reason for this is presumably simply that the translators felt that ܚܓܐ was the idiomatic verb to use in this context. In Hb i 10 משחק is rendered ܡܒܙܚ, while the cognate ישחק is rendered ܐܓܚܟ; in the only other occurence of this root in the Dodekapropheton (Sa viii 5) the sense is different, and the Peshiṭta uses a third and appropriate word (ܡܫܬܥܝܢ) to render it. In Na iii 15 the repetition התכבד ... התכבדי is surely deliberate, but the Peshiṭta uses different verbs (ܘܡܣܟܝ̈ܢ ..., ܚܒܨܘ) in company with LXX^{Mss} V T. In Sa i 13 the Peshiṭta uses two words (ܡܠܟ ... ܦܬܓܡ̈ܐ) to render the repeated דברים. The word אמלל occurs five times in the Dodekapropheton. In Hs iv 3 it is rendered ܬܠܐ. In Jl i 10, 12 it is rendered by ܐܬܒ ... ܐܬܒ. In Na i 4 it occurs twice, being rendered the first time by ܐܠܐ and the second time by ܢܪܒ. In this case three different words are used to render the five occurrences of the same Hebrew word in the Dodekapropheton. It is clear that the Peshiṭta translators were not always embarrassed by a paucity of lexical resources.

There are on the other hand a number of instances where this is the most likely explanation for the repeated use of a single Syriac word to render two different Hebrew words. In Hs ii 11 בעתו and במועדו are used synonymously, and it is hardly surprising that the Peshiṭta renders both by ܒܙܒܢܗ (cf V). In the same and the following verse ܦܐܪ̈ܘܗܝ is used twice to render ערותה ... נבלתה (cf T). In Jon ii 6–7 ܐܬܚܕ is used twice; the first is not really apposite, but may have been suggested by the homographic סוף ('end') in place of סוף ('rushes'). In Mi v 9 ܐܘܒܕ is used twice, to render והכרתי ... והאבדתי, again with synonymous meaning. It is not surprising that the cognate ܐܘܒܕ is used to render the other two occurrences of the Hiph'il of אבד (Ob 8, Zf ii 5) and the one occurrence of its Pi'el (Zf ii 13). The word is however also used uniformly to render the seventeen other occurrences of the Hiph'il of כרת in the Dodekapropheton. This seems to be a clear instance where Syriac has only the one verb available to render the two Hebrew verbs meaning 'destroy'. This can hardly be the explanation however for the double use of the verb ܛܘܣ in Hb i 8 to render ופשו and יעפו. In the four other instances of עוף (Hs ix 11, Na iii 16, Sa v 1, 2) it is rendered by ܦܪܚ, while פוש is rendered elsewhere by ܪܒܐ (Na iii 18) and ܪܗܛ (Ml iii 20). In the light of this it can hardly be claimed that the translators were constrained by the paucity of lexical resources to use ܛܘܣ twice in Hb i 8.

In Jl i 4 four different words for 'locust' occur. Of these גזם is consistently rendered by ܙܚܠܐ (also in Jl ii 25, Am iv 9) and חסיל by ܙܚܠܐ (Jl ii 25). ארבה is rendered ܩܡܨܐ ܓܘܒܐ (also in Jl ii 25), and simply by ܩܡܨܐ in Na iii 15, 17. ילק is rendered ܩܡܨܐ ܘܣܠܐ on the first occurrence in Jl i 4, but simply ܣܠܐ in Jl i 4$^{2°}$, ii 25, Na iii 15 *bis*, 16. The variants in 7a1 at Jl i 4 and 6h9 at Na iii 15 are most unlikely to be original. This indicates an almost consistent pattern of lexical equivalents, but this may be due partly to the fact that apart from the one word in Am iv 9 these words for 'locust' are concentrated in two contexts (Jl i 4, ii 25 and Na iii 15-17). It is in any case clear that Syriac has the lexical resources to match the four different Hebrew terms in Jl i 4, though it does have to use ܩܡܨܐ again to render a fifth term גבי in Am vii 1 and Na iii 17.

The case is not the same with the four different Hebrew words for 'lion' which occur in various passages in the Dodekapropheton. As might be expected ארי (twice) and אריה (ten times) are rendered consistently by the cognate ܐܪܝܐ. This word is also used to render שחל in both its occurrences (Hs v 14, xiii 7). כפיר occurs six times: three times it is rendered by ܓܘܪܝܐ ܕܐܪܝܐ (Hs v 14, Mi v 7, Na ii 12), once by ܓܘܪܝܐ alone (Na ii 14), and twice by ܐܪܝܐ alone (Am iii 4, Sa xi 3). לביא occurs three times and the *fem pl* לבאות once (Na ii 13), where it is rendered ܐܢܫܘܗܝ̈ ('his mates'). In Na ii 12 the Peshitta translators read לביא as the Qal (rather than the Hiph'il, *cf* LXX V) infinitive of בוא and rendered it accordingly ܠܡܐܬܐ. Of the other two occurrences of לביא one (Hs xiii 8) is rendered by ܐܪܝܐ and the other (Jl i 6) by ܓܘܪܝܐ ܕܐܪܝܐ. It is clear that the Syriac translators had only the single word ܐܪܝܐ at their disposal to render the four Hebrew words for 'lion', but they made use of ܓܘܪܝܐ ('whelp'), often in combination with ܐܪܝܐ, for some of their renderings of כפיר and לביא.

In Na i 6 ܚܡܬܐ is used twice, to render חרון and חמתו, and ܪܘܓܙܐ is used twice, to render זעמו and אפו. It is of interest to trace the Syriac equivalents used for each of these four Hebrew words for 'anger' in the Dodekapropheton. חרון, occurring four times in addition to Na i 6, is uniformly rendered by ܚܡܬܐ. Two of the six occurrences of the cognate verb חרה (Hs viii 5, Sa x 3) are rendered by the verb ܚܡܬ. Only two however of the other five occurrences of חמה (Mi v 14, Sa viii 2) are rendered by ܚܡܬܐ; in two of the others (Na i 2, Hb ii 15) ܪܘܓܙܐ is used, and in the remaining one (Hs vii 5) ܠܒܫܢܝ. There are three further occurrences of זעם; in Zf iii 8 ܪܘܓܙܐ is again used, but in Hs viii 16 the rendering is ܡܫܚܠܦܬܐ and in Hb iii 12 it is ܚܡܬܐ. אף is the commonest of the four nouns. Discounting Am iv 10 where it is used to denote literal 'nostrils' and the three occurrences of the phrase ארך אפים (Jl ii 13, Jon iv 2, Na i 3) where ܢܓܝܪܐ is used, there are fourteen occurrences in addition to Na i 6. In one (Mi vii 18) it is rendered by ܐܠܬܐ, and in the remaining thirteen by ܪܘܓܙܐ. Two conclusions emerge from these data. One is that the Syriac translators confined themselves practically to the two nouns

ܚܡܬܐ and ܪܘܓܙܐ, though Mi vii 18 shows that ܐܟܬܐ was also available to them. The other is that while ܚܡܬܐ is consistently used to render חרון and never used to render אף , both Syriac words are used to render חמה and זעם. It is a curious fact that it is חרון and not the cognate חמה which is consistently rendered by ܚܡܬܐ.

The verb פקד occurs eighteen times in the Dodekapropheton, and is rendered by the cognate ܦܩܕ in fifteen of these. ܬܒܥ is used twice (Hs i 4, xii 3) and ܣܥܪ once (Hs iv 14). The cognate noun פקדה occurs twice; in Hs ix 7 it is rendered by ܬܒܥܬܐ, but in Mi vii 4 by ܦܘܪܥܢܟ, which Sebök (*cf* p. 100 *supra*) suggests may be an inner-Syriac corruption of ܦܘܪܢܣܟ, since a positive sense of פקד is unlikely in this context. At least it is pertinent to note that the semantic range of Syriac ܦܩܕ does not include the positive sense of gracious visitation which is sometimes found in the Hebrew פקד, and ܦܪܩ is used to render פקד in this sense in Psalm cvi 4.

Further evidence of inconsistency on the part of the translators may be found in their renderings of דחק, רחק and נדח. דחק occurs in the Dodekapropheton only at Jl ii 8, where it is rendered by the cognate ܕܚܩ. רחק occurs eight times, and in six of them it is rendered by the cognate ܪܚܩ (Jl iv 6, 8, Mi iv 3, Hb i 8, Sa vi 15, x 9). Unaccountably it is rendered in Mi vii 11 by ܕܬܬܥܠܡ, while in Jl ii 20 it is rendered by ܕܚܩ, which is also used in the same verse for נדח, which in turn is rendered apparently by different roots at each of its two other occurrences in the Dodekapropheton, *viz* by ܒܕܪ in Mi iv 6 and by ܪܚܩ in Zf iii 19. It will however be necessary to return to this last point in the next section.

Finally we may note what can only be regarded as loose equivalents. The substitution of ܒܢܝ for בית before the proper name 'Israel' in Am vi 1 is an instance of this, and it is of interest that the same substitution occurs in some Mss in Am v 25 and ix 9. Another example may be found in the use of ܐܪܥܐ rather than the more usual ܚܩܠܐ or ܕܒܪܐ to render שדה in Ml iii 11, despite the fact that ܐܪܥܐ has already been used in this verse to render אדמה. The only other instance of the rendering of שדה by ܐܪܥܐ in the Dodekapropheton is at Hs xii 13, where the reference is to the plain of Aram and 'land' may be regarded as a reasonable equivalent, though the Targum uses חקלא in both these passages, and the Peshiṭta itself uses ܚܩܠܐ for the 'land' (שדה) of Edom in Genesis xxxii 4.

These last examples confirm the impression that the Peshiṭta translators made little effort to be consistent in rendering particular words, that they were sometimes content with an approximate equivalent even when a more precise one was available, and that the restricted range of vocabulary sometimes employed was not always due to the paucity of the lexical resources of the Syriac language.

We must now turn to the special problems posed by homonymous or very similar Hebrew roots, to which SEBÖK paid particular attention; many of the examples listed below were noted already by him. The nature of the problems which arise is well illustrated by the rendering in the several versions of חלה in Mi i 12, which, if the text is correct, is probably to be derived from חול ('writhe' in the sense 'wait anxiously'). It is derived however by the Peshitta translators, in company with Aquila and the Vulgate, from חלה ('be weak'), by Theodotion, Symmachus and the Targum from יחל ('wait'), and by the LXX from חלל ('begin'). A similar confusion occurs in Hs xi 6 where וחלה is probably again to be derived from חול, this time in the sense 'whirl' (*cf* A? T), but is derived by the Peshitta translators once more, this time in company with LXX, from חלה ('be weak'), but by Symmachus from חלל ('wound') and by the Vulgate from חלל ('begin').

In the following seven instances the Peshitta translators have probably chosen the incorrect one of two possible homonymous roots or of disparate meanings of the same root, generally in company with one or more of the other versions:

Hs vii 6	ישׁן 'be old' rather than 'sleep'	(T)
Hs x 5	גור 'sojourn' rather than 'be afraid'	(LXX)
Hs x 11	שׁדד 'despoil' (שׂ) rather than 'harrow' (שׁ)	
Jl ii 17	משׁל 'rule' rather than 'taunt'	(LXX V T)
Am v 11	ברר 'select' rather than 'grain'	(LXX V)
Hb iii 9	עור 'awake' rather than 'be naked'	(LXX[Barb] V)
Zf iii 1	גאל 'redeem' rather than 'defile'	(LXX V T)

The fact that the meaning chosen by the translators is generally the more common no doubt largely accounts for such misinterpretations.

In the following ten instances the Peshitta translators seem to have confused two similar Hebrew roots:

| Hs x 12 | ניר 'freshly till'—נור 'give light' | (LXX) |
| *Hs xiii 15 | בושׁ 'be ashamed'—יבשׁ 'be dried up' | (LXX V T) |

* The Qumran fragment 4QXII(?) attests a Hebrew text without a vowel between *beth* and *shin*, although only the three letters יבשׁ survive. This may represent a reading identical with

Hs xiv 1	מרה 'be rebellious'—מרר 'be bitter'	(V)
Am iii 10	נכח 'be straight'—יכח 'reprove'	
*Am iv 6	נקה 'be clean'—קהה 'be blunt'	(LXX A V T)
Am v 24	גלל 'roll'—גלה 'reveal'	(V T)
Mi vi 9	יעד 'appoint'—עוד 'bear witness'	
Hb i 16	ברא 'be fat'—ברר 'select'	(LXX V)
Sa iv 7	שוא 'make a noise'—שוה 'be like'	(LXX A V)
Sa xiii 5	קנה 'acquire'—קנא 'be zealous'	(T)

These nineteen instances may be held to indicate limitations in the translators' knowledge of biblical Hebrew, and we now turn to further evidence of such limitations.

The Hebrew קיץ can mean simply 'summer' or more specifically 'summer fruit'; the cognate Syriac ܩܝܛܐ has only the first of these two meanings. The use of ܩܝܛܐ therefore to render קיץ in Am iii 15 and Sa xiv 8, where it means 'summer', presents no problems. This is not the case however in Am viii 1, 2 and Mi vii 1, where קיץ means 'summer fruit'. In the latter passage the use of ܩܝܛܐ thus amounts to a mistranslation, while in the former passage the word ܩܨܐ is used, although the same word is also and more naturally used to render the Hebrew קץ, the word-play between the two Hebrew words thus being lost in the Syriac. In the same passage the word כלוב ('basket'), though recognized by LXX A Th S(?) and T, is rendered in the Peshiṭta by ܐܬܐ ('sign, portent'), suggesting that the translators missed the literal sense of the phrase altogether.

In Mi ii 1 the translators do not seem to have understood the idiomatic כי יש־לאל ידם, rendering ܡܥܠܝܢ ܐܝܕܝܗܘܢ ܠܘܬ ܐܠܗܐ in an attempt to make sense of the individual words which must be deemed less successful than the similar attempts of LXX and V, since it results in a clause strikingly at variance with its context. A similar failure to recognize the idiomatic meaning of לפי in Hs x 12 and כפי in Sa ii 4 presumably accounts for the literal renderings ܦܘܡܗ (ܐܝܟ), although the similar כפי אשר in Ml ii 9 is correctly rendered ܐܝܟ ܕ. The translators seem on occasion to have assumed that the Hebrew preposition ל can denote the direct object as *lamadh* commonly does in

---

MT but written defectively, or alternatively a reading וְיִיבַשׁ (imperfect Qal of יבשׁ), which would make a good parallel to וְיחרב, and might be regarded as the common *Vorlage* of the Peshiṭta and, if vocalized as a Hiph'il, of LXX V and T. The uncertainty of the vocalization of the Qumran fragment precluded the consideration of this reading in the previous chapter.

* This is probably due to the influence of Jeremiah xxxi 29f. and Ezekiel xviii 2.

Syriac, and this has sometimes led to a recasting of the syntax, as in Hs i 6 (להם), v 2 (לכלם) and probably x 12 (לצדקה). The two instances in Hs xi 1 (לבני) and xi 2 (להם) may be explained in the light of the greater readiness in Syriac to construe the verb ܩܪܐ with a direct object.

There is no doubt that on a number of occasions the Peshiṭta translators found their Hebrew *Vorlage* very difficult to understand. In Ob 20 for example they rendered the obscure החל by ܡܪܕܘܬܐ, presumably in the light of the Hiph'il verb החל ('begin') (*cf* LXX), while the other versions seem to have vocalized the Hebrew word as הַחַיִל. In Mi v 5 they rendered בפתחיה by ܒܙܝܢܗܘܢ, a rendering which finds no support in any of the other versions and which SEBÖK finds inexplicable. Unless it be regarded as an inner-Syriac corruption of ܒܙܝܕܘܬܐ (which would indicate agreement with the Hebrew *Vorlage* presupposed by 8HevXII gr noted on p. 117 *supra*), although it is not easy to see how such a corruption might have occurred, this is presumably to be explained as a sheer guess to fill the place of a word which the translators found unintelligible.

Other methods adopted to deal with words which the translators found unintelligible may include the occasional choice of a similar sounding word in Hebrew or even in Syriac, despite the fact that the meaning was quite different. For instance in Na ii 4 מתלעים ('clad in scarlet') is rendered by ܡܫܬܥܝܢ, which might well have been used to render מתעללים ('playing') (*cf* LXX), and in Na iii 19 כהה ('alleviation'?) is rendered ܕܟܐܒ ܠܗ ('who grieves') as if it were connected with the root כאב (so T). This phenomenon is not confined to words which the translators might have been expected to find unintelligible. This can hardly be the explanation of the rendering of אדניהם in Zf i 9 by ܚܕܝܘܗܘܢ, which is peculiar to the Peshiṭta, and might have been suggested by assonance between the Hebrew and Syriac words, though it has the happy effect of removing the difficulty in the Hebrew that the thieves fill their masters' houses rather than their own storerooms with stolen goods! The use of ܫܩܠ to render נסע in Sa x 2 might appear *prima facie* to be the result of a similar confusion with נשא, but it is in fact a judicious substitution of a Syriac idiom (literally to 'pack up') for a Hebrew idiom (literally to 'pull up' the tent-pegs).

Further evidence of the limitations of the Peshiṭta translators' knowledge of biblical Hebrew will be provided in the next chapter under the category of passages where they turned to the LXX for help in interpreting their Hebrew *Vorlage*. One further method of dealing with unintelligible words and phrases in the *Vorlage* may however be included here. This was the simple expedient of omission. In contrast with the minuses considered in the previous section the following, most of which are peculiar to the Peshitta, are probably to be accounted for in this way:

Hs iv 18	סר סבאם	
Am iii 12	ערש	
Mi ii 4	ימיש לי	
Mi vii 4	ישר ממסוכה	
Hb i 12	צור	
Hb ii 5	ואף כי היין	
Hb iii 16	יגודנו	
Zf iii 10	עתרי בת־פוצי	(cf LXX*)
Hg i 2	עת¹°	(LXX V T)
Hg ii 16	לחשׂף .. פורה	
Hg ii 19	עד	
Ml i 12	ניבו	(T)

It has become clear that the Peshitta translators' knowledge of biblical Hebrew was subject to certain limitations in the area of idiom as well as in that of the semantic range of particular lexical equivalents. Sometimes they were hampered by comparative paucity of lexical resources in Syriac, but at other times they failed to make full use of the resources that were available. They were by no means always consistent in employing a particular lexical equivalent for a particular Hebrew word or root. On a number of occasions they confused homonymous or similar roots. Occasionally they seem to have despaired of interpreting a particular Hebrew word or phrase and simply omitted it from their translation. All of this has the effect of reducing the confidence with which we can reconstruct the Hebrew *Vorlage* of the Peshitta. Inevitably however we have been concerned largely with the evidence for inconsistency, inaccuracy, confusion and ignorance. It remains true that the greater part of the Peshitta of the Dodekapropheton is a faithful though far from pedantic version of a Hebrew *Vorlage* closely similar to MT, and the degree of ignorance or inaccuracy on the part of the translators should not be exaggerated. They certainly had to work from an unvocalized Hebrew text, and it is probable that sometimes at least they had to work independently of any tradition of vocalization. It is hardly surprising that they were sometimes mistaken in identifying the root of an unusual Hebrew word!

Despite these limitations the Peshitta translators' knowledge of biblical Hebrew was on occasion superior to our own, and to that extent the expectations raised by Goshen-Gottstein in the passage quoted at the beginning of the Introduction to this monograph are likely to be realized. Further progress in this area will be facilitated by the completion of the critical edition of the whole of the Old Testament in Syriac and the provision of a concordance to the complete text. Already however we may note that it is fortunately the case that the Peshita translators did on occasion identify correctly quite rare roots, e.g. the ἅπαξ λεγόμενον נהג ('moan') in Na ii 8 (cf V T) in distinction from the common נהג ('drive, conduct') with which it is confused in LXX and a doublet in T. Another ἅπαξ λεγόμενον is כפיס in Hb ii 11, whose rendering in the Peshitta by ܣܟܬܐ ('peg, nail') is noted though rejected by Theodore of Mopsuestia in his commentary on the Dodekapropheton; this rendering is however probably closer to the meaning of the Hebrew than the interpretation of LXX defended by Theodore (cf RUDOLPH).

An interesting further dimension is suggested by LANE, who points out that where there are significant variants within the Peshitta tradition they may reflect "different and equally valid" attempts to produce a Syriac version of a single Hebrew *Vorlage*. One of his illustrations is of particular interest. At Hs xi 8 the אמגנך of MT is rendered ܐܥܕܪܟ ('will I help you?') in the standard text of the Peshitta and ܐܝܩܪܟ ('will I give you honour?') in 9a1 *fam* (9a1 *vid*). Lane points out that these are two possible interpretations of the Hebrew, and it is interesting that others are chosen by the other versions: 'shield, protect or surround' by LXX A Th V, 'destroy' by T and 'give up' by S!

While therefore considerable uncertainty must attend any attempt to reconstruct a Hebrew *Vorlage* of the Peshitta distinct from MT, we can look hopefully to the Peshitta tradition for some lexical insights which will enrich our own knowledge of biblical Hebrew.

3. Exegetical and theological modifications

It is not always possible to distinguish clearly between merely stylistic and exegetical modifications on the part of the Peshitta translators, but in this section we are concerned primarily with those which have definite significance for the interpretation of the text.

The insertion of ܐܡܪܘܢ in Hs vi 1 (LXX T) serves to identify the speakers in vi 1–3 as the subject of the three plural verbs in v 15. The insertion of ܘܐܡܪ in Hs xiv 9 (T) is even more significant, making it clear that Ephraim and not Yahweh is now the speaker. These insertions must however be set alongside the similar insertions of ܘܐܡܪܘ in Hs viii 2 (LXX^Mss T), Hs xiv 4 and Jl i 14, of which the last two are peculiar to the Peshiṭta, and none of which is necessary since the identity of the speakers is clear in each case. These insertions seem therefore to be of an essentially stylistic nature, but nevertheless serve an exegetical purpose in Hs vi 1 and xiv 9.

The similar insertion of ܘܐܡܪ at the end of Zf ii 15, peculiar to the Peshiṭta, leads to the mistaken exegesis of Zf iii 1 ff as the taunt against Nineveh mentioned in ii 15 instead of a Woe oracle addressed to Jerusalem. This also accounts for the rendering of the last two words of iii 1 as ܕܚܛܝܬܗ ܕܝܘܢܢ, where the translator has mistaken היונה for an allusion to the prophet Jonah, failing to observe that were this the meaning of the Hebrew the preceding noun would have to be in the construct state and therefore without the article. This exegesis is also mentioned and rejected by Theodore of Mopsuestia in his commentary on the Dodekapropheton.

Another passage mentioned by Theodore is Zf i 5, though his evidence for the respective readings of the LXX and the Peshiṭta (if this is indeed the Syriac version to which he refers, as seems to be the case in Hb ii 11 and Zf iii 1) is not clear, cf WEITZMAN, p. 277, n. 2. In fact the Peshiṭta recognizes in מלכם in Zf i 5 an allusion to the deity Milcom in company with LXX^L V and implicitly also T; the same identification is made by the Peshiṭta in Am i 15 in company with LXX^L and V (cf p. 124 supra).

The insertion of ܡܛܠ ܕ before the last two words in Na ii 1, peculiar to the Peshiṭta, serves to improve the sequence of the passage by making it clear that the two final statements of the sentence are causally related. Perhaps this should be regarded simply as an attempt to avoid the abruptness of the Hebrew parataxis, but it may be more than a purely stylistic embellishment.

The substitution of the first singular personal pronoun for the divine name in Na ii 3 is also peculiar to the Peshiṭta and has the effect of making the verse, and presumably also the preceding one and a half verses, into a Yahweh-speech. Another interesting change of person occurs at Hb i 3, where the 2 masc sg תביט is rendered by the 1 sg ܘܚܙܐ

EXEGETICAL AND THEOLOGICAL MODIFICATIONS

אנא. This is presumably an attempt at consistency, making the subject of the verb תביט the same as the object of the preceding Hiph'il תראני. The other versions obviate the difficulty in different ways, LXX and V by using an infinitive to render תביט and T by using the 1 *sg* for both verbs. The effect of both these modifications of person in the Peshiṭta is to secure a greater smoothness and consistency.

In Mi iv 6f. and Zf iii 19 הצלעה is used metaphorically of the personified Judah in a state of exile. In Mi iv 6 and Zf iii 19 it is used in parallel with הנדחה, and in Mi iv 7 in parallel with הנהלאה. If for the moment we may ignore the possibility of inversion the equivalents in the Peshiṭta are as follows:

Mi iv 6	הצלעה] ܬܘܚܡܐ
	הנדחה] ܒܕܕܪܐ
Mi iv 7	הצלעה] ܒܕܕܪܐ
	הנהלאה] ܬܘܚܡܐ
Zf iii 19	הצלעה] ܒܚܒܬܐ
	הנדחה] ܬܘܚܡܬܐ

Our present concern is to note that in each of these pairs of terms the metaphorical הצלעה is "decoded" and replaced with a word expressing the literal condition of the population described in a way similar to that of the other term in the pair. As the text stands it appears that הצלעה is rendered by a different term on each of the three occasions, while the two instances of הנדחה are also rendered by different terms as already noted (p. 142 *supra*). In the light however of the occasional tendency to invert the order of pairs of words (*cf* pp 135f. *supra*) one might speculate in particular whether there has been such an inversion in Mi iv 6. If so, then it would appear that originally both instances of הנדחה had been rendered by the root ܢܘܚ, which would also naturally have been chosen to render הנהלאה in Mi iv 7, while הצלעה would at least have been rendered consistently by ܒܕܕܪܐ in the two consecutive verses in Micah. The use of ܚܒܬܐ to render הצלעה in Zf iii 19 would still be inconsistent with this, but the translators might have felt that ܚܒܒ was a more suitable root to use for the interpretation of the metaphor in this passage in the light of the preceding reference to מעניך. The translators' practice is hardly consistent enough to render the hypothesis of an inversion in Mi iv 6 probable, but the possibility of such an inversion is at least worth considering. An alternative possibility is simply that the translators adopted a chiastic pattern in Mi iv 6f. for stylistic reasons, regarding the three terms used in the Hebrew as virtually synonymous descriptions of the exiled and dispersed Judaeans.

Assimilation to other passages may be a further factor on occasion. The addition of ܘܒܒܪܕܐ in Am iv 9, peculiar to the Peshiṭta, is best explained as an assimilation to Hg ii 17, a passage in all probability consciously echoing Am iv 9. The rendering of הצרים נתצו in Na i 6 by ܛܘܪܐ ܐܬܦܪܩܘ seems inexplicable until it is recalled that the similar ܘܢܬܦܪܩܘܢ ܛܘܪܐ has already occurred in Mi i 4 where it correctly renders ונמסו ההרים. The other versions found no difficulty in rendering the two words in Na i 6, and unless we are to infer that the Peshiṭta translators' *Vorlage* was very obscure assimilation to Mi i 4 seems the most probable explanation of this rendering.

A particularly interesting example of assimilation to another passage is to be found at Jon iv 8, where in place of the last three words of the Hebrew, which are rendered accurately though not literally ܦܩܘܕ ܠܝ ܠܡܡܬ ܛܒ ܡܢ ܕܐܚܐ where they occur earlier in the chapter at the end of v. 3, the Peshiṭta reads ܡܛܐ ܒܐ̈ܢܝܢ ܡܪܝܐ ܠܡܣܒ ܢܦܫܝ ܡܢܝ. ܡܛܠ ܕܠܐ ܗܘܝܬ ܛܒ ܡܢ ܐܒܗ̈ܝ. This is clearly the result of assmilation to 1 Kings xix 4, which after the words וישאל את־נפשו למות ויאמר which the two passages have in common continues רב עתה יהוה קח נפשי כי־לא־טוב אנכי מאבתי. The Peshiṭta renders this fairly literally ܣܦܩ ܠܝ. ܗܫܐ ܡܪܝܐ ܣܒ ܢܦܫܝ ܡܢܝ. ܡܛܠ ܕܠܐ ܗܘܝܬ ܛܒ ܐܢܐ ܡܢ ܐܒܗ̈ܝ, the additions ܠܝ, ܡܢܝ and ܗܘܝܬ being stylistic. The last nine words of 1 Kings xix 4 and Jonah iv 8 are identical in the Peshiṭta, while in place of ܣܦܩ ܠܝ. ܗܫܐ ܡܪܝܐ ܣܒ in 1 Kings xix 4, Jonah iv 8 reads ܡܛܐ ܒܐ̈ܢܝܢ ܡܪܝܐ ܠܡܣܒ. The only parallel to this assimilation in the tradition is the addition in the LXX Ms 239 *μὴ κρείττων ἐγώ εἰμι ὑπὲρ τοὺς πατέρας μου*, which apart from the negative is identical with the end of 1 Kings xix 4 LXX. The parallel with the Peshiṭta is only partial, and attested only in this single Catena Ms of the LXX, dated 1046. It is most probable that a similar assimilation has taken place independently, and in the case of the Peshiṭta it is probably based on recollection rather than on a written text of Kings.

We shall return later in this section to the question of possible assimilations to passages in the New Testament. In the meantime we note that assimilation of a much less specific kind may also perhaps account for some other renderings. The choice of the root ܗܦܟ for instance to render והכה in Sa x 11 may perhaps reflect the overtones

EXEGETICAL AND THEOLOGICAL MODIFICATIONS   151

of the Exodus in this passage. Comparison may be made with Psalm lxvi 6 where this root is used in both MT and the Peshitta in a similar context.

The same root ܗܦܟ is used in a very different sense in Mi iii 4 to render the Hebrew יסתר. This is an interesting passage, for the use of ܗܦܟ has been thought to suggest a *Vorlage* יסר, rather than יסתר, and the LXX might be thought to afford additional evidence for such a *Vorlage*, or alternatively to have influenced the Peshitta translators here (*cf* p. 127 *supra*). In the light of BALENTINE's recent study (chapter IV), however, it appears more probable that we have here an instance of a tendency in the late biblical and post-biblical period to substitute סור for סתר; it is in any case clear that ܗܦܟ is the normal rendering of הסתיר (פנים) in the Peshitta, ܟܣܝ also being used on occasion. One possible but by no means certain explanation of this interesting phenomenon is that of deliberate theological modification; this particular modification is however unlikely to have originated with LXX or the Peshitta, dependence on a Jewish tradition of interpretation seeming the most probable of the possible explanations considered by Balentine.

The modification of anthropomorphic and anthropopathic language in relation to God has often been detected in the versions, particularly in the Targums. It is however never consistently carried out in a version, and it is now widely questioned whether this is always the most natural explanation of linguistic phenomena of this kind. The avoidance of terms denoting the parts of the body in relation to God may seem a natural instance of this kind of reverential modification, yet the rendering of מידכם by a simple ܡܢܟܘܢ in Ml i 10, when the hands are human and there can be no question of avoidance of anthropomorphic language being the reason for the modification, indicates that caution is appropriate in detecting the presence of this particular motive. In Ml iii 16 ויכתב ספר זכרון לפניו the verb is vocalized as a Niph'al in the Masoretic tradition, but in LXX and the Peshitta it is translated in the active (*v.* p. 125 *supra*), and the Peshitta (in common with T, which however retains the passive verb) prefixes the preposition *beth* to ܩܕܡܘܗܝ. There is clearly no avoidance of anthropomorphism on the part of the Peshitta translators here!

One regular device employed in the Targum is the use of the preposition קדם, and this is occasionally introduced into the Peshitta. Reverential motives may underlie its substitution for את in Hs xii 4²⁰ (where T surprisingly renders עָם), Mi v 6 and Sa vii 12^ult, for אֶל in Jon ii 2 and for עַל in Sa iv 14 and vi 5; the same substitution occurs in T in all these passages except the first. A more interesting and more substantial modification involving the introduction of ܩܕܡ occurs in Sa vii 2, viii 21f., where the phrase לְחַלּוֹת אֶת־פְּנֵי יהוה is thrice rendered ܠܡܨܠܝܘ/ܠܐ܌ܗܘܢ ܩܕܡ ܐܠܗܐ, again in close agreement with T (cf also Ml i 9). In all these passages LXX and V (except in Hs xii 4) seem unembarrassed by the theological crudities of the Hebrew literally understood. What is striking however in a study of the Dodekapropheton as a whole is the rarity of this kind of device in comparison with its frequency in T.

Turning to anthropopathisms the concept of God "changing his mind" and relenting occurs at Jl ii 13 and Jon iii 10. In both cases the Peshiṭta modifies the Hebrew נִחָם עַל הָרָעָה by using the Aph'el of ܗܦܟ; in Jl ii 13 it reads ܘܡܗܦܟ ܒܝܫܬܐ and in Jon iii 10 it reads ܘܐܗܦܟ ܐܠܗܐ ܪܘܓܙܗ. The second passage is instructive, since it actually introduces a different anthropopathism, that of God's anger, which we have already seen to arouse no regular susceptibilities in the minds of the Peshiṭta translators. The previous verse is also instructive. For here the Hebrew expresses the idea of a divine "change of mind" no less than three times: יָשׁוּב וְנִחַם הָאֱלֹהִים וְשָׁב מֵחֲרוֹן אַפּוֹ. This is rendered in the Peshiṭta: ܕܬܟܦܐ ܐܠܐ ܘܢܬܒܥܐ ܒܠܒ. ܘܡܗܦܟ ܡܢ ܐܠܗܐ ܪܘܓܙܗ. Here again the concept of God's relenting from his anger is modified into his diverting it from its intended objects, but in view of ܬܟܦܐ it can hardly be maintained that there is a fundametal objection to the concept of God relenting. The rewriting of both these passages in T is much more drastic, but even T can render וְיָתוּב מִתְּקוֹף רוּגְזֵיהּ in Jon iii 9 and וְתָב יוי מן בִּשְׁתָּא in Jon iii 10. It seems that neither version is concerned consistently to avoid this kind of anthropopathic language, and it may perhaps be suggested that the use of נחם in biblical Hebrew in the sense of 'comfort' as well as in that of 'relent' may have influenced the rendering of this verb in the Peshiṭta of Jon iii 9. The same phenomenon occurs in Jl ii 14. In addition to these two passages SEBÖK cites Na i 2 as another passage where the desire to avoid anthropopathic language has affected the translation. The MT includes among the attributes of God נֹקֵם יהוה וּבַעַל חֵמָה, which is rendered in the Peshiṭta ܐܚܒܕ ܐܢܘܢ ܒܚܡܬܗ. Sebök claims that this reduces the reference of the description from that of a permanent characteristic to that of a specific attitude on a particular occasion,

EXEGETICAL AND THEOLOGICAL MODIFICATIONS

but the rendering of the previous נקם by ܬܒܥܐ suggests that no embarrassment was felt about this concept, and that the modification should be regarded as stylistic rather than as theological.

Two modifications of a different kind however may well be theologically motivated. In Sa xiii 2 the threat to remove the prophets from the land is modified by the addition of the qualification ܕܓܠܐ to the word ܢܒܝܐ; similar modifications are made in LXX and T. In view of the immediate sequel this is no doubt a correct exegesis, but it is a substantial modification in the text. The same qualification is added in T and the Peshitta in v.4. Even more interesting is Zf ii 11 where את כל־אלהי הארץ is rendered ܠܛܥܘܬܐ ܕܟܠܗܘܢ ܥܡܡܐ. One possibility is that ܛܥܘܬܐ is an inner-Syriac corruption of ܐܠܗܐ, cf Psalm xcvii 7 where precisely this substitution occurs for אלהים denoting gods other than Yahweh. GERLEMAN however draws attention to Psalm cxxxviii 1 where in most Mss אלהים in a similar sense is rendered ܛܥܘܬܐ. Either reading would constitute a significant modification of the text, peculiar to the Peshitta, and presumably the result of a deliberate theological motivation.

The question of possible assimilation to passages in the New Testament, to which we now turn, is of particular interest in view of its relevance to the much debated question whether the Peshitta is of Jewish or Christian origin. There are a number of direct citations from the Dodekapropheton in the New Testament, and a much larger number of indirect allusions; it is not always easy to distinguish between citations and allusions, and the problem is complicated by the presence of conflate citations and by the varying pattern of agreement or disagreement with the LXX text in the New Testament citations. Considerations of space alone preclude any thorough examination of these questions in the present monograph. Such an examination will in any case be more practicable when the critical edition of the Peshitta Old Testament is complete.

As a preliminary sounding in this area the following citations have been examined in the text of the Peshitta New Testament and where applicable also in the Old Syriac Gospels:

Hs ii 25, 1	cited in	Romans ix 25f.
Hs vi 6		Matthew ix 13, xii 7
Hs xi 1		Matthew ii 15
Hs xiii 14		1 Corinthians xv 55
Jl iii 1–5		Acts ii 17–21
Am v 25–27		Acts vii 42f.

Am ix 11f.	Acts xv 16–18
Mi v 1	Matthew ii 6
Hb i 5	Acts xiii 41
Hb ii 3	Hebrews x 37
Hb ii 4	Romans i 17, Galatians iii 11, Hebrews x 38
Sa ix 9	Matthew xxi 5, John xii 15
Sa xi 13	Matthew xxvii 9f.
Sa xii 10	John xix 37
Sa xiii 7	Matthew xxvi 31, Mark xiv 27
Ml i 2f.	Romans ix 13
Ml iii 1	Matthew xi 10, Mark i 2, Luke vii 27

Three of these citations raise points of interest. That of Am ix 11 at Acts xv 16 suggests that the insertion of ܐܢܐ in 7a1 8a1* vid (reading no 52 in Chapter 3) may have originated as an assimilation to the form of the citation in Acts. That of Hs xiii 14 in 1 Corinthians xv 55 agrees with the Old Testament Peshitta in the significant detail that ܙܟܘܬܐ is the word used to render the Hebrew דבריך, in agreement with a minority LXX reading (νίκη for δίκη, cf νῖκος in 1 Corinthians). A direct relation between the Peshitta of Hosea and 1 Corinthians is less than probable however in view of the inversion of the two nouns ܙܟܘܬܐ and ܥܘܩܣܐ in the Peshitta (though not the Greek) of 1 Corinthians.

Exact verbal agreement is confined to one of the three New Testament citations of the last three words of Hb ii 4, viz that in Galatians iii 11. The three citations are all different, ܢܚܐ being replaced by ܢܐܚܐ in Romans and Hebrews, and these very differences make it probable that the exact agreement between the Peshitta of Habakkuk and Galatians is fortuitous. There is a further point of interest in this citation: MT has a 3 masc sg suffix in באמונתו, which is not represented in the Peshitta. Unfortunately the citation of the text is not extant in 1QpHab, although as BROWNLEE (p. 44) points out the pesher אמנתם in viii 2 confirms the suffix, which is reflected also in A S Th V and implicitly T. LXX however implies a 1 sg suffix, which is also reflected in the Peshitta of Hebrews x 38. The reading without any suffix (as in the Old Testament Peshitta) is reflected in the Greek text in all three New Testament citations (though some Mss assimilate to LXX in Romans and Hebrews) and in the Peshitta in the two Pauline citations. The total evidence for the text of the citation of Hb ii 4 in the Peshitta New Testament thus hardly indicates any direct

EXEGETICAL AND THEOLOGICAL MODIFICATIONS

relation to the text of the Old Testament Peshitta.

Two New Testament allusions to passages in the Dodekapropheton may also be noted. The first five words of the Peshitta of Ml iii 24 are exactly reproduced in the Peshitta of Luke i 17; the Old Syriac is not extant for this verse. There is an allusion to the last six words of Hs x 8 in Luke xxiii 30, where however there appears to be an inversion of כסונו and נפלו עלינו, although both LXX (except cod A) and the Peshitta Old Testament agree with MT. The Old Syriac and Peshitta of Luke agree with the Greek New Testament against the Peshitta of Hosea.

The general impression resulting from the examination of these citations from and allusions to the Dodekapropheton in the Syriac versions of the New Testament is that they were translated into Syriac directly from the New Testament without any specific reference to the text of the Peshitta Old Testament. The extent of exact verbal agreement has been seen to be very small. There is little to suggest that the Syriac versions of the New Testament have had any influence on the wording of the Peshitta, and in any case this is hardly likely in view of the respective dates of the versions. The only two details susceptible of explanation as the result of Christian influence are the use of ܘܒܗܘܢ to render דבריך in Hs xiii 14 and the loss of the suffix in the Peshitta rendering of באמונתו in Hb ii 4; in neither case is this a compelling explanation. It becomes even less probable in the light of the Peshitta rendering of Hs vi 2, where ܚܝܘܬܐ eliminates both the preposition *min* and the dual sense of MT מימים; the effect of this is that it is far less easy to detect an allusion to Christ's resurrection in the Peshitta than in the MT or LXX of this verse. Reverting to the wider question of the Jewish or Christian origins of the Peshitta, while we shall see in the next two chapters evidence of familiarity on the part of the Peshitta translators with Jewish exegetical traditions, we have looked in vain for any clear traces of a Christian origin.

The modifications examined in this section vary in degree and significance. Some appear to be simple attempts at exegetical clarification, while others are clearly of more positively theological significance. The introduction however of reverential terminology or the avoidance of anthropomorphic or anthropopathic language in relation to God is at best occasional and cannot be said to characterize the version as a whole. Assimilation to other passages in the Old Testament has influenced the rendering on several occasons. It must be remembered that our attention has been directed to passages where modifications occur, and it should not be assumed that these are characteristic of the version as a whole. They are sufficient however to add to the difficulties already noted in the previous sections in the way of reconstructing the Hebrew *Vorlage* of the Peshitta of the Dodekapropheton, and in most if not all of the passages considered in this section there is little to suggest that the *Vorlage* is different from MT.

4. Conclusion

In this chapter we have been taking preliminary soundings to determine the nature of the Peshitta of the Dodekapropheton as a version. It is quite clearly not a slavish translation. Considerable liberties were taken by the translators in respect to the syntax and vocabulary. They were rarely wholly consistent in their choice of lexical equivalents, and were sometimes hindered by the limitations of their knowledge of biblical Hebrew. They were not afraid to make minor additions or adjustments either in order to explicate the meaning of the text as they understood it or occasionally for theological reasons; nor were they afraid to leave some elements in the *Vorlage* untranslated, either for stylistic reasons or because they simply found them unintelligible. The effect of all these characteristics is to increase the difficulty of reconstructing the Hebrew *Vorlage*, though this difficulty must not be exaggerated: in the last chapter it was often found possible to be reasonably certain which of two variant Hebrew texts was to be assumed to have belonged to the *Vorlage* of the Peshitta. Nor must the degree of divergence of the Peshitta from the Hebrew be exaggerated. Any perusal of the three versions of the Dodekapropheton over a sample of thirty to fifty verses will make it clear beyond question that the Peshitta is closer to MT than either LXX or T. The fact that it is not a slavish translation reduces its direct value as a witness to the Hebrew text, but by no means makes it an unfaithful or poor translation. The slavishness of Aquila's version may be a boon to the modern textual critic of the Hebrew Old Testament as it may also have been to Greek-speaking beginners in biblical Hebrew in antiquity (*cf* JELLICOE, p. 314) but the Peshitta will have stood well in comparison with it as an idiomatic and essentially faithful version of the Scriptures for reading in public worship.

Before we conclude this chapter three general points may be made. Some apparent divergences from the Hebrew are probably best

CONCLUSION

explained by the hypothesis that the particular exemplar of the *Vorlage* used by the translators was either damaged or in some other way difficult to decipher. This is suggested in a number of passages by SEBÖK; we may be content here with a single illustration. At Mi i 15 עד־עדלם is rendered ܥܕܡܐ ܠܥܠܡ, suggesting a *Vorlage* עד־עולם. It should not however be too readily assumed that this was an actual Hebrew reading; the misreading of *daleth* as *waw* could easily be the result of fading, poor initial writing or subsequent damage in the Hebrew exemplar used by the Peshitta translators. A place-name is more appropriate to the general context, and Adullam is recognized here by LXX S V and T.

A second general point concerns the multiple explanations of particular readings which are often possible. A single example will again suffice. In Sa xiv 18 corresponding to the Hebrew ולא$^{2°}$ the Peshitta reads ܐܦ. Three explanations are theoretically possible. One is that the Hebrew *Vorlage* was different from MT, reading perhaps (ו)גם. A second possibility is that the Peshitta translators have assimilated their version to that of the LXX. The third possibility is that they understood the Hebrew as a negative question, and in accordance with the examples noted on p. 137 *supra* modified it by rendering it as a positive statement. The last of these possibilities is in this case the most likely, but it is by no means always so easy to determine which of several possible explanations is the most probable, and it is seldom possible to attain certainty.

The third general point concerns the question of the consistency and homogeneity of the Peshitta as a translation. We have seen sufficient evidence of inconsistency of practice in each of the preceding sections to make us suspect that we are dealing with several translators rather than one. This again is hard to prove definitively since inconsistency could be characteristic of a single translator! The balance of probability seems however to be in favour of several translators having been at work, and this impression is reinforced by the observation that the degree of freedom exercised in the translation varies considerably in different parts of the Dodekapropheton. While it is true in general that the greater the obscurity of the Hebrew the greater is the freedom shown in the translation, this is by no means always the case. We may conclude this chapter therefore by drawing attention to three sample verses to illustrate the different degrees of closeness to the original to be found within the Peshitta of the Dodekapropheton. Like so many other questions this will be capable of a more systematic examination when the whole of the Peshiṭta Old Testament is available in the critical edition.

A good example of a verse which is rendered faithfully word by word into the Syriac idiomatic equivalent of MT is Ob 15. The additions of enclitic ܗܘ, the suffix in ܠܚܘܠܗ, the ܘܗܕܐ to balance and bring out the full force of ܐܝܟ ܕ, and the copula before ܗܦܟܝܢ are all illustrations of the idiomatic differences between the two languages, while the choice of ܥܠ to render the Hebrew preposition *beth* in the final word may be regarded as the substitution of an equivalent (*cf* Esther ix 25 in MT), though the Peshiṭta does retain the preposition *beth* in the similar passages 1 Kings ii 33 and Psalm vii 17.

Hs ix 6 will serve as an example of a verse which the Peshiṭta translators found difficult to interpret, but which they attempted to render as faithfully as possible while making certain modifications in order to secure a rendering which was intelligible. The rendering of הִנֵּה by ܗܢܘܢ may be the result of an obscure exemplar (confusion with הֵמָּה), and the modification of the preposition *mem* to *beth* may reflect the common confusion between these letters in the older Hebrew script. The awkward preposition *lamedh* before כספם is simply ignored. The rare קמוש is replaced by ܣܚܕܐ, probably as a simple substitution for a word unknown to the translator. It seems also to have been unknown to the Peshiṭta translator at Proverbs xxiv 31, but is interpreted correctly as ܩܘܪܛܒܐ in the Peshiṭta at Isaiah xxxiv 13; these three are the only occurrences of the word in MT. The suffix to יירשם is modified to a singular, indicating that the translator regarded מחמד as the antecedent. Finally the generic חוח is rendered in the plural. None of these modifications are likely to reflect a Hebrew *Vorlage* different from MT, but they indicate the kind of manner in which the Peshiṭta translators handled a passage which they found obscure.

As a final illustration we turn to Hb i 15. This is a verse which is readily intelligible in the Hebrew, but one in which the Peshiṭta translator has exercised much more freedom than in Ob 15. The most striking modification is that the opening כלה is made the subject instead of the object. The Hiph'il העלה is accordingly replaced by the Pe'al ܣܠܩ, while יגרהו and ויאספהו are rendered by passive verbs and the suffixes to בחרמו and במכמרתו are omitted. The conjunction על־כן is then replaced with the more specific ܡܛܠ ܗܢܐ in order to facilitate the change of subject in the two final verbs, which are rendered in agreement with the Hebrew, except that they are in the perfect rather than the imperfect tense. All these modifications are peculiar to the Peshiṭta, and it is improbable that they were occasioned by any difficulty in construing or deciphering the Hebrew *Vorlage*. They simply illustrate an unusual degree of freedom in the Peshiṭta translation.

These three sample verses suffice to illustrate the varying degree to which the Peshiṭta translators of the Dodekapropheton were prepared to depart from a strict word for word rendering of their Hebrew *Vorlage*, ranging from the merely idiomatic and stylistic modification, through attempts to render a *Vorlage* they found difficult to interpret, to a style which is content to reproduce the substance of the original with little regard for detailed accuracy. The variety of translation method employed exacerbates the difficulty of reconstructing the Hebrew *Vorlage*; each passage must be considered in its own right, and the burden of proof must rest in every case on those who claim that the *Vorlage* of the Peshiṭta is distinct from MT.

7

The Peshiṭta and the Septuagint

1. Introduction

AGREEMENTS of LXX and the Peshiṭta against MT may theoretically be evaluated in a number of ways. The purpose of this chapter is to try to determine the relationship between LXX and the Peshiṭta and to assess its bearing on the significance of exclusive agreements between the two versions.

One theoretically possible relationship is that the Peshiṭta was translated not from MT or any other Hebrew *Vorlage* but directly from LXX. This may be discounted at once. We have already noted that a comparison of the two versions over a reasonable number of verses consistently indicates that the Peshiṭta is closer to MT than is LXX, and this could not be the case if the Peshiṭta were a translation of LXX. A comparison between the Peshiṭta and the Syrohexapla, which is a direct translation of the hexaplaric LXX, will make the point even clearer. The many instances in which LXX deviates from MT while the Peshiṭta remains faithful to it put the matter beyond doubt. Three may be given to illustrate the nature of the evidence.

In Hs ii 14 LXX reads μαρτύριον for יער, probably at least confusing the *resh* with a *daleth*. The Peshiṭta however renders the Hebrew accurately with ܥܒܐ, and could not have done so on the basis of LXX without recourse to the Hebrew. In Hs viii 10 the LXX has an interesting reading τοῦ χρίειν for the Hebrew ממשא, and this has often been thought to reflect a Hebrew *Vorlage* ממשח. The Peshiṭta however reads ܡܢ ܫܥܝܐ, which is a straightforward rendering of MT and could not have been derived from LXX alone. In Am v 26 LXX renders כיון צלמיכם 'Ραιφαν, τοὺς τύπους αὐτῶν and inverts this phrase and כוכב אלהיכם which immediately follows it in the Hebrew. The Peshiṭta however not only adheres here to the order of MT but renders ܟܗ ܘܝܠܚܗܐ, which again could not have been derived from LXX alone. It introduces a slight modification of its own in the syntax of the remainder of the verse by making ܟܘܟܒܐ emphatic and placing ܐܠܗܟܘܢ (without suffix) as predicate at the end of the clause.

INTRODUCTION

To these three examples we add a more complex illustration. In Zf iii 7 the Peshitta agrees with LXX in rendering the 2 *fem sg* verbs at the beginning in the 2 *masc pl* and in rendering מעונה as if it were מֵעֵינֶהָ (*v.* p. 116 *supra*), but retains the 3 *masc sg* in its rendering of יכרת and the 3 *masc pl* in its rendering of השחיתו, and it recognizes the correct meaning of עלילותם while LXX confuses it with עוללות ('gleaning'). Both versions seem to have misunderstood אכן in a similar way, while LXX's rendering of השכימו is closer to the meaning of the Hebrew despite the change of person and number than the Peshitta's ܢܘܩܒܘ. While this verse thus shows a more complex pattern of agreements and disagreements, it is hardly possible that the Peshitta of this verse could have been translated solely from the Greek without reference to the Hebrew.

Another theoretical possibility is that if they were Christian the Peshitta translators might have regarded LXX as the authoritative text and for this reason on occasion preferred its readings to those of MT. This too is to be discounted, and for two reasons. In the first place one would expect a much more consistent preference for the readings of LXX in such a case. In the second place we have already seen little reason to suggest that the Peshitta translators were in fact Christian.

A third theoretical possibility is that the exclusive agreements between LXX and the Peshitta are the result of pure coincidence. This may occasionally be the case, but the evidence to be presented in the next section shows that as a general explanation of the relation between the two versions this too is to be discounted.

There are further theoretical possibilities. Exclusive agreements between LXX and the Peshitta against MT may on occasion indicate the independent use of a common Hebrew *Vorlage* distinct from MT. Where this can be shown to be probable it is of considerable potential significance as evidence for the Hebrew text. Caution must however be exercised in inferring the existence of a common distinctive Hebrew *Vorlage* on the basis of LXX and the Peshitta alone, especially in view of the evidence to be presented in the next section to prove the use of LXX by the Peshitta translators. Dependence on common exegetical traditions may account for some of the exclusive agreements between LXX and the Peshitta, while the possibility of occasional correction of an earlier Syriac translation to agree with particular LXX readings cannot be excluded, though in the absence of evidence of the existence of such an earlier Syriac reading it must remain hypothetical, and in view of the sporadic distribution of exclusive agreements it appears rather improbable.

Fortunately the nature of some of the agreements between LXX and the Peshitta is such as to make it certain that the Peshitta translators on occasion made direct use of LXX. This affords one certain fact as a basis for our further examination of the relationship between the two versions. This evidence must now be examined.

2. The dependence of the Peshitta on LXX

The actual use of LXX by the Peshitta translators can be proved by a number of passages in which the Peshitta rendering is explicable only in the light of that of LXX.

In Hs ii 17 LXX renders תקוה σύνεσιν αὐτῆς, having evidently vocalized the previous word as an infinitive (לִפְתֹּחַ). As has been pointed out (by VOLLERS, cf SEBÖK and RUDOLPH) the Greek translators probably used σύνεσις in the sense 'coming together' relating it to the root קוה ('collect') rather than the homonymous root קוה ('wait for'). The Peshitta translators appear to have consulted LXX and assumed that the Greek translators used σύνεσις in its common sense of 'understanding'; accordingly they rendered תקוה ܣܘܟܠܗ, a rendering that could hardly have suggested itself on the basis of the Hebrew. It is interesting to note that at Mi v 6 the Peshitta recognizes the sense 'wait for', while at Sa ix 12 it renders ܕܟܢܘܫܬܐ in close agreement with LXX τῆς συναγωγῆς.

In Zf ii 2 לדת חק is rendered ܬܗܘܘܢ. This is problematic, but GERLEMAN is probably right in regarding LXX γενέσθαι (ὑμᾶς) as a rendering of (כם)לדת (however inappropriate in the context), which has been followed by the Peshitta translators. The link is again provided by LXX, γενέσθαι meaning both 'be born' (לדת) and 'be' (ܬܗܘܘܢ). Similarly the rendering of או by ܗܠܝܢ at the beginning of Ml iii 16 is explicable only as the result of the influence of LXX ταῦτα, which itself may have arisen as a corruption of τότε (cf RUDOLPH)! Another instance of double meaning in a Greek word which may have influenced the Peshitta translators is that of LXX ὀξύτεροι for חדו in Hb i 8; both the Greek adjective and the Syriac participial adjective ܚܪܝܦܝܢ mean 'sharp' (as MT) and 'swift' (cf the parallel קלו). This example however is less certain than the previous ones.

We proceed now to consider six passages where the close agreement of the Peshitta with LXX points strongly to dependence of the former on the latter. The rendering of ישרה in Hb ii 4 by ܣܒܪ seems explicable only in the light of LXX εὐδοκεῖ. In Zf ii 14 קול ישורר is rendered ܢܬܘܡ ܐܚܘܬܐ, which exactly follows LXX καὶ θηρία φωνήσει, and seems hardly likely to have arisen independently from the Hebrew. In Zf iii 9 the idiomatic שכם אחד, to which Syriac has the exact equivalent ܟܬܦܐ ܚܕ, is surprisingly rendered ܚܒܠܐ ܚܕ, a rendering which as GERLEMAN states demonstrates the dependence here of the Peshitta translators on the LXX ὑπὸ ζυγὸν ἕνα. In Zf iii 18 נוגי ממועד is rendered ܐܝܟ ܕܒܝܘܡܐ ܕܥܐܕܐ, which exactly follows LXX ὡς ἐν ἡμέρᾳ ἑορτῆς. If GERLEMAN is right in regarding LXX here as a conjectural rendering rather than as deriving from a *Vorlage* כביום מועד, this passage affords another example of the dependence of the Peshitta translators on LXX. In Sa vii 7 LXX seems to have failed to recognize the proper names הנגב והשפלה, rendering ἡ ὀρεινὴ καὶ ἡ πεδινή, where the first adjective seems to be a guess to provide a counterpart to the second. It is difficult to resist the conclusion that the Peshitta rendering ܛܘܪܐ ܘܦܩܥܬܐ is dependent on LXX. Finally in Sa ix 12 in place of גם־היום מגיד the Peshitta reads ܘܣܠܟ ܚܕ ܝܘܡ, which would suggest a Hebrew *Vorlage* ותחת יום אחד. It is much more probable however that the Peshitta is dependent on LXX καὶ ἀντὶ μιᾶς ἡμέρας παροικεσίας σου, simply omitting the last two words. Both versions seem to have found the Hebrew unintelligible; LXX improvised and the Peshitta followed it.

Not all of the above examples are equally cogent, but in the light of this evidence it is impossible to deny at least the occasional dependence of the Peshitta translators on LXX. We now proceed to review a series of further instances where, especially in the light of the evidence already presented, dependence of the Peshitta on LXX seems the most likely explanation of the agreements between the two versions. The force of this evidence is cumulative.

In Jl i 1 the name of the prophet's father is given as Bethuel in LXX and the Peshitta, possibly in unconscious assimilation to the patriarchal name, rather than Pethuel as in MT V and T. In Jl ii 27 the emphatic addition ܠܗܘ ܒܠܚܘܕ finds a counterpart only in LXX. In Jl iv 16 it is probable that מחסה and מעוז are to be taken as synonyms denoting 'refuge'. LXX however has rendered both words as verbs, deriving the first from the root חוס ('spare') instead of חסה ('seek refuge'), and the second from the root עזז ('be strong') instead of עוז ('seek refuge'). The fact that the Peshitta agrees with both these renderings suggests strongly that it does so under the influence of

LXX.

In Am i 15 the addition ܘܚܕܐܝܗܘܢ is found also in LXX. In Am iv 8 ונעו is rendered somewhat freely ܘܢܬܟܢܫܘܢ, a rendering which agrees closely with LXX συναθροισθήσονται. In Am vii 7f. the word אנך occurs four times, and is uniformly rendered ܐܕܡܢܣ, a loan-word from the very Greek term used here in LXX. In Am vii 9 the proper name Isaac is treated in both versions as a common noun 'laughter'. In Am ix 6 אגדה is rendered ἐπαγγελίαν in LXX; SEBÖK suggests that this rests on a derivation from the root נגד (הגיד). In this case the LXX translators may have used ἐπαγγελία in the sense of 'announcement', while the Peshiṭta translators understood it in the sense 'promise' and accordingly used ܡܘܠܟܢܐ to render it. In Ob 5 the second אם is rendered by LXX in the sense 'or' as if it introduced a disjunctive question, a rendering in which the standard text of the Peshiṭta concurs, although 12a1 has a reading closer to a literal equivalent to MT (reading no 130 in Chapter 3).

In Mi ii 4 the counterpart of ימיר in LXX is κατεμετρήθη ἐν σχοινίῳ, and this may have suggested the Peshiṭta rendering ܒܡܫܘܚܬܐ ܕܚܒܠܐ; both versions seem to have been influenced by the reference to חבל in the following verse, and the Peshiṭta introduces ܒܡܫܘܚܬܐ again at the end of verse 4 to render יחלק, where LXX is closer to the Hebrew with its διεμερίσθησαν. In Mi ii 11 מטיף is rendered ܡܢ ܢܛܘܦܝܬܗ, which agrees with LXX ἐκ τῆς σταγόνος, both versions interpreting the *mem* as the preposition and the rest of the word as a noun rather than taking the whole word as a Hiph'il participle in accordance with the Masoretic vocalization. In Mi v 6 both versions assimilate to the following verse by introducing ἐν τοῖς ἔθνεσιν/ܒܥܡܡܐ before בקרב עמים; the singular of the Peshiṭta is consistent with its rendering of בגוים in verse 7 where LXX renders in the plural with MT.

In Na i 12 אם־שלמים is rendered ܥܠ ܪܝܫ ܡܝܐ, which suggests dependence on LXX κατάρχων ὑδάτων, particularly if the first word were read as two words κατ' ἀρχῶν. The LXX rendering seems to be the result of an attempt to wrest sense from the Hebrew by detecting in it the root משל and the noun מַיִם, while that of the Peshiṭta seems to be a further development from that of LXX.

In Sa ii 2 the addition of ܟܝ is exclusively common to LXX and the Peshiṭta. RUDOLPH points out that the rendering of צמח in Sa iii 8 and vi 12 by ܕܢܚܐ may be a literal equivalent of LXX's ἀνατολή in its more usual sense of 'sunrise' (*cf* V). In Sa ix 4 the opening הִנֵּה is rendered ܗܘܐ ܚܪܒܐ in exclusive agreement with LXX. In Sa xi 6 וכתתו is rendered ܘܦܣܩܝܢ ܗܘܘ (with an anticipatory suffix); this may reflect a misunderstanding of LXX κατακόψουσι in the sense 'cut up' rather than 'destroy'. In Sa xiv 13 עלתה is rendered ܐܬܟܒ, a rendering which represents a substantial modification of the Hebrew from a hostile to a friendly sense; this may have arisen from a misunderstanding of LXX συμπλακήσεται.

In Ml i 14 the omission of נוכל in the Peshitta, already noted at p. 133 *supra*, may have been due to the influence of its rendering in LXX by δυνατός, a concept which the Peshitta translators may have felt was already adequately represented in the rest of the clause. In Ml iii 10 the rendering of והריקתי by ܘܐܫܦܥ may reflect the influence of LXX ἐκχεῶ.

Some of these passages are patient of more than one explanation, but the cumulative force of the evidence presented in this section is amply sufficient to establish the fact that the Peshitta translators did on occasion make use of LXX in their attempt to interpret their Hebrew *Vorlage*, and that the rendering of LXX, though sometimes misunderstood, did influence that of the Peshitta in some passages. We have been concerned here primarily to establish some degree of dependence on LXX on the part of the Peshitta translators; its implications for the limitations of their knowledge of biblical Hebrew and their understanding of the biblical text will be considered more fully in the next section.

We may conclude this section with an ambiguous case. The noun גֵּר occurs twice in the Dodekapropheton, at Sa vii 10 and Ml iii 5. On both occasions LXX renders it by προσήλυτος, which is the word it most commonly uses for the purpose, and which in itself need mean no more than 'stranger, sojourner'. SEBÖK states that the usual renderings in the Peshitta are ܥܡܘܪܐ and ܬܘܬܒܐ, the former of which is used in Ml iii 5. In Sa vii 10 however the Peshitta renders ܕܐܬܟܢܫ ܠܗ, and it seems that the Peshitta plus in Ml iii 5 noted on p. 135 *supra* must be regarded as a doublet rendering of גר in that verse, ܥܡܘܪܐ drawing out the literal and the plus the derived meaning of the Hebrew term. SEBÖK implies that the Peshitta translators at Sa vii 10 were following the Jewish tradition, first attested in the Talmud, whereby גר denotes a proselyte to Judaism. It is equally possible that the Peshitta translators were influenced by the same meaning which had come to be attached to the LXX rendering. The full evaluation of the Peshitta's treatment of the noun גר in the Old Testament must await the completion of the critical Edition.

3. The use of LXX by the Peshiṭta translators

The demonstration that the Peshiṭta translators made use of LXX in some passages does not prove that every agreement between the two versions against MT must be the result of direct use of LXX by the Peshiṭta translators, though it does create a certain presumption in favour of such an explanation. Perhaps the agreements which are least likely to be the result of deliberate consultation of LXX are those where the translation methods of the two versions are similar. For example the following cases of exclusive agreement between the two versions fall into the same general categories of stylistic modifications which we noted as characteristics of the Peshiṭta in the first section of the previous chapter.

Characteristic pluses include the copula at the beginning of Sa i 4, ܐܘ in Mi iv 13, ܗܘ in Hg i 9, the ethic dative ܠܗ in Hb ii 6 and the suffixes to ܒܗܘܢ and ܪܓܠܝܗܘܢ in Na ii 10. Modifications include the change of preposition in מצרה in Jon ii 3 to *beth* ($\dot{\epsilon} \nu$), the change from singular to plural in ܐܠܗܐ ܘܢܦܫܗܘܢ in Na i 14, and the change of person from 3 *masc sg* to 1 *sg* in ישא in Ml i 9 and ונשא in Ml ii 3. The omission of והיה at the beginning of Sa xiv 6 also belongs to this category, and has occurred in Symmachus as well as in LXX and the Peshiṭta. Modifications of this kind may well have occurred independently in more than one version.

We turn now to some more substantial syntactical modifications. The phrase באחרית הימים occurs twice in the Dodekapropheton, at Hs iii 5 and Mi iv 1. On both occasions it is rendered $\dot{\epsilon} \pi'$ $\dot{\epsilon} \sigma \chi \acute{a} \tau \omega \nu$ $\tau \hat{\omega} \nu$ $\dot{\eta} \mu \epsilon \rho \hat{\omega} \nu$ in LXX and ܒܚܪܬܐ ܕܝܘ̈ܡܬܐ in the Peshiṭta. In Hs vi 5 the preposition *beth* is omitted before נביאים with the effect of making the prophets the object rather than the instrument of God's destruction. The last two words of Hs viii 9 are rendered in such a way as to suggest that the functions of the noun and the verb have been reversed; this is probably the result of an attempt to make sense of a difficult *Vorlage*, התנו being derived mistakenly from the root נתן. A similar misunderstanding seems to underlie the treatment of יתנו in the following verse, where LXX renders it $\pi a \rho a \delta o \theta \acute{\eta} \sigma o \nu \tau a \iota$ and the Peshiṭta ܢܬܝܗܒܘܢ (v. p. 123 *supra*). In Hs xi 2 both versions supply a correlative ($\kappa a \theta \acute{\omega} s$/ܐܝܟ) to the following כן; the same prepositions are prefixed to בראשון in Jl ii 23. In Hs xii 1 Judah is taken in close conjunction with the house of Israel in the first part of the verse.

In Jl i 7 the first letter of הלבינו seems to have been read as a suffix to the previous word and the verb taken in a transitive sense (contrary to Hebrew usage) and modified as a 3 *masc sg*. In Jl ii 22 the order of the fig and the vine is inverted (*cf* pp 135f. *supra*). In Am v 25 the inversion of במדבר and ארבעים שנה is common to LXX$^{C\,L}$ and the Peshitta. In Mi ii 8 מעברים בטח is rendered τοῦ ἀφελέσθαι ἐλπίδα in LXX. We have already noted (p. 122 *supra*) that the Hebrew participle was vocalized as a Hiph'il by the LXX and Peshitta translators. We observe now further that in LXX the participle is modified to an infinitive introduced by the genitive of the article. The Peshitta rendering ܣܒܪܗܘܢ ܕܢܓܒܘܢ seems to be based on that of LXX, the infinitive of LXX being understood as denoting purpose and a suffix being gratuitously added to בטח. The addition of ܗܠܝܢ in Mi iii 1 in the standard text of the Peshitta (but not in 7a1 8a1*— reading no 9 in Chapter 3) seems to be due to assimilation to the reading ταῦτα of LXX^{Mss} and is probably not original to the Peshitta. In Sa vi 10 אשר באו is modified, the verb being changed into a participle and into the singular; according to this interpretation אשר is the subject of the verb and its antecedent is Josiah, whereas MT can be taken in a different sense, אשר meaning 'where' and the subject of the verb being indefinite.

In many ways the most interesting area of dependence on LXX on the part of the Peshitta translators is that of lexical equivalents. Not all of the following renderings of the Peshitta may be due to the influence of LXX, but in view of the evidence presented in the previous section and section 2 of the previous chapter it seems probable that many of them represent cases where the Peshitta translators turned to LXX for help in interpreting their Hebrew *Vorlage*.

Hs ii 8	ܐܪܝܘܬܐ	
Hs iv 2	ܚܠܛܘ	
Hs iv 14	ܐܦܩ	
Hs v 11	ܣܪܝܩܘܬܐ	
Hs v 12	ܕܥܘܠܐ	
Hs vi 9	ܚܒܪܘܗܝ	(*v.* p. 123 *supra*)
Hs viii 6	ܛܥܝܘܬܐ	
Hs x 1	ܒܗ	
Hs x 4	ܐܠܘܬܐ ܕܓܠܬܐ	
Hs x 5	ܫܘܢ ܬܘܪܬܐ	

Hs x 7	ܐܙܠ	
Hs xi 5	ܠܐ ܝܗܒ	
Hs xi 6	(ܡܢ) ܐܚܝܢܘܗܝ	
Hs xii 15	ܐܬܐܫܕ	
Hs xiii 7	ܕܐܬܘܪ	(v. p. 123 supra)
Hs xiii 15	ܒܝܬ ܐܚܐ ܘܐܝܒܐ	(cf p. 122 supra)
Hs xiv 9	ܚܒܒܬܗ	
Jl i 17	ܘܗܦܟܘ ܥܓܠܬܐ ܥܠ ܐܘܪܝܗܘܢ	
Jl i 17	ܚܡܪܝܐ	
Jl ii 23	ܡܐܟܘܠܬܐ	
Am ii 7	ܪܓܙܝܢ	
Am ii 8	ܕܚܛܝܢ ܣܝܡܝܢ ܗܘܘ	(cf p. 124 supra)
Am iv 2	ܐܢܐ	
Am iv 12	ܕܐܬܘܪ	
Am vi 5	ܢܦܫܢ	
Am vi 6	ܘܐܠܝܚ	
*Am viii 5	ܐܘܨܪܐ	
Jon i 6	ܩܪܝ	
Mi i 8	ܢܣܦܕ	
Mi i 11	ܚܡܬܗ	
Mi ii 8	ܩܕܡܬ	
Mi v 7	ܦܘܡ	(cf Rudolph)
Mi vi 8	ܗܐ ܐܡܪܬ ܠܟ	
Mi vii 4	ܐܘܪܝܚܬܐ ܕܐܟܠ ܣܡܐ	
Na ii 14	ܚܝܠܟܝ	
Na iii 1	ܥܘܠܐ	
Hb ii 1	ܐܠܗܐ	
Zf i 12	ܕܫܠܝܢ ܒܛܠܝܗܘܢ	
Zf i 14	ܘܐܣܪܗ	
Zf ii 1	ܠܐ ܨܒܝܐ	
Sa i 8	ܕܫܠܝܛܝܢ	
Sa i 8	ܩܫܝܐ	(cf Rudolph)
Sa iii 7	ܩܘܪܒܢ	
†Sa iii 9	ܐܟܘܣܐ	

* This word can mean 'storehouse' or 'corn' and the Peshiṭta uses it again for בר in v. 6 where LXX is quite different; it is possible that the Peshiṭta intends a deliberate play on the two meanings.

† This may illustrate the tendency of the Peshiṭta translators to read the Hebrew in the light of their own language. Of the two Hebrew roots מוש they have selected the one meaning 'feel' which has a Syriac cognate rather than the one meaning 'remove' which is required in this context.

Sa iv 10	ܘܣܢܝ
Sa iv 14	ܗܡܠܟ
Sa ix 17	ܡܚܒܠ
Sa xi 8	ܢܚ,
*Sa xiii 7	ܢܥܠܒ
Sa xiv 1	ܚܒ

In the light of this evidence it is surprising and unfortunate that the Peshiṭta translators did not consult LXX for the meaning of כלוב in Am viii 1f. (*cf* p. 144 *supra*).

We turn now to a smaller group of passages where the agreement between LXX and the Peshiṭta consists in a common exegesis of the Hebrew text, and where it is reasonable to suppose that in at least some cases the Peshiṭta translators deliberately consulted LXX in their attempt to understand the Hebrew text before translating it.

In Am vii 14 modern commentators have been much exercised over the interpretation of the nominal sentence לא־נביא אנכי: should the verb 'to be' be supplied in the present or in the past tense? LXX and the Peshiṭta answer this question by inserting the past tense of the verb 'to be' in contrast to V which inserts it in the present tense and T which retains the ambiguity of the Hebrew. The verb תטפו which occurs in various forms three times at the beginning of Mi ii 6 is interpreted by LXX and the Peshiṭta in terms of weeping, although both versions recognize its special sense in relation to prophecy in Am vii 16. Both versions agree in making the explanatory addition κατὰ σοῦ/ܥܠܝܟ after יעץ in Mi vi 5. Both versions agree in the false rendering of מדון in Hb i 3 as 'judge', and the Peshiṭta goes further than LXX in supplying an object (ܫܘܚܕܐ, 'a bribe') for ישא, though it is probably doing no more than make explicit the meaning intended by LXX.

The verb תכהה at the end of Sa xi 17 is rendered appropriately but much more specifically 'will be blind' in both versions. In Sa xii 13 the tribe of Shimei becomes that of Simeon in both versions; the further assimilation to the context by prefixing 'house of' which is found in the Peshiṭta and LXX^C has already been noted on p. 121 *supra*, but this could have occurred independently and is found also in T. At the end of Sa xiii 4 למען כחש means 'in order to deceive'; while ܡܛܠ can be used to render למען, the following perfect tense ܕܓܒ suggests here the

---

* i.e. 'pastors', not ܢܥܠܐ ('exalted') as implied by SEBÖK, SAEBØ and RUDOLPH.

interpretation 'because they were deceptive', which is exactly that conveyed by LXX ἀνθ' ὧν ἐψεύσαντο. In Sa xiv 4 the repetition of τὸ ἥμισυ αὐτοῦ/ܦܠܓܗ before the western direction is a clarification introduced in both versions. In Ml iii 3 ὡς/ܐܝܟ is inserted before the first כסף to make it clear that the expression is metaphorical.

We may also consider here three passages which have already been noted, but which raise wider points of interest. Two of them concern readings where the consonantal Hebrew of MT has been vocalized in a way different from that of the Masoretic tradition. The pointing of ויחו in Sa x 9 as a Pi'el rather than a Qal (v. p. 125 supra) carries with it the corollary that the following את is interpreted as the nota accusativi rather than as the preposition 'with'. This interpretation is peculiar to LXX and the Peshitta and contrasts with that of V and T which concurs with that of the Masoretic pointing. The pointing of בצרה in Mi ii 12 as בְּצָרָה, 'in distress' (v. p. 124 supra) is also peculiar to LXX and the Peshitta, although the other versions also fail to recognize the proper name. This kind of misunderstanding may also have occurred in Mi iv 8, where עדר and עפל are treated as common nouns and interpreted in the same way in both versions in common with V (and A for עפל), but may well in fact be proper names. Another misunderstanding of this kind gave rise to a variant within the Peshitta tradition at Am iv 1 (no 48 in Chapter 3, cf p. 74 supra), where LXX recognizes the proper name.

The third passage is Ml iii 6, where the Peshitta plus has already been noted on p. 135 supra. The relationship between the Peshitta and LXX here is however more complex. LXX renders the verb at the end of v. 6 ἀπέχεσθε and takes it with the beginning of the following verse, continuing ἀπὸ τῶν ἀδικιῶν τῶν πατέρων ὑμῶν, where ἀπὸ τῶν ἀδικιῶν seems to replace MT למימי. The Peshitta agrees with V and T in rendering מימי straightforwardly (although like V it ignores the difficult initial lamedh) and in beginning a new sentence with this word. Its plus at the end of v. 6 however seems to derive from LXX, and like LXX it connects these words with the verb at the end of v. 6, which it renders ܬܬܪܚܩܘܢ in broad agreement with LXX ἀπέχεσθε.

While there is room for different judgements in particular cases the evidence presented in this section as a whole suggests that the Peshitta translators did turn to LXX fairly frequently if by no means continuously or slavishly for help in understanding the Hebrew text they were trying to render into Syriac. The number of exclusive agreements between the two versions, some of a quite striking nature, is too large to be attributed to coincidence. Such a conclusion is in any case improbable in view of the demonstration in the previous section that certain renderings of the Peshiṭta are explicable only with reference to LXX. In some respects its influence was pervasive. This may be seen particularly in the consistent use of ܣܒܐܘܬ to render the divine name צבאות, which surely reflects its regular rendering in LXX by παντοκράτωρ.

The implications of this indebtedness to LXX on the part of the Peshiṭta translators are important. In the first place it provides considerable further evidence of the limitations both of the translators' knowledge of biblical Hebrew and of their understanding of the text of the Old Testament. In the second place it reduces the probability that exclusive agreements between the two versions are the result of common dependence on a Hebrew *Vorlage* distinct from MT. Where there is such a *Vorlage* it is perhaps generally more likely that only LXX is directly dependent on the *Vorlage*, the Peshiṭta rendering being the result of reading MT in the light of LXX. Reconstructions of a Hebrew *Vorlage* distinct from MT based solely on agreements between LXX and the Peshiṭta must therefore be scrutinized most carefully.

4. Some further agreements between LXX and the Peshiṭta

We must now revert to the question of agreements between LXX and the Peshiṭta which might be thought to derive from a Hebrew *Vorlage* distinct from MT. All the probable cases were reviewed in chapter 5, and in section 4 of that chapter a list of agreements between the two versions was given (pp 126f.). In the light of the evidence considered in the present and previous chapters it must be recognized that some even of those agreements may be explained rather as the result of licence on the part of the LXX translators and their influence on the Peshiṭta translators. The addition of a suffix in Hs xiv 9 (p. 127, *cf* pp 137, 166), the change of verb in Mi iii 4 (p. 127, *cf* p. 151), the change of a suffix in Na iii 9 (p. 127, *cf* p. 137), the change of tense in Zf ii 11 (p. 127, *cf* p. 136) and the change of preposition in Sa viii 9 (p. 127, *cf* pp 136, 166) are all explicable in this way rather than by derivation from a Hebrew *Vorlage* distinct from MT. It is difficult to determine in such cases which of the two explanations is the more likely.

We turn now to some further agreements between the two versions which are unlikely to derive from a Hebrew *Vorlage* distinct from MT. We have already noted some agreement between LXX and the Peshiṭta in Mi ii 4 (*v.* p. 164 *supra*); we may add the rendering of אִיךְ by καὶ οὐκ ἦν/ܘܠܐ, which seems to presuppose a Hebrew *Vorlage* אֵין. This may be the result of misreading an obscure or damaged *Vorlage* which was in fact identical with MT, or of a desperate attempt to make sense of a difficult passage by substituting a word of similar appearance. The agreement between the two versions is most likely to be due to use of LXX by the Peshiṭta translators, and the possibility of the existence of a Hebrew *Vorlage* אִי as the source of the LXX reading must be considered remote.

The divine name ܐܠܗܐ is added in these two versions alone at Am ix 6 (for its omission in 7k10* *cf* p. 80 *supra*, reading no 114). Assimilation to LXX is perhaps an improbable explanation for this Peshiṭta reading, since LXX inserts also ὁ θεός and it is not easy to see why the Peshiṭta translators should have borrowed only one of the two additional divine titles in LXX. It is of course possible that the Peshiṭta translators' *Vorlage* contained צבאות, but in view of the omission of this title at Hg i 9 (*v.* p. 133 *supra*) and its addition at Hg i 13 (*v.* p. 134 *supra*), both peculiar to the Peshiṭta, it seems most likely that the addition in Am ix 6 is to be attributed to the Peshiṭta translators themselves. We have already reached a similar conclusion about the addition of ܐܠܗܐ in these two versions except LXX^C in Sa viii 17 (*v.* p. 135 *supra*), while the case of Mi i 13 2° is complicated by the evidence of a few Hebrew Mss for a *Vorlage* with צבאות (*v.* p. 121 *supra*), the reading τῶν δυνάμεων for παντοκράτωρ in LXX^V, and the omission of ܐܠܗܐ in 6h9 and 7a1 (*cf* pp 69 and 121 *supra* for comments on reading no 24). Clearly the evidence for a Hebrew *Vorlage* צבאות is strongest in Ml i 13, but even there the possibilities of assimilation to LXX or independent modification by the Peshiṭta translators cannot be discounted.

In Sa xii 3 מֶעְמַסָּה ... עֲמָסִיָה is rendered καταπατούμενον ... ὁ καταπατῶν αὐτήν in LXX and ܕܪܝܫܐ ... ܘܪܡܣܗ in the Peshiṭta. These renderings might suggest that the root עמס was misread as עסס (*cf* Ml iii 21) or even רמס (*cf* Daniel viii 10), or alternatively that it was interpreted in the light of either of these. It is hardly probable that they derive from a *Vorlage* distinct from MT.

We turn now to some agreements between the two versions which find further support in one or more of the other versions. Agreements between LXX and V are probably to be explained in terms of the influence of LXX on V, but agreed readings of LXX and the Peshitta which find support in T or the later Greek versions require examination to see whether they are likely to depend on a common Hebrew *Vorlage* distinct from MT. The probable cases were reviewed in section 4 of chapter 5, but a few further ones are listed here.

The addition of πασῶν/ܟܠܗܘܢ in Am vi 2 is an expansion similar to those at Hg ii 2 and Sa xiv 17 noted on p. 135 *supra*, and differs from them only in that it appears to be reflected also in V. The correction of וְתַשְׁלִיךְ in Mi vii 19 to the 3 *masc sg* is found also in LXX V and T, but is so appropriate to the context that it might readily occur to several translators independently. In Hg i 9 וְהִנֵּה is rendered ܘܗܘܐ as if it were וַיְהִי, and this rendering is found also in LXX and T, while V combines both in its conflate reading *et ecce factum est*; it is however more likely that LXX T and the Peshitta are giving an idiomatic equivalent than that their *Vorlage* actually read ויהי. In Mi i 5 במות is rendered in LXX T and the Peshitta as if it were חטאת, while S and V reproduce MT; this rendering is more probably a conscious assimilation to the first part of the verse than the result of dependence on an actual *Vorlage* חטאת. In the formula which forms the first five words of both Hs xii 10 and Hs xiii 4 the Peshitta inserts ܐܪܥܐ ܕܡܨܪܝܢ before מארץ מצרים, and similar insertions are made in LXX and T; these again are natural interpretative expansions, and there is no reason to suspect their derivation from a distinctive Hebrew *Vorlage*.

There is even less reason to suspect the existence of a Hebrew *Vorlage* distinct from MT behind the further agreements between the versions which we now list. Dependence on a common tradition of interpretation seems by far the most likely explanation of these agreements. We consider first some interpretative syntactical modifications. In Hs xi 1 the initial כי is rendered twice in the Peshitta: ܟܕ ܓܝܪ. The first of these renderings ('because') is common to LXX V and T, while the second ('when') is peculiar to the Peshitta and may be thought more appropriate to the context. LXX V and the Peshitta agree in taking the last word of Ob 9 with the following verse. In Ob 21 LXX A Th and the Peshitta interpret משעים as a passive rather than an active with S V and T in agreement with the Masoretic pointing. In Mi ii 12 הדברו is rendered ܪܕܝܗܘܢ in the Peshitta in essential agreement with LXX V and T, despite the anomalous combination of the article and a pronominal suffix in the interpretation of the Hebrew which this presupposes. In Mi vii 8 אור is paraphrased ܡܚܘܝܢ in the Peshitta in agreement with LXX and T.

The interpretation of שב in Na ii 3 in a transitive sense as if it were a Hiph'il is common to LXX V T and the Peshitta and may be held to be implicit in the use of את in MT.

The remaining agreed interpretations are of a lexical nature. The obscure עושו at the beginning of Jl iv 11 is interpreted by LXX T and the Peshitta in the sense 'assemble'. The obscure מזור in Ob 7 is interpreted by LXX V and the Peshitta as an 'ambush'. The rendering of the obscure נעלמה in Na iii 11 in the Peshitta as ܥܠܬܐ is similar to that of LXX and V. The rendering of the proper name Shinar in Sa v 11 as Babylon is common to LXX T and the Peshitta, although the Peshitta renders it ܣܢܥܪ in Genesis x 10, xi 2, xiv 1, 9 and Daniel i 2. In Sa xii 8 הנכשל is interpreted in the Peshitta as ܕܢܨܚܘܢ in common with LXX and T. In Sa xiv 20 the ἅπαξ λεγόμενον מצלות is rendered ܦܓܘܕܬܗܘܢ ('bridle') in agreement with LXX and V. In Ml i 3 תנות is rendered ܢܕܪܐ, and this interpretation is probably that of LXX (if δόματα = δώματα as Rudolph suggests) and is certainly found in Ms c of T. The interpretation of התרומה in Ml iii 8 as the more specific 'firstfruits' is common to LXX V and the Peshitta.

Finally we may note the treatment of the obscure פארור which occurs in the Hebrew Bible only at Jl ii 6 and Na ii 11. In both passages the Peshitta paraphrases without specifically rendering the verb קבצו (*cf* p. 133 *supra*); its rendering of the last four words of Jl ii 6 is ܩܕܡ ܐܦܝ̈ܗܘܢ ܐܝܟ ܐܘܟܡܘܬܐ ܕܩܕܪܐ, and its rendering of the last four words of Na ii 11 is ܘܐܦ̈ܐ ܕܟܠܗܘܢ ܐܝܟ ܐܘܟܡܐ ܕܩܕܪܐ. The use of ܩܕܪܐ suggests confusion with פרור ('a pot'), while ܐܘܟܡܐ ('blackness, soot') probably represents an attempt to wrest sense from such an identification by drawing attention to a colouring which might serve as a point of comparison between faces and pots! At all events this interpretation agrees with that of LXX (ὡχ πρόσκαυμα χύτρας), V (*in ollam, sicut nigredo ollae*) and T (אכרום אוכמין כקדרא). Clearly a common exegetical tradition underlies all these renderings.

None of the agreements between LXX and the Peshitta reviewed in this section, whether or not supported by any other version, have been found to point with any probability to the existence of a Hebrew *Vorlage* distinct from MT. They do serve however to draw attention not only to the direct influence of LXX on V and the Peshitta, but also to the presence of certain common traditions of interpretation which are to be found even in versions which are not likely to have been connected by any direct influence, such as LXX and T.

It remains only to consider briefly the question whether any special affinity can be traced between the Peshiṭta and any particular recension or individual Ms of the LXX of the Dodekapropheton. We have already observed (*cf* pp 117f. *supra*) that there is no reason to suppose any direct link between 8ḤevXII gr and the Peshiṭta. There is however one curious exclusive agreement between the Peshiṭta of Jon iv 10 and the citation of the Greek text of this passage in Justin, *Dialogue with Trypho* cvii 4. This concerns the addition of αὐτοῦ to the phrase ὑπὸ νύκτα on both occasions, and the double rendering ܒܗ ܠܠܝܐ in the Peshiṭta. The only other evidence for the suffix is in Syh, which reads it only on the second occasion, reading ܠܠܝܐ in the emphatic state on the first.

Within the LXX tradition a special affinity has often been noted between the Lucianic readings and the Peshiṭta (*cf* JELLICOE, p. 346). Among such agreements in the Dodekapropheton may be noted the recognition of the name of the deity Milcom at Am i 15 and Zf i 5 (*cf* pp 124, 148 *supra*), the preposition *lamadh* in ܘܠܡܘܪܬܐ in Am v 16 which may however be purely stylistic, the addition of the suffix in ܚܠܕܬܚܒܪ in Na iii 11 which Theodotion also reflects, and the *pl* וידעתם in Sa iv 9 (p. 120 *supra*), which is also found in a Cairo Geniza Hebrew Ms as well as in V and T. Other agreements with LXX^L may be found at Hs xiii 13 (p. 122 *supra*), Sa iv 2 (p. 120 *supra*), Sa vi 11 (p. 121 *supra*) and Sa x 7 (p. 135 *supra*), but in none of these passages is the LXX reading purely Lucianic.

Agreements between the Peshiṭta and the Catena recension of LXX are to be found at Sa xii 13 (pp 121, 169) and, in agreement with LXX^L, at Hs xiii 13 and Sa vi 11 (*v. supra*); against these however must be set agreements between LXX and the Peshiṭta against MT at Hb i 13 and Sa viii 17 (p. 135 *supra*) where the Catena Mss agree with MT.

Agreements between the Peshiṭta and individual LXX^{Mss} may be found at Sa i 16 (LXX^A, p. 121 *supra*) and Sa xii 7 (LXX^Q, p. 135 *supra*), but the first of these readings is found also in one Hebrew Ms and the second is found also in T. Two further agreements between the Peshiṭta and LXX^Q have been noted, one at Sa iii 3 (p. 135 *supra*) in conjunction with LXX^W and LXX^V (which also shares the Lucianic reading at Sa x 7 noted above) and the other at Sa x 1 in conjunction with LXX^W and LXX^A, where these three LXX Mss and the Peshiṭta invert the order of the Hebrew words מיהוה מטר.

The most striking agreements however are to be found between the Peshiṭta and the Barberini LXX text of Hb iii 9, 14. In addition to those already noted on pp 116, 124 and 143 we may observe the interpretation of מטות in v. 9 in the sense of 'arrows, bolts' and perhaps also the rendering of כמו־לאכל in v. 14 by ἕνεκεν τοῦ καταφαγεῖν/ܕܢܐܟܠܘܢ. Most of these agreements are in matters of interpretation rather than of text, but the relation of τοὺς πεποιθότας/ܪܫܐ ܕܚܝܠܬܢܐ to יסערו להפיצני in v. 14 (p. 116 *supra*) remains obscure.

Very few of these agreements between the Peshitta and individual LXX Mss or recensions are exclusive, and in many cases they may be due to a distinctive Hebrew *Vorlage*, dependence on a common exegetical tradition or independent editorial activity on the part of translators or copyists rather than to the direct influence of a particular LXX reading on the Peshitta translators. The slightly greater degree of agreement with LXX^L than with any other LXX recension or individual Ms is only to be expected for geographical if for no other reasons, while none of the cases listed is sufficient to establish proof of dependence specifically on LXX^L on the part of the Peshitta translators or conversely of the use of the Peshitta by LXX^L. The only striking agreements are those with Justin's citation of Jon iv 10 and the Barberini LXX text of Hb iii 9, 14.

Assimilation to LXX has also given rise to some of the variants within the Peshitta tradition. We may instance readings nos 9, 16 and 36 in chapter 3 (*cf* pp 70f., 167), in each of which the standard text of the Peshitta seems to have been assimilated to LXX, and also agreements with LXX noted in some of the readings of individual Mss such as 9a1 (p. 83), though it is often impossible to distinguish agreements with LXX from those with Syh.

The evidence reviewed in this section thus corroborates and complements the picture of the relationship between LXX and the Peshitta which has already emerged in the earlier sections of this chapter, without yielding any further instances of agreement between the two versions which might with any probability suggest derivation from a Hebrew *Vorlage* distinct from MT.

5. Conclusion

Many of the specific agreements between LXX and the Peshitta which have been examined in this chapter are patient of more than one interpretation, but a fairly clear general picture of the relationship between the two versions has emerged. The many passages in which

LXX is more distant from MT than the Peshitta prove that the latter is a translation of the Hebrew text, while the existence of a number of Peshitta renderings which are explicable only by reference to LXX prove that the Peshitta translators made use of LXX. While the Peshitta is more often in agreement with Lucianic readings than with those of any other recension or individual Ms of LXX, in no case is the agreement of such a nature as to prove dependence of the Peshitta translators on a specifically Lucianic recension of LXX. The striking agreements are those with Justin's quotation of Jon iv 10 and the Barberini LXX text of Hb iii 9, 14.

The Peshitta translators seem to have turned to LXX frequently though not consistently for help in understanding the Hebrew text which they were attempting to translate, and the fact that they needed to do so constitutes additional evidence of the limitations both of their knowledge of biblical Hebrew and of their own understanding of the text of the Dodekapropheton. No agreements between the two versions were found additional to those examined in chapter 5 which point with any probability to the existence of a common Hebrew *Vorlage* distinct from MT. The chief importance of the Peshitta thus lies in the history of exegesis rather than in the evidence it affords for the establishment of the Hebrew text (*cf* LANE).

8
The Peshiṭta and the Targum

1. Introduction

Despite the many uncertainties attending the exact content of the LXX text known to the Peshiṭta translators there is no doubt that they had access to a written text of LXX. One of the major difficulties attending any examination of a possible relationship between the Peshiṭta of the Dodekapropheton and the Targum is that of identifying what if any Targum text was accessible to the Peshiṭta translators. There has moreover been a massive development in Targumic studies during the last quarter of a century, and it is impracticable to enter here into any detailed investigation of Targumic origins. All that is attempted in this chapter is a brief comparison of the Peshiṭta of the Dodekapropheton with the text of Targum Jonathan in SPERBER's edition to examine the nature of agreements between the two versions and to consider what inferences may reasonably be drawn from them. A few preliminary remarks however are necessary.

It is clear from the Mishnah (Megillah iv 4) that the Targums originated in the context of the worship of the Synagogue, where a running oral translation was made into the vernacular Aramaic of the Hebrew Scriptures read during the service. In the nature of the case it is hardly possible to envisage a fixed original text of the Targum which came to be written down at a later stage. Internal evidence supports the inference from general probability that the written Targums represent the culmination of a process of editorial work, and contain strata of different age. CHILTON gives a useful summary of recent discussion of the highly complex problem of the date and provenance of Targum Jonathan, and concludes that the Targum of Isaiah, with which he is primarily concerned, contains two levels of interpretation (Tannaitic and Amoraic), the earlier level being subdivided into material earlier and later than A.D. 70. In an appendix Chilton investigates the theme of 'Messiah' in the remaining Targums of the Latter Prophets, tentatively suggesting that the Hosea and Micah Targums may represent a later and the Habakkuk and Zechariah Targums an earlier period than the earlier stratum of the Isaiah Targum. GORDON had earlier inferred a basic date before A.D. 70 for the Targums of Nahum–Malachi on the basis of seven passages (Na i 9, Hb iii 17, Sa viii 19, xi 1, xii 11, Ml i 11, iii 6). The most therefore that can be said at present is that there is a fair possibility that at least some strata in Targum Jonathan on the Dodekapropheton derive from a period before A.D. 70, in which case the possibility exists that the renderings enshrined in them may have been accessible to the Peshitta translators. The relative dates of the two versions, so far as they can be approximately determined, thus allow at least the theoretical possibility of direct influence of either version on the other. On the one hand the emerging Targum, whether still oral or already in an incipient written stage, may have influenced the Peshitta translators in forming their own version; on the other hand the written text of the Peshitta may have influenced the formation of the later strata within the Targum. In the main however it is more probable that we should think in terms of common familiarity with particular exegetical traditions rather than of the direct influence of a written text, not least because of the relative paucity of exact verbal agreement between the two versions.

It is in any case only to be expected that there would be considerable agreement between the Targum and the Peshitta even if there were no direct link between them. Translations made into dialects of the same language at approximately the same period might indeed have been expected quite independently of each other to have produced almost identical versions rather more often than is in fact the case. As we shall see many of the agreements are the result of the application of similar translation methods, which we have already examined in the case of the Peshitta in Chapter 6. Agreements of this kind hardly constitute evidence for a direct relationship between the two versions. Lexical agreements in the rendering of particular Hebrew words may also be coincidental, though they may also have at least the potential value of throwing light on the meaning of an obscure Hebrew term. The strongest evidence for a connection, direct or indirect, between the two versions arises from passages where they present a common exegesis, though even here the lack of sustained verbal agreement and the occasional appearance of the same exegesis in another version often makes it more probable that the connection is indirect, consisting of mutual dependence on common exegetical traditions. In the following sections of this chapter agreements between the two versions will be examined broadly under these three categories, though it is sometimes difficult to differentiate clearly between them. The question whether such agreements indicate derivation from a common Hebrew *Vorlage* distinct from MT must generally be answered in the negative, though this possibility will be considered in a few cases. All the probable cases of such a basis for agreements between the two versions have already been examined in Chapter 5.

The Peshitta's independence of the Targum may be illustrated by two passages in Micah. As we have already seen (p. 144 *supra*) the Peshitta translators failed to recognize the Hebrew idiom of the last four words of Mi ii 1; the Targum however has understood the clause correctly, and had the Peshitta translators been following the Targum at this point it would have helped them to make sense of their Hebrew *Vorlage*. At Mi iii 11 both versions employ the participle ܡܚܠܦ, but the Peshitta applies it to the priests and the Targum to the prophets, each version using the term cognate to the respective Hebrew to render the other verb. As in the case of the LXX independence in one passage by no means precludes dependence in another, but these examples, which could be multiplied almost indefinitely, demonstrate that there is no close and continuous relationship between the two versions.

2. Stylistic modifications

In this section we shall be concerned with minor modifications, mainly of a grammatical or syntactical nature, which do not greatly affect the sense, and which belong to the same general kind as those discussed in Chapter 6, section 1. Most of those considered here are exclusively common to the Targum and the Peshitta.

We may begin with participles and prepositions. The introduction of כען/ܗܫܐ in Hs ix 9 serves to link the two halves of the verse more closely; assimilation to viii 13 may also have been a factor. The introduction of כען/ܗܫܐ in Hs xiii 14 may be regarded as similar. The substitution of ܘ ܥܠ for the *waw consecutive* of וישימו in Sa vii 14 similarly makes the sequence of thought clearer. A more substantial modification is that of the repeated כי ... כי in Mi v 5 into ܘ... ܐܠܐ ולא ... ולא/ܘܠܐ; this takes up the conditional sense implicit in the Hebrew כי ('when, if') and enhances the effectiveness of the divine protection promised in the first part of the verse by making it clear that the Assyrians will not even gain entry into Israelite territory. Prepositions are introduced at Am v 8 (*lamadh* before ܠܐܠܠ, *cf* LXX), Jon iii 9 (ܥܠ with suffix, in consequence of the interpretation of נחם as 'be compassionate', *cf* pp 152f. *supra*) and Sa ix 15 (*beth* in place of the construct relation of אבני־קלע). Modification of prepositions occurs at Hs xii 11 (ܚܡ for על), Mi vii 17 (ܒ for אל) and Sa ix 7 (*dalath* for *beth*).

We turn next to modifications of mood, number and person in verbs and nouns. Both versions seem to have vocalized תמטיר towards the end of Am iv 7 as a Niph'al rather than a Hiph'il and paraphrased accordingly; this could well have arisen by assimilation to the previous תִּמָּטֵר. In Mi i 7 both versions in company with the Vulgate render קבצה by a passive. Conversely ובאו in Hg ii 7 is rendered transitively as if the verb were a Hiph'il. A 1 *sg* (ואעשר) is modified to 3 *masc sg* in Sa xi 5 (and a 1 *pl* suffix added). Plural nouns are modified to the singular in Hs xiii 10 (שפטיך, possibly in assimilation to the previous מלכך), Zf i 10 (הגבעות) and Sa xiii 2 (שמות). Conversely singulars are rendered in the plural in Na ii 4 (the first three words, in agreement with Symmachus) and Na iii 2 (אופן, in agreement with LXX). Further modifications of singular into plural occur at Hg ii 19 (the verb נשא, in agreement with LXX), Ml i 4 (where 'Edom' is rendered 'the Edomites' and the accompanying verb is made plural) and Ml iii 18 (the four general classes). Suffixes are added at Hs vi 7 (ܥܒܕܝ), Mi v 5 (ܥܡܗܝ), Sa xiv 5 (ܡܕܥܟܗ, in agreement with Basilius Neopatrensis, *cit* ZIEGLER) and Ml i 13 (ܗܢܘܢ), and omitted at Jon i 3 (שכרה), Sa xi 10 (בריתי) and Sa xiv 5 (הרי).

Turning to more specifically synactical modifications we note the replacement of the slightly awkward nouns with suffixes (טובו ... יפיו) at Sa ix 17 with adjectives, the introduction of ܒ/ܐܝܟ before (ܐ)ܝܟ in Sa ii 9 to make it clear that this is a simile, and the avoidance of a rhetorical question by the replacement of מי with ܠܐ at Mi vii 18. Verbs are introduced at Mi ii 1 (ܚܡܕܝܢ), Ml i 6 (ܢܣܠܝ ... ܚܡܢܝ), Ml ii 17 (עביד/ܐܢ, avoiding the construct relationship in MT's אלהי המשפט) and Ml iii 10 (ܐܠܗܐܘܗܝ, replacing בלי). The last of these is a substantial and striking modification.

Two further stylistic modifications claim our attention. A characteristic of Malachi is the series of disputations between the prophet and his hearers, in which he anticipates their objections with the *waw consecutive* ואמרתם, "and if you say..." in order to refute them before his hearers have a chance to voice them. This idiom occurs in Ml i 2, 6, 7, 13, ii 14, 17, iii 7, 8, 13, and the Targum uniformly renders ואם תימרון, while the Peshitta generally renders ܘܐܢ ܐܡܪܝܢ ܐܢܬܘܢ, but in i 2, 13 simply ܘܐܡܪܝܢ ܐܢܬܘܢ. GORDON infers that the Peshitta is dependent on the Targum and that this dependence is literary, but it may be argued that the explicit recognition of the conditional note in a recurrent phrase could have arisen independently in the two versions, and that the Peshitta's preference for the participal construction and its failure to use the conditional particle ܐܢ in two of the passages discount the probability of at any rate literary dependence.

The Targum has a tendency to insert בית before the proper names Israel, Judah, etc. when used in a tribal sense (cf SPERBER, vol IV B, p. 346 ad Mi i 5), and this is occasionally found also in the Peshitta. In Mi i 5 the Peshitta, like MT, reads בית only before Israel, while the Targum adds it also before Jacob (twice) and Judah. In Am vii 16 MT reads בית only before Isaac, while both Targum and Peshitta add it also before the preceding Israel, though this could easily have arisen through independent assimilation to the following clause. A similar instance, paralleled in LXX^Q, at Sa xii 7 (where assimilation to the earlier 'house of David' may be a factor) has already been noted at p. 135 *supra*. A further complication is that the Targum characteristically prefixes בית in phrases denoting tribe or nation with the preposition *dalath*, a practice which is sometimes but much less frequently found in the Peshitta. Unusually the Peshitta has *dalath* twice in Am vii 16 and the Targum not at all, and twice in Sa xii 7 where the Targum has it only at the second occurrence. Some other passages where the Peshitta has *dalath* are: Hs i 4, 6 (Israel), Hs v 12, 14 (Judah), Ob 17 (Jacob), Sa x 6 (Joseph), Sa xii 10, xiii 1 (David), the Targum agreeing in all but the first two and last two cases. Variants have also arisen in the Mss over this practice. For instance 7a1 adds a *dalath* at Hs v 1 (Israel) and Am v 6 (Bethel), and omits *dalath* in company with 6h9 (reading no 80 in Chapter 3) at Sa viii 15 (Judah). This reinforces the impression that the addition of *dalath* is a merely stylistic device, found in various passages in both versions, but occurring quite independently.

The nature of the modifications considered in this section is such that they reflect the idiom of Aramaic-Syriac, and it is only to be expected that similar modifications of this kind would arise in both Targum and Peshitta at numerous points. The frequent lack of verbal identity between the two versions weakens any hypothesis of direct dependence of one version on the other. The most suggestive instances are those where the modification is striking and substantial (as in Ml iii 10) or where it results in a modification of the actual sense of the passage (as in Mi v 5). In these passages there may well be at least dependence on the part of both versions on a common exegetical tradition.

3. Lexical agreements

A high incidence in the vocabulary used by the Targum and the Peshitta to render the same Hebrew *Vorlage* is to be expected, and the use for instance of ܦܝܓܐ in both versions to render אפיקי in Jl i 20 should not therefore be regarded as a significant agreement between the two versions. Earlier in the same chapter (v. 4) there is an interesting difference between the two versions in the nouns used to render the four kinds of locusts (*cf supra* pp 140f.). This may be set out in tabular form:

MT	Targum	Peshitta
גזם	זחלא	ܙܚܠܐ
ארבה	גובא	ܩܡܨܐ
ילק	פרחא	(ܩܡܨܐ) ܐܝܠ
חסיל	שמוטא	ܓܙܪܐ

Not only does the Targum employ two terms which are foreign to the Syriac dialect, but it employs the two terms which are common to the two versions to interpret different terms in the Hebrew. Nor is the Targum as consistent as the Peshitta, for in Na iii 15 f. it uses two distinct terms (**זחלא** twice and **קמצא**) to render the Hebrew ילק, for which it had used **פרחא** in Jl i 4. One can only conclude that the two versions are independent in their treatment of the nouns denoting different kinds of locusts.

A number of lexical agreements may reflect a common style of translation rather than the direct influence of one version on the other. For instance, a preference for an ordinary rather than an obscure or technical word may account for the common rendering of מניף in Sa ii 13 by ܩܪܒ, to which the Vulgate's *levo* may also be compared. A more striking agreement is the weakening of the specific notion of 'kindling' the altar in Ml i 10 to the more general 'offering' upon it, but this too could have resulted from the independent use of the same method and style of translation. Somewhat similar is the double avoidance of metaphor in Sa x 11, where both versions render the verb הורד by the root ܢܚܬ and the noun שבט by the abstract ܫܘܠܛܢܐ, though in this case the double agreement may be felt to point more strongly to a direct relationship between the two versions. Both versions also use ܢܚܬ to render the more specifc אשבור in Hs ii 20, and this does not therefore necessarily point to a common Hebrew *Vorlage* אשבית as suggested by Sebök. Another example of agreement between the versions which may rest on the characteristic practice of each is the use of the root ܟܢܫ to render קבץ in Jl iv 11, Mi ii 12 and Mi iv 6; in each of these passages the two versions have already used ܚܒܪ, which might be felt more appropriate, to render another word earlier in the verse. In none of the agreements reviewed in this paragraph can the case for the direct influence of one version on the other be said to be strong; the most suggestive instances are Ml i 10 and Sa x 11, but in neither of these can the possibility of coincidental agreement be excluded.

Some further examples may be listed. The use of the root ܥܠ for נכמרו in Hs xi 8, of ܚܒܪ for הנעותי in Am ix 9, of ܣܘܦ for קצות in Hb ii 10 (*cf* also p. 124 *supra*), of the Aph'el of ܩܘܡ for ידרכני in Hb iii 19 and of ܢܣܒ for נשא in Hg ii 19 may well have arisen independently in the two versions. The choice of ܐܓܪܝ/ܐܓܪܝ to render אשלח in Sa viii 10 may well have been occasioned by the desire to provide an assonance with ܐܓܪܐ earlier in the verse; this is certainly a more significant agreement. Agreements in imprecise renderings of nouns include ܘܐܕܐ for שריך in Am v 23, ܡܫܚܠܛܐ/ܦܛܡܝܢ for כרים in Am vi 4 and ܚܠܐ for פתחי in Mi vii 5.

A further possible cause of lexical agreement is the common confusion of two similar Hebrew roots, *cf* pp 143f. *supra*. To the examples listed there may be added two further exclusive agreements between the Targum and the Peshiṭta:

Jl iv 11   נחת 'go down'—חתת 'be shattered'
Ml i 4   רשש 'beat down'—רוש 'be in want'

Less specific examples may also be found. The use of ܘܡܐ to render ותמוג in Am ix 5 finds an indirect parallel in LXX καὶ σαλεύων αὐτήν. In Ob 5 נדמיתה seems to have been derived by both versions from דמה 'be silent' (so V), though different Aramaic/Syriac roots are used, and this has resulted in the rendering of the following הלוא¹° by עד/ܥܕܡܐ ܕ. The verbal disagreement in this passage suggests a common but independent interpretation of the Hebrew. In Na i 10 סירים has been read as if it were סרים = שרים, though again the renderings do not agree verbally.

There are a number of agreements between the two versions which are most probably to be explained as reflecting a common tradition of interpretation of particular Hebrew words. Three of these may be paralleled in the Vulgate: the interpretation of מעוז in Na iii 11 in the sense 'help', of ברורה in Zf iii 9 in the sense 'chosen' (inappropriate in this context), and of חרף in Sa xiv 8 as 'winter' rather than 'autumn'; in the first two of these the Targum and Peshitta use different roots to express their common interpretation. In Na iii 18 both versions employ ܟܢܫ to render נפשו; this has sometimes been thought to indicate confusion with the root פוץ, but it may equally reflect knowledge of the true meaning of the Hebrew (cf RUDOLPH). The common use of the root ܣܚܦ to render קדרנית in Ml iii 14 may simply be a guess. In several other passages the versions differ verbally in expressing a common interpretation: they both understand שאה in Zf i 15 as meaning 'tumult, confusion', the root עלז in Zf ii 15 and Zf iii 11 as meaning 'strong' and the obscure גרמו in Zf iii 3 as meaning 'wait'; the last may again be simply a guess.

Finally we note a few more suggestive agreements. The double agreement in Hs vi 1, where טרף is rendered by ܚܒܠ and יך by ܐܬܟ, is the more striking in that ܚܒܠ would be the natural equivalent of יך. In Hs vii 13 the exclamation שד להם is paraphrased ܒܚܘܬ ܐܬܝ ܥܠܝܗܘܢ/בזחין איתי עליהון ܐܬܘܬܐ ܠܗܘܢ; the insertion of ܐܬܘܬܐ is peculiar to these two versions, and one is tempted to speculate whether the Peshitta's ܒܚܘܬ may be a corruption of ܒܚܘܬ, in which case the double agreement would be more striking. It is worth noting that the two versions agree in using the root ܒܙ to render ישדד in Hs x 2. Curiously they also agree in a common rendering of שד 1° at Am v 9, though this time by the root ܢܒܠ, where they also agree in interpreting the obscure המבליג in the improbable sense 'cause to triumph over', though their renderings of the second half of the verse are quite different. The interpretation of חיל in Sa ix 4 as 'wealth' has also occasioned the rendering of הכה by ܢܣܒ; once again the double agreement may suggest a closer relationship between the two versions.

In none of the passages reviewed in this section can the agreement between the two versions be held to prove a direct dependence of one on the other. The most suggestive instances are those where there is a double agreement in a single passage in an interpretation peculiar to these two versions (Hs vi 1, Am v 9, Sa ix 4, x 11 and possibly Hs vii 13), or a single exclusive agreement of a striking nature (Ml i 10). On the other hand the not infrequent verbal disagreement in rendering a common interpretation suggests dependence on a common tradition of interpretation rather than the direct influence of one version on the other.

4. Exegetical Traditions

It is in the area of exegesis that agreements between the Targum and the Peshiṭta are likely to be most significant, and to these we now turn. One of the characteristic features of the Targum is the paraphrastic gloss, though it is probable that the more expansive and midrashic examples derive from the later strata in the Targum. Three instances, where the Peshiṭta does not follow suit, will illustrate the point: the universal scope of Yahweh's kingdom in Ob 21, the introduction of the Messiah in Mi iv 8 and the expansion of the reference to Moses, Aaron and Miriam in Mi vi 4. There are however a number of passages where the two versions agree in simple modifications or insertions of an exegetical nature. At a simple level there are agreements in identification, such as the rendering of ספרד in Ob 20 as 'Spain' and of הדד־רמון in Sa xii 11 as ܟܕ ܐܟܣ, i.e. Josiah, who is actually named in the Targum, where further paraphrastic details are supplied. These certainly suggest dependence on a common exegetical tradition. Among modest expansions to clarify the sense we may note the additions of ܡܝܐ in Hs ii 10, ܕܓܘܠܐ ܠܢ in Hs ii 11 and ܣܩܬܐ in Jl iv 4. These two versions are accompanied by Aquila only in their recognition of the *beth pretii* in בזונה in Jl iv 3, where they both clarify the sense by expanding the *beth* into ܒܐܓܪ.

A few explanatory or expansive glosses of this nature, peculiar to the Peshiṭta and not previously noted, are:

Hs iv 16   ܡܢ ܫܠܝ
Am ii 10   ܘܐܘܒܠܬܟܘܢ ܐܪܥܐ ܗܝ
Am iii 2   ܡܢ ܟܠܗܘܢ ܫܒܛܐ ܕ
Am ix 11   ܘܐܩܝܡ ܡܫܟܢܗ ܕܢܦܝܠ
Mi iv 7   ܘܒܐܘܪܫܠܡ
Zf ii 10   ܥܠ ܐܠܗܐ

The chief significance of these glosses is their confirmation that this characteristic of the Targumist was also to be found in the Peshiṭta translators even if less frequently, and it is therefore possible that some agreements at least between the two versions in such glosses may be coincidental.

Turning now to questions of interpretation, we note a few suggestive agreements between the Targum and Peshitta in this area. In Hb i 2 the prophet's exclamation חמס is rendered indirectly ܡܢ ܚܛܘܦܐ, 'on account of (the) extortioners', a paraphrase which, as SEBÖK points out, occurs also in both versions in the similar passage at Jeremiah xx 8. In Hb iii 9 it is perhaps hardly surprising that both versions render אמר by ܐܡܪܝܢ, where the suffix has no basis in the Hebrew, and at least in the Targum the use of this term with the suffix may have theological overtones of the Memra.

An interesting example is to be found in the treatment of בלי הפוכה at the end of Hs vii 8. The Peshitta renders ܕܠܐ ܐܬܐܟܠ ܐܟܘܠܬܐ, 'which is eaten before it is fully baked', losing sight altogether of the concept of 'turning' the cake. The Targum however renders דעד לא אתאכלת אתהפכת, although several Mss reverse the order of the last two words, probably correctly. This then would mean 'which is eaten before it is turned over', a rendering much closer to the Hebrew. One is tempted to speculate whether the Peshitta's ܐܟܘܠܬܐ is a corruption of ܐܬܗܦܟܬ, but its reading is perfectly intelligible as it stands and may simply be a rather free translation.

The first six words of Hs xii 12 are far from easy to construe. The Targum retains the opening אם and renders אך by ברם, while the Peshitta omits both particles. Both versions prefix the preposition *beth* to the place-name Gilead. The Peshitta interprets און in the sense of 'trouble, sorrow' rather than 'wickedness', while the Targum replaces it with a *nomen agentis* אנוסין, 'oppressors', which at least bears some graphical similarity to the Hebrew. Both versions take שוא with the following clause, prefixing the preposition *lamadh*: "in Gilgal you/they sacrificed oxen to vanity/idols". The Peshitta omits the verb היו altogether, while the Targum takes it before the previous two words and in conjunction with און. The agreement between the two versions is thus confined to the construction of שוא with the following clause, ignoring the intervening היו, and the addition of the prepositions *beth* and *lamadh*. This suggests at most dependence at these points on a common exegetical tradition, and is hardly compatible with a theory of literary dependence.

At Sa xi 17 MT describes the shepherd as האליל, a reading which appears to be corroborated by LXX and V. The Targum however renders it by טפשא, and the Peshiṭta by ܟܒܗܐ, in each case using the same term as that with which אולי had been rendered at the end of v. 15. It is of course possible that they had a common *Vorlage* האולי, but it seems more probable that they independently 'emended' their text or simply interpreted it by assimilation to v. 15. The fact that they used different equivalents again militates against the theory of literary dependence; this modification could have occurred independently in the two versions, or it may have arisen from a common exegetical tradition.

These last two passages have brought us finally to the category of common modifications of the Hebrew text. Seven further passages fall to be considered here.

In Hs vii 11 קראו is rendered אתקרבו in the Targum and ܐܬܐ in the Peshiṭta, and SEBÖK conjectures a Hebrew *Vorlage* קרבו. This is in fact unlikely, because neither version offers a straightforward rendering of such a *Vorlage*, and it is in any case improbable in the context. The Targum renders the following הלכו by גלו, suggesting a paraphrastic approach to the passage, and its rendering of קראו by אתקרבו might be explained in more than one way. It might simply be the result of misreading the *Vorlage*, or it might be intended as a suggestion that קראו might be interpreted in a special sense 'claim relationship' as an allusion to the political intrigues of Israel with Egypt. The reading of the Peshiṭta on the other hand seems to be merely a simplification of the text, based on assimilation to the following הלכו which it renders straightforwardly by ܐܙܠܘ. No link between the two versions seems likely in this passage.

At the end of Jl i 10 the failure of corn, must and oil is lamented. The Targum and Peshiṭta agree in the strange replacement of 'oil' by 'olive trees' and the consequent rendering of the accompanying verb in the plural, though they use different roots for the verb. In Am iv 2 the two versions agree in rendering the final דוגה by 'hunters' (though the Targum has rendered the preceding סירות by דגוגית ('fisher-boat'). In Mi vii 5 the pair רע ... אלוף becomes in both versions רחים ... קריב, although קריב might be thought a more natural equivalent of רע. LXX however renders רע by φίλοις and V by *amico*, while both versions interpret אלוף as 'leader'. The Targum and Peshiṭta are alone in interpreting אלוף as 'neighbour'.

At Sa xiv 4 both Targum and Peshiṭta omit the phrase ביום־ההוא, and it is just possible that they reflect a *Vorlage* without this phrase, since the eleventh century Judah ben Balaam records that it was omitted by the Babylonians (*cit* CERIANI, p. 17; *cf* also SAEBØ *ad loc*). On the other hand the phrase interrupts the natural sequence of thought where it occurs, and it is to be found several times in the same context (vv 6, 8, 9). It is possible that the Targum (if R represents the original text) and Peshiṭta translators felt that it could be omitted without loss in v. 4, and that its omission would clarify and improve the flow of the prophecy. The omission is certainly not uncharacteristic of the Peshiṭta (*cf* pp 133f., 146 *supra*).

Two striking modifications are to be found in Ml ii. In v. 12 the obscure ער וענה is rendered inexplicably ܒܪ ܘܒܪ ܒܪ/ܒܪܐ ܘܒܪ ܒܪܗ. Literary dependence is unlikely because the Targum has recognized the force of the preposition *lamadh* in the preceding לאיש, while the Peshiṭta has misinterpreted it as a *nota accusativi*, hence its repetition and the additional copula in the phrase with which we are concerned. The interpretation of the two nouns as denoting son and grandson is however peculiar to the Targum and Peshiṭta and must surely rest on a common exegetical tradition. The other striking modification occurs in v. 16 of the same chapter and consists in the insertion of the negative ܠܐ before the rendering of כסה, resulting in exactly the opposite sense from that of the Hebrew. This again very probably rests on a common exegetical tradition.

Some of the passages considered in this section point strongly to dependence of the Targum and Peshiṭta on a common exegetical tradition, but the very limited extent of verbal agreement between the two versions makes it hazardous to think in terms of a direct literary relationship between them. Dependence on a common Hebrew *Vorlage* distinct from MT is possible at Sa xi 17 and xiv 4, but in neither case does the evidence point strongly to such a conclusion.

5. Conclusion

Our soundings in the agreements between Targum Jonathan and the Peshiṭta have produced little in the way of firm conclusions. There has been no compelling evidence of a dependence of either version on the other, and no further agreements have been found to derive with any great probability from a common Hebrew *Vorlage* distinct from MT. On the other hand there have been not a few suggestive agreements between the two versions, which point to a certain similarity of method and approach on the part of the translators and, more significantly, to a probable dependence on common exegetical traditions. This is probably as much as we can hope to conclude from our soundings in the present state of Targum and Peshitta studies, but it does tend to confirm the hypothesis of a Jewish rather than a Christian origin of the Peshitta of the Dodekapropheton, without providing any decisive evidence to prove this hypothesis.

Note. Two readings of 7a1 involving diacritic points result in agreements with the Targum. The reading ܕܢܟܒܪ in place of ܕܢܟܒܪ at Am v 17 we have already judged (pp 78f. *supra*) to be most probably an inner-Syriac corruption; it is found in no other Ms earlier than the seventeenth century, while the reading of the standard text is found in 7k10 and 8a1. The paraphrastic rendering of the Targum clearly presupposes a *daleth* in place of the *resh* in the Hebrew, but there is no further connection between 7a1 and the Targum in this verse, and this agreement is most probably coincidental. In Zf iii 15 7a1 has a diacritic point above ܕܢܟܬܒ, indicating the meaning 'judges' rather than 'judgements', as already noted in the Introduction to the EDITION. The earliest Ms to share this point is 13d1; 8a1 has the diacritic point below the word to indicate the meaning 'judgements', while 6h9 has no diacritic point at all. The Targum also interprets the word as 'judges', though it adds 'of falsehood'. Once again in the absence of any further link between 7a1 and the Targum in this verse we must regard this agreement as a coincidence.

9
The Origins of the Peshitta

It is well known that already in the time of Theodore of Mopsuestia there was no tradition relating to the origins of the Peshitta version of the Old Testament (*cf* Theodore's Commentary on Zf i 5, JELLICOE, p. 247 and WEITZMAN, pp. 277f.). It is not our purpose here to trace the history of the modern debate about this question, but rather to summarize the bearing on it of the researches carried out in Part 2 of this monograph. In the nature of the case we cannot expect conclusive evidence for the date or milieu of the version, but it is to be hoped that the conclusions which we have been able to reach will contribute something to the quest for the origins of the Peshitta.

The chief interest of the ordinary Old Testament scholar in the Peshitta is in its potential value as a witness to the Hebrew text. Accordingly we made it our first business in Chapter 5 to explore the alignment of the Peshitta in passages where actual variant readings are attested within the transmission of the Hebrew text. Only five passages were found where the Peshitta presupposes a significant extant non-Masoretic reading; they are listed on p. 118, the most important being the two striking agreements with 1QpHab in Hb i 5 and ii 16, though even here we must allow for the possibility that the Peshitta reading derives from the LXX rather than from a Hebrew *Vorlage* in agreement with 1QpHab.

The general result of our analysis in Chapter 5 was that the Hebrew *Vorlage* presupposed by the Peshitta of the Dodekapropheton was closely similar to MT, though the word-division occasionally and the vocalization more often differed from that of the later Masoretic tradition. In the light of our soundings into the translation methods adopted in the Peshitta (Chapter 6) it is likely that some of the apparent agreements of the Peshitta with variant readings attested in later Hebrew Mss, the *Tiqqune sopherim* or *Kthibh/Qre* variants are to be attributed rather to the initiative of the translators than to derivation from a Hebrew *Vorlage* distinct from MT. Others are probably to be attributed to the influence of the LXX or of exegetical traditions attested also in the Targum. Thus the somewhat meagre list of passages where a Hebrew *Vorlage* distinct from MT seems to be presupposed by the Peshitta certainly needs to be reduced still further to obtain a true impression of the relation of the Hebrew *Vorlage* of the Peshitta to the MT. In a fairly limited number of passages the Peshitta, alone or in company with one or more of the other ancient versions, may reflect a Hebrew *Vorlage* distinct from MT, but it is seldom possible to be confident that this is so in a specific case. The Peshitta of the Dodekapropheton has thus only a limited contribution to make to the reconstruction of a putative original Hebrew text. To this extent the expectations voiced in the quotation from M.H. Goshen-Gottstein at the beginning of the Introduction have been largely disappointed.

In Chapters 7 and 8 we examined the relation of the Peshitta to the LXX and Targum Jonathan. It proved possible to demonstrate beyond reasonable doubt that the Peshitta translators knew and made selective use of the LXX. The relation of the Peshitta to Targum Jonathan proved much less easy to determine, but in general the agreements between the two versions, when not reflecting a common distinctive *Vorlage*, seemed to reflect a common exegetical tradition or common linguistic factors rather than to suggest a relationship of direct literary dependence on either side.

In the light of these conclusions what inferences may be drawn concerning the origins of the Peshitta of the Dodekapropheton? The proven dependence of the Peshitta translators on the LXX yields a *terminus post quem* of the middle of the second century B.C., by which date the LXX version of the Prophets had already been made, as is known from the translator's Preface to Ben Sirach. Aphrahat's knowledge of the standard text of the Peshitta yields a *terminus ante quem* of the first half of the fourth century A.D. The only way in which we can delimit the date of the Peshitta more precisely is by drawing inferences from the nature of its Hebrew *Vorlage*.

The standardization of the MT is traditionally associated with the name of Rabbi Aqiba, and this indicates a date in the early part of the second century A.D. The close but not exclusive agreement of the Hebrew *Vorlage* presupposed by the Peshitta with the MT suggests as most probable a date for the version shortly before the standardization of the MT. It is necessary however to remember both that much uncertainty still attends the question of the standardization of the MT, and also that what may be called proto-Masoretic Hebrew Mss existed at an earlier period. Perhaps the most that we can reasonably infer is that the Peshiṭta version is unlikely to have been made much later than 100 A.D., and that while it may have been made at any time within the previous two hundred and fifty years it is most likely to belong to the later stages of that period, the middle or later part of the first century A.D.

This tentative conclusion about the date of the Peshiṭta version has the advantage of compatibility with the theory popularized by KAHLE (pp. 270–272), following Marquart, that the version was made for the Jewish community in Adiabene in the middle of the first century A.D. The Jewish origin of the Peshiṭta Pentateuch has been demonstrated by Y. Maori (*The Peshiṭta Version of the Pentateuch in its Relation to the Sources of Jewish Exegesis*, Jerusalem, 1975). We have borne in mind the question whether the Peshiṭta of the Dodekapropheton is of Jewish or Christian origin, and while we have found no conclusive evidence we have found nothing positively to suggest a Christian origin and nothing to make a Jewish origin improbable. Our examination of citations of and allusions to passages from the Dodekapropheton in the New Testament (pp 153–155) has yielded only two cases where assimilation to the New Testament might have occurred in the Peshiṭta of the Dodekapropheton, and in neither of these was this a compelling explanation of the agreement between the respective passages. Much more significant was the negative fact that the Peshiṭta rendering of Hs vi 2 was less susceptible of a Christian interpretation than either the MT or the LXX. The fact that the Peshiṭta translators showed no consistent preference for readings of the LXX rather than those of the MT also favours a Jewish rather than a Christian origin for the version. Finally the dependence of Targum Jonathan and the Peshiṭta on a common exegetical tradition at a number of points also generally favours a Jewish origin for the Peshiṭta. While none of this evidence is conclusive, it all points in favour of a Jewish rather than a Christian origin for the Peshiṭta of the Dodekapropheton, and, like our conclusions about its date, it is at least compatible with the theory that the version was made for the Jewish community in Adiabene.

To the question whether the Peshiṭta of the Dodekapropheton is the work of a single translator the evidence for variety of approach and inconsistency of practice reviewed in Chapter 6 (*cf* especially pp 138f., 157–159) suggested a negative answer. To this general argument we should possibly add the occasional occurrence of what appear to be doublets, though it is not always easy to distinguish these from the kind of expansive gloss noted on p. 186. The example quoted there from Am iii 2 for instance might have originated as a doublet, in the sense that it was an original loose rendering of the Hebrew to which a more literal rendering was subsequently added. If however the intention was to revise the version to achieve closer conformity with MT, why was the original rendering not replaced rather than merely supplemented, and why was this revision of the version not carried out more systematically? It is also possible that ܫܘܒܚܐ and ܓܠܐ ܣܬܪ are doublet renderings of the obscure תלאבות in Hs xiii 5, the second reflecting the interpretation of the LXX, and this raises the possibility of modification of an original text of the Peshiṭta towards greater conformity with the LXX. Another passage where this explanation might be offered for an expansion in the Peshiṭta is the addition of ܐܠܗܢ in Hs xiv 3, which is certainly in agreement with the LXX. Assimilation however to יהוה אלהיך in the previous verse is an equally plausible explanation, and this might account for the same expansion having occurred independently in the two versions. Perhaps the clearest example of a doublet is the rendering of the obscure ולעו in Ob 16 by two verbs ܘܬܗܘܢ ܘܢܬܬܙܝܥܘܢ ("and they shall be dazed and stagger/reel"), yet in this passage none of the other versions renders by more than one word and neither of the Syriac words agrees with any of the terms employed in the other versions. A simpler explanation is that the Peshiṭta translators were unsure of the meaning of the Hebrew verb and incorporated into their version two traditional interpretations of it. Yet another example is the double rendering of גר in Ml iii 5 already discussed on p. 165. We may also recall the fact that variants within the Peshiṭta tradition on occasion offer an alternative interpretation or rendering of the Hebrew (*cf* the example given by LANE, cited on p. 147). It seems however that some copyists were not averse to substituting alternative renderings for those in the standard text (*cf* the relatively large number of such readings peculiar to 17d5 listed on p. 62). On the whole the occasional tendency to expansion and a desire not to suppress one of alternative traditions of interpretation seem more probable explanations for such doublets as we find in the Peshiṭta of the Dodekapropheton than any theories of revision of an earlier text to greater conformity with either the MT or LXX. Any theory of different strata within the Peshiṭta version would need to be sustained by much more consistent and unambiguous evidence.

Our tentative conclusions about the origin of the Peshitta of the Dodekapropheton are therefore these. The version was most probably made within a Jewish community in the middle or late first century A.D. Several translators contributed to the work, and on occasion alternative traditional interpretations were incorporated into the text of the version. Others may have survived only in particular Mss or families or groups of Mss. Unfortunately the paucity of early Mss of the Peshitta of the Dodekapropheton prevents us from tracing the emergence of the standard text, or from assessing whether it represents any conscious or deliberate attempt at revision of an earlier form of the text. There is certainly insufficient evidence at present to establish with any probability a hypothesis of deliberate revision to secure greater conformity with either the MT or the LXX, although such motives may have been at work on occasion in the minds of particular copyists.

Before we draw this monograph to a close we must attempt some assessment of the value of the Peshitta of the Dodekapropheton and indicate some directions in which future Peshitta studies may be developed. SEBÖK's three main conclusions (p. 9) have been confirmed by the results of the present study. His judgement that there was no substantial difference between the Hebrew *Vorlage* of the Peshitta of the Dodekapropheton and the MT has been vindicated; we have indeed seen reason to question some of the instances where Sebök inferred a Hebrew *Vorlage* distinct from MT, so that the *Vorlage* of the Peshitta appears now to have been even closer to the MT than Sebök thought. With his second conclusion, that the Peshitta was a faithful and accurate though not a slavishly literal translation, our own analysis of the translation methods adopted fully concurs. Sebök's third conclusion, that the chief value of the Peshitta is as a monument of ancient exegesis, we also affirm; it has relatively little to offer directly to the textual critic of the Hebrew Bible, but it does offer occasional insights in the area of lexicography (*cf* pp 147, 185 *supra*), and it seems probable that the interrelationships between the Peshitta and the other ancient versions will open up a rich area for exploration of the early strata of Old Testament exegesis. It is indeed in the field of early Jewish exegetical traditions that the richest harvest is to be expected.

For too long the Peshitta has been viewed primarily as a quarry for potential readings distinct from the MT. This has often led to retroversions into a putative distinctive Hebrew *Vorlage* which will hardly bear close examination. Paradoxically it is only when we cease to look to the Peshitta in the first instance for direct information about the Hebrew text, and begin to study it as a version in its own right, that its true value and significance begin to emerge. The lesson which has been grasped by scholars of the LXX and the Targums is only beginning to be applied to the study of the Peshitta.

How then should future research into the Peshitta develop? We have already outlined at the end of Part 1 some directions for further research into the text of the Peshitta itself. The most urgent need in the evaluation of the Peshitta is for more extensive and more detailed investigations into the nature of the Peshitta as a version of the Hebrew. The preliminary soundings we took in Chapter 6 offer some indication of the work to be done in this area. Studies are needed of the stylistic modifications introduced by the Peshitta translators, of their lexical choices and the reasons for them, of the exegetical traditions incorporated into the version, of the interrelationships with the other versions, and of the pluses and minuses in relation to the Hebrew *Vorlage* and the reasons for them. In the course of such studies it should begin to be possible to investigate the plurality of translators in a way that has not been possible within the present monograph. How far do the inconsistencies point to different strata within the version? Is it possible to assign particular sections of the text to different translators? Is there any evidence for sporadic revision of an earlier text to secure greater conformity with either the MT or the LXX? If so, why was such revision carried out only sporadically?

The present monograph has been concerned almost exclusively with the Peshitta of the Dodekapropheton. This has been a necessary limitation for two reasons. In the first place there is the sheer volume of material involved. A detailed study of the one thousand and fifty verses of this Book alone would vastly exceed the scope of a single book, as may be seen from a glance at the volume of such studies of small portions of it as those of GERLEMAN, JANSMA and SAEBØ. The other reason is that only about half of the Peshitta of the Old Testament is yet available in the critical edition. The future researches projected in the last paragraph need to be carried out on a broader basis, and the time is approaching when it will be necessary to determine how far particular characteristics apply to the version as a whole, and how far the Peshitta versions of individual Books or groups of Books of the Old Testament differ from one another. It is to be hoped that investigations on such a broader basis will both illuminate the question of the homogeneity of the Peshitta version of the Old Testament as a whole, and help to bring a sharper focus to bear on the question of possible strata within that version. For the present research can proceed only in particular Books, as the critical edition becomes available, but it must be remembered that this entails a provisional character to the results of such studies as those of the present monograph, and it cannot be assumed that any conclusions about the nature of the Peshitta of the Dodekapropheton are equally valid for the Peshitta of other Books of the Old Testament. The most urgent need therefore is for the completion of the critical text of the Peshitta of the Old Testament, together with a concordance to the whole version. Only then will the necessary tools be available to carry out the programme of research outlined above; only then will it be possible to attempt a well-founded evaluation of the Peshitta as a version of the Hebrew Old Testament, and only then will a fully critical use of the version as a witness to the text of the Hebrew Bible be possible.

It is necessary finally to underline once more the provisional nature of the researches presented in this monograph. Not only have considerations of space frequently necessitated the presentation of a selection only of the data available. The lack as yet of a critical edition of half of the Peshitta of the Old Testament has imposed further limitations on the evaluation of data within the Dodekapropheton. Furthermore the not infrequent possibility of multiple interpretation of the data inevitably leaves room for considerable differences of opinion in particular cases, and it is hardly possible to avoid an element of subjective judgement. Is a particular rendering of the Peshitta to be evaluated as evidence of a distinctive Hebrew *Vorlage*, of the influence of the LXX, or simply of the independence of the translators? It is to be hoped that the more broadly based studies of the future will both clarify prevailing patterns and also bring to light a sufficient number of instances where a specific conclusion is possible to give a clearer perspective to the wider questions as a whole. In the meantime the present study is offered as a contribution to the continuing quest for a true evaluation of the relationship between the Peshitta and its Hebrew original.

INDEXES

READINGS DISCUSSED
References are to the serial numbers assigned to each reading.

CHAPTER 3

HOSEA			
i 2	37	ix 6	114
ii 18	103	ix 11	52
iv 3	123		
iv 6	38	**OBADIAH**	
iv 14$^{2°}$	39	5	130
iv 14$^{4°}$	124	13	131
iv 15	40	16	53
iv 16	5		
v 14	41	**JONAH**	
vi 5	42	i 16	8
vii 3	104	ii 3	134
vii 6	127	ii 5	25
vii 14	43	iv 5	120
vii 15	44		
vii 16	125	**MICAH**	
viii 4	45	i 8	54
ix 15	46	iii 1	9
xi 11	126	iv 3$^{3°}$	100
xii 12	1	iv 3$^{4°}$	101
xiii 10	128	v 6	108
xiii 14	129	vi 8	55
xiv 3	47	vi 13	109
xiv 8	2	vii 12	10
xiv 9	3	vii 15	26
		vii 17	27
JOEL		vii 20	110
i 15	105		
ii 10	106	**NAHUM**	
ii 27	107	i 4	56
		i 14	57
AMOS		ii 1	58
i 14	99	ii 2	34
ii 8	4	ii 3	59
iv 1	48	iii 3	28
iv 6	6	iii 19	11
v 20	49		
v 22	50	**HABAKKUK**	
vi 2	7	i 4	94
vi 14	119	i 5	12
vii 8	51		

HABAKKUK (cont.)

i 14	60
iii 1¹°	35
iii 1²°	61
iii 1²°	116
iii 6	117
iii 8	95
iii 10	115
iii 11	132
iii 17	62
iii 19	63

ZEPHANIAH

i 1	64
i 11	111
i 18¹°	65
i 18²°	66
i 18³°	67
ii 5	68
ii 9	69
ii 11	90
ii 12	70
iii 1	33

HAGGAI

i 11	13
i 14	14
ii 11¹°	29
ii 11²°	121
ii 16	71
ii 18	15
ii 20	72

ZECHARIAH

i 2	16
i 4	73
i 9	74
ii 17	75
iii 4	17
iii 7	76
iii 8	102
iv 6	91
iv 12	77
v 1	30
v 8	36
viii 6	78
viii 10	79
viii 15	80
viii 17	122
ix 8¹°	96
ix 8²°	18
ix 9	118
ix 11	97
ix 12	92
ix 13	19
x 4²°	98
xi 2	81
xi 4	20
xii 2	112
xii 3	21
xii 4	22
xii 10	31
xiv 9	82
xiv 10	32
xiv 16	83
xiv 17	93
xiv 18	84
xiv 21	23

MALACHI

i 4	85
i 13	24
ii 9	86
ii 16	87
ii 17	88
iii 2	133
iii 11	113
iii 13	89

CHAPTER 4

HOSEA

xi 10	1
xiv 8	7

JOEL

ii 20	11
iv 13	8

AMOS

v 10	2
vi 13	3

JONAH

ii 5	5

MICAH

iii 4	9

NAHUM

ii 1	6
ii 5	15
ii 12	12
iii 11	13

INDEXES 201

HABAKKUK		ZECHARIAH	
i 13	14	xi 4,7	10
iii 4	4	xii 13	16

REFERENCES TO THE DODEKAPROPHETON
References in this index are to page numbers.

CHAPTER 5

HOSEA				
i 2	123	xiii 8		123
iii 1	123	xiii 9		122, 126
iii 4	126	xiii 10		126
iv 7	119	xiii 13		122
iv 8	120	xiii 14		126
iv 12	120	xiii 15		122
iv 16	116, 118	xiv 8		122, 123
iv 19	126	xiv 9		127, 128
v 1	123			
v 5	123	**JOEL**		
v 10	115	ii 23		120
vi 3	127	iv 2		123
vi 5	122	iv 16		128
vi 9	115, 123			
vii 1	122	**AMOS**		
vii 5	120			
vii 6	123, 126	i 2		128
vii 10	123	i 7		123
vii 12	122	i 11		128
vii 14	120, 122	i 15		124
viii 4	122	ii 1		124
viii 6	115	ii 2		120
viii 7	115	ii 8		124
viii 10	120, 123, 128	ii 15		124
viii 11	123	iii 4		128
viii 12	119	iii 8		128
ix 1	123	iii 11		120, 122
ix 2	120	iii 12		124
x 5	126	iv 3		124
x 9	120	v 6		127
x 10	119	v 9		122
x 11	123	v 26		122
xi 2	122	vi 1		124, 127
xi 3	120, 126	vi 3		124
xi 6	123	vii 1		122
xi 10	128	vii 2		122
xi 11	122	vii 5		122
xii 1	123	vii 15		113
xii 2	122	vii 16		114
xii 9	127	viii 1		122
xii 11	123	viii 2		122
xiii 5	126	viii 3		122
xiii 7	123	viii 4		127

AMOS (cont.)

viii 8	119, 120, 124
viii 11	120, 124
ix 1	124
ix 5	114, 124

OBADIAH

11	114
17	113

JONAH

ii 1	127
iii 7	121
iii 8	114

MICAH

i 1	117
i 2	115
i 9	122
i 10	114
i 15	120
ii 4	120
ii 6	122
ii 8	117, 122, 124
ii 12	124
iii 1	124
iii 4	127
iv 4	116
iv 9	124
iv 12	122
v 1	122
v 3	116, 117
v 5	117
vi 5	122, 127
vi 8	127
vi 10	124
vi 13	122
vii 2	115
vii 4	124
vii 5	113
vii 12	114, 127
vii 14	124
vii 19	120

NAHUM

i 2	115
i 10	122, 124
i 11	124
i 12	123
ii 4	127
ii 5	123
ii 6	117, 120
ii 8	117
ii 10	122
ii 12	123
ii 13	115
ii 14	127
iii 3	115
iii 5	115
iii 6	115
iii 7	115, 120, 127
iii 8	115, 117
iii 9	115, 117, 127
iii 10	113, 115
iii 11	115
iii 16	117, 120
iii 18	124

HABAKKUK

i 5	114, 118
i 7	123
i 8	117 f.
i 12	115, 119
i 13	114
i 14	115
i 15	114, 115
i 17	114 f., 117
ii 3	114, 117
ii 5	128
ii 6	115, 116, 117, 122
ii 8	117
ii 10	124
ii 13	114, 124
ii 16	114, 118
ii 17	116, 117, 118
ii 18	117, 124
iii 2	123, 127
iii 3	126, 129
iii 4	124
iii 5	123
iii 9	117, 124, 129
iii 10	113
iii 13	129
iii 14	114, 116

ZEPHANIAH

i 1	120
i 2	124
i 3	124
i 4	120
i 5	124
ii 7	120
ii 9	120
ii 10	116
ii 11	123, 127
ii 14	124
iii 3	128
iii 5	123
iii 7	116, 117, 118, 124
iii 8	120, 124

INDEXES

iii 9		vii 9	121
iii 10		vii 12	128
iii 15	113	viii 9	127
iii 17	124	viii 17	121
iii 19	113, 120	ix 1	125
iii 20	127	ix 10	123
	124, 128	ix 12	123
	120	x 1	121
HAGGAI		x 6	123
i 2	124	x 9	125
i 11	120, 124	xi 3	128
i 12	121	xi 4	125
ii 1	114	xi 5	121
		xi 7	125
ZECHARIAH		xi 13	121
i 4	121	xi 16	126
i 15	128	xii 7	121
i 16	121	xii 10	121
i 17	127	xii 13	121
ii 4	121	xiii 7	115
ii 12	119, 121	xiii 8	121
iii 4	128	xiv 5	121
iii 7	125	xiv 6	120, 127
iii 9	123	xiv 10	120
iv 2	120, 121	xiv 18	121
iv 9	120		
v 6	121	MALACHI	
vi 7	127	i 10	115
vi 11	121	i 13	119, 121, 125
vi 12	121	iii 7	128
vi 14	125	iii 16	125
vii 4	121	iii 19	121

CHAPTER 6 (SELECTIVE)

HOSEA		x 14	137
i 6	137, 145	xi 1 f.	145
ii 10	138	xi 6	143
ii 11 f.	140	xi 8	133, 147
iv 3	140	xii 13	142
iv 18	146	xiii 14	154 f.
v 2	145	xiii 15	143 f.
vi 1	148	xiv 1	144
vi 2	155	xiv 9	148
vii 6	143		
vii 10	133	JOEL	
viii 1	133	i 9	135
viii 6	138	i 10	140
ix 1	133	i 12	140
ix 6	158	ii 6	133
ix 10	133	ii 13	138
x 5	143	ii 13 f.	152
x 8	155	ii 17	143
x 11	133, 143	ii 20	142
x 12	143, 144, 145	ii 27	135

INDEXES

AMOS

i 15	148
iii 10	144
iii 12	146
iv 6	144
iv 9	150
iv 13	138
v 11	143
v 24	144
vi 1	142
viii 1 f.	144
ix 11	154

OBADIAH

15	158
20	145

JONAH

i 9	134
i 12	134
ii 6 f.	140
ii 7	134
iii 9 f.	152
iv 1	134
iv 2	138
iv 6	134
iv 8	150

MICAH

i 12	143
i 15	157
ii 1	144
ii 4	146
iii 4	151
iv 6 f.	149 f.
v 5	145
v 9	140
vi 9	144
vii 1	144
vii 2	133
vii 4	142, 146
vii 11	134
vii 17	133

NAHUM

i 2	152 f.
i 3	138
i 4	140
i 6	141, 150
ii 1	139, 148
ii 3	148
ii 4	145
ii 5	132
ii 8	135, 147
ii 11	133
iii 9	138
iii 15	139 f.
iii 17	133, 138
iii 19	145

HABAKKUK

i 3	148 f.
i 6	135
i 8	140
i 10	139
i 12	146
i 13	135
i 15	158 f.
i 16	144
ii 4	154 f.
ii 5	146
ii 9	133
ii 11	147
ii 19	133
iii 9	137, 143
iii 16	146

ZEPHANIAH

i 5	148
i 9	145
ii 11	153
ii 15	148
iii 1	143, 148
iii 10	146
iii 19	135, 149

HAGGAI

i 1	133
i 2	146
i 9	133
i 13	134
ii 2	135
ii 3	134
ii 6	135
ii 16	146
ii 19	134, 146

ZECHARIAH

i 13	140
ii 4	144
ii 6	136
ii 9	134
iii 2	135
iii 3	135
iii 4	134
iv 3	134
iv 5	134
iv 7	144

INDEXES

vi 3	134	xiv 17	135
vi 8	133	xiv 18	157
vii 2	152	xiv 21	136
vii 5	134		
viii 4	134	MALACHI	
viii 5	139		
viii 10	135	i 10	151
viii 17	135	i 11	137
viii 21 f.	152	i 12	146
ix 1	133	i 13	135
x 2	135, 145	i 14	133
x 7	135	ii 2	133
x 11	150 f.	ii 3	134
xi 17	134	ii 9	144
xii 7	135	ii 11	134, 135
xiii 1	136	ii 12	134
xiii 2	135, 153	ii 15	133, 134
xiii 5	144	ii 16	134
xiii 9	134	iii 5	135, 136
xiv 4	134	iii 6	135
xiv 5	135	iii 11	134, 142
xiv 6	134	iii 16	151
xiv 8	133	iii 24	155
xiv 13	133		

CHAPTER 7 (SELECTIVE)

HOSEA		xiii 15	168
ii 8	167	xiv 9	168, 171
ii 14	160		
ii 17	162	**JOEL**	
iii 5	166		
iv 2	167	i 1	163
iv 14	167	i 7	167
v 11	167	i 17	168
v 12	167	ii 6	174
vi 5	166	ii 22	167
vi 9	167	ii 23	166, 168
viii 6	167	ii 27	163
viii 9 f.	166	iv 11	174
viii 10	160	iv 16	163 f.
x 1	167		
x 4	167	**AMOS**	
x 5	167		
x 7	168	i 15	164, 175
xi 1	173	ii 7	168
xi 2	166	ii 8	168
xi 5	168	iv 1	170
xi 6	168	iv 2	168
xii 1	166 f.	iv 8	164
xii 10	173	iv 12	168
xii 15	168	v 16	175
xiii 4	173	v 25	167
xiii 7	168	v 26	160
xiii 13	175	vi 2	173

AMOS (cont.)

vi 5	168
vi 6	168
vii 7 f.	164
vii 9	164
vii 14	169
vii 16	169
viii 1 f.	169
viii 5 f.	168
ix 6	164, 172

OBADIAH

5	164
7	174
9	173
21	173

JONAH

i 6	168
iv 10	175 f.

MICAH

i 5	173
i 8	168
i 11	168
ii 4	164, 172
ii 6	169
ii 8	167, 168
ii 11	164
ii 12	170, 173
iii 1	167
iii 4	171
iv 1	166
iv 8	170
v 6 f.	164
v 7	168
vi 5	169
vi 8	168
vii 4	168
vii 8	173
vii 19	173

NAHUM

i 12	164
ii 3	174
ii 11	174
ii 14	168
iii 1	168
iii 9	171
iii 11	174, 175

HABAKKUK

i 3	169
i 8	162
i 13	175
ii 1	168
ii 4	163
iii 9	175 f.
iii 14	175 f.

ZEPHANIAH

i 5	175
i 12	168
i 14	168
ii 1	168
ii 2	162
ii 11	171
ii 14	163
iii 7	161
iii 9	163
iii 18	163

HAGGAI

i 9	172, 173
i 13	172

ZECHARIAH

i 8	168
i 16	175
ii 2	164
iii 3	175
iii 7	168
iii 8	164
iii 9	168
iv 2	175
iv 9	175
iv 10	169
iv 14	169
v 11	174
vi 10	167
vi 11	175
vi 12	164
vii 7	163
vii 10	165
viii 9	171
viii 17	172, 175
ix 4	164 f.
ix 12	162, 163
ix 17	169
x 1	175
x 7	175
x 9	170
xi 6	165
xi 8	169

INDEXES

xi 17		169	MALACHI		
xii 3		172	i 3		174
xii 7		175	i 13		172
xii 8		174	i 14		165
xii 13		169, 175	iii 3		170
xiii 4		169 f.	iii 5		165
xiii 7		169	iii 6 f.		170
xiv 1		169	iii 8		174
xiv 4		170	iii 10		165
xiv 13		165	iii 16		162
xiv 20		174			

CHAPTER 8 (SELECTIVE)

HOSEA			MICAH		
ii 10		186	i 5		182
ii 11		186	ii 1		180
ii 20		184	ii 12		184
iv 16		186	iii 11		180
vi 1		185 f.	iv 6		184
vii 8		187	iv 7		186
vii 11		188	v 5		180 f.
vii 13		185 f.	vii 5		184, 188
x 2		185			
xi 8		184	NAHUM		
xii 12		187	i 10		185
			iii 11		185
JOEL			iii 15 f.		183
i 4		183	iii 18		185
i 10		188			
iv 3		186	HABAKKUK		
iv 4		186	i 2		187
iv 11		184	ii 10		184
			iii 9		187
AMOS			iii 19		184
ii 10		186			
iii 2		186	ZEPHANIAH		
iv 2		188	i 15		185
v 9		185 f.	ii 10		186
v 17		190	ii 15		185
v 23		184	iii 3		185
vi 4		184	iii 9		185
vii 16		182	iii 11		185
ix 5		184	iii 15		190
ix 9		184			
ix 11		186	HAGGAI		
			ii 19		184
OBADIAH					
5		184			
20		186			

ZECHARIAH

ii 13	183
viii 10	184
ix 4	185 f.
x 11	184, 186
xi 17	187 f.
xii 7	182
xii 11	186
xiv 4	188 f.
xiv 8	185

MALACHI

i 4	184
i 10	183 f., 186
ii 12	189
ii 16	189
iii 10	181
iii 14	185